Advancing Media Production Research

Global Transformations in Media and Communication Research

Series Editors: **Marjan de Bruin**, The University of the West Indies, Jamaica and **Claudia Padovani**, University of Padova, Italy

Advisory Board:

Pradip Thomas, Vice-President of IAMCR, University of Queensland, Australia, **Antonio Pasquali**, Universidad Central de Venezuela, **Daya Kishan Thussu**, University of Westminster, UK, **Francesca Musiani**, CSI, MINES ParisTech, France, **Gerard Goggin**, University of Sydney, Australia, **Liu Liqun**, Communication University, China, **Hillel Nossek**, The College of Management Academic Studies, Israel, **Ibrahim Saleh**, University of Cape Town, South Africa, **Kaarle Nordenstreng**, University of Tampere, Finland, **Karin Wilkins**, University of Texas, Austin, **Marc Raboy**, McGill University, Canada, **Martin Becerra**, Universidad Nacional de Quilmes, Argentina, **Robin Mansell**, London School of Economics, UK, **Ruth Teer-Tomaselli**, University of KwaZuluNatal, South Africa, **Todd Holden**, Tohoku University, Japan, **Usha Raman**, University of Hyderabad, India.

This series contributes to exploring, in creative and trans-disciplinary manners, the challenges posed by fast-evolving communication developments in an increasingly connected world. It provides a venue for collecting state of the art, sound and innovative scholarly perspectives on specific aspects of communication transformations.

Due to ever-increasing global interactions amongst individuals, communities and communication devices, scholars face the challenge to rethink the very categories – of space, time, boundaries and technology – through which communication and media studies have evolved, thus contributing to identifying and refining concepts, theories and methods to explore the diverse realities of communication in a changing world.

The IAMCR has a long tradition of being a truly international academic association, with members working in all corners of the globe. This unique feature makes it possible to include in the Palgrave/IAMCR series contributions from highly diverse geo-cultural and disciplinary traditions.

The series fosters and generates research that explores critical communication and media concerns from a variety of theoretical and methodological approaches. Outstanding contributions from non-Anglophone areas will also be made available to a global readership, after translation into English.

Titles include:

Claudia Padovani and Andrew Calabrese (*editors*)
COMMUNICATION RIGHTS AND SOCIAL JUSTICE
Historical Accounts of Transnational Mobilizations

Luis Albornoz (*editor*)
POWER, MEDIA, CULTURE
A Critical View from the Political Economy of Communication

Maria Way (*translator*)
THE THEORY OF THE SOCIAL PRACTICE OF INFORMATION

Chris Paterson, David Lee, Anamik Saha and Anna Zoellner (*editors*)
ADVANCING MEDIA PRODUCTION RESEARCH
Shifting Sites, Methods, and Politics

Global Transformations in Media and Communication Research
Series Standing Order ISBN 978–1–137–43370–1 (Hardback)
                978–1–137–43371–8 (Paperback)
(*outside North America only*)

You can receive future titles in this series as they are published by placing a standing order. Please contact your bookseller or, in case of difficulty, write to us at the address below with your name and address, the title of the series and one of the ISBNs quoted above.

Customer Services Department, Macmillan Distribution Ltd, Houndmills, Basingstoke, Hampshire RG21 6XS, England

Advancing Media Production Research

Shifting Sites, Methods, and Politics

Edited by

Chris Paterson
University of Leeds, UK

David Lee
University of Leeds, UK

Anamik Saha
Goldsmiths, University of London

and

Anna Zoellner
University of Leeds, UK

Selection and editorial matter © Chris Paterson, David Lee, Anamik Saha and Anna Zoellner 2016
Epilogue © C.W. Anderson 2016
Remaining chapters © Individual authors 2016

All rights reserved. No reproduction, copy or transmission of this publication may be made without written permission.

No portion of this publication may be reproduced, copied or transmitted save with written permission or in accordance with the provisions of the Copyright, Designs and Patents Act 1988, or under the terms of any licence permitting limited copying issued by the Copyright Licensing Agency, Saffron House, 6–10 Kirby Street, London EC1N 8TS.

Any person who does any unauthorized act in relation to this publication may be liable to criminal prosecution and civil claims for damages.

The authors have asserted their rights to be identified as the authors of this work in accordance with the Copyright, Designs and Patents Act 1988.

First published 2016 by
PALGRAVE MACMILLAN

Palgrave Macmillan in the UK is an imprint of Macmillan Publishers Limited, registered in England, company number 785998, of Houndmills, Basingstoke, Hampshire RG21 6XS.

Palgrave Macmillan in the US is a division of St Martin's Press LLC, 175 Fifth Avenue, New York, NY 10010.

Palgrave Macmillan is the global academic imprint of the above companies and has companies and representatives throughout the world.

Palgrave® and Macmillan® are registered trademarks in the United States, the United Kingdom, Europe and other countries.

ISBN: 978–1–137–54193–2

This book is printed on paper suitable for recycling and made from fully managed and sustained forest sources. Logging, pulping and manufacturing processes are expected to conform to the environmental regulations of the country of origin.

A catalogue record for this book is available from the British Library.

Library of Congress Cataloging-in-Publication Data

    Advancing media production research : shifting sites, methods, and politics / Chris Paterson, University of Leeds, UK ; David Lee, University of Leeds, UK ; Anamik Saha, Goldsmiths, University of London ; Anna Zoellner, University of Leeds, UK.
       pages cm
    Includes bibliographical references and index.
    ISBN 978–1–137–54193–2
    1. Mass media – Research – Methodology. I. Paterson, Chris, 1963 – editor. II. Lee, David, 1975 – editor. III. Saha, Anamik, 1977 – editor. IV. Zoellner, Anna, editor.

P91.3.A39 2015
302.23072—dc23   2015023916

Contents

Acknowledgements vii

Notes on Contributors ix

Part I Debates and Transitions

1 Production Research: Continuity and Transformation 3
   Chris Paterson, David Lee, Anamik Saha, and Anna Zoellner

2 On the Vagaries of Production Research 20
   Philip Schlesinger

3 The Importance of Time in Media Production Research 38
   David M. Ryfe

Part II Theory and Research

4 Field Theory and Media Production: A Bridge-Building Strategy 53
   Ida Willig

5 Studying News Production: From Process to Meanings 68
   Daniel A. Berkowitz and Zhengjia Liu

6 News Media Ecosystems and Population Dynamics: A Cross-Cultural Analysis 79
   Wilson Lowrey and Elina Erzikova

7 Micro vs. Macro: A Reflection on the Potentials of Field Analysis 95
   Tore Slaatta

Part III Matters of Method

8 Applying Grounded Theory in Media Production Studies 115
   Astrid Gynnild

9 The Qualitative Interview in Media Production Studies 131
   Hanne Bruun

10 When You Can't Rely on Public or Private: Using the Ethnographic Self as Resource   147
Michael B. Munnik

11 Investigating the Backstage of Newswriting with Process Analysis   161
Daniel Perrin

Part IV Beyond the Newsroom

12 From 'Poetics' to 'Production': Genres as Active Ingredients in Media Production   181
Ana Alacovska

13 Production Studies and Documentary Participants: A Method   200
Willemien Sanders

14 A Cultural Biography of Application Software   217
Frederik Lesage

Epilogue   233
C.W. Anderson

Index   237

Acknowledgements

This book arises from a one-day conference amongst scholars with an interest in improving our understanding of how the products of information and culture are created: 'Advancing Media Production Research' was simultaneously an International Association of Media and Communication Researchers (IAMCR) pre-conference and an International Communication Association (ICA) post-conference, conceived to take advantage of a unique opportunity to tap the expertise of well over a thousand media scholars from around the world who had converged on the British Isles in the summer of 2013 to attend one or both of the conferences of those associations (ICA in London, IAMCR in Dublin).

The event was sandwiched between those large conferences and drew about 60 scholars to the University of Leeds. It was initiated and co-sponsored by the IAMCR Media Production Analysis Working Group along with the Journalism Studies section of the ICA and the Media Industries and Cultural Production Working Group of ECREA (European Communication Research and Education Association) – yielding an unprecedented international and inter-associational collaboration. The event was organized primarily by editors Chris Paterson, Anamik Saha, and David Lee, along with University of Leeds Institute for Communication Studies (now School of Media and Communication) colleagues Toussaint Nothias, Daniel Mutibwa, and research administrator Liz Pollard.

It is suitable, then, for this book to be published as part of the IAMCR's series 'Global Transformations in Media and Communication Research', launched in 2014, and this anthology is an important milestone in over 15 years of IAMCR facilitated scholarship combining that organization's history of critical, and very international, scholarship with advocacy of direct, exhaustive, and rigorous researcher engagement with complex and fast-changing media production environments, as is manifest in work of the Media Production Analysis Working Group.

Prominent scholars from around the world who participated in that conference included C.W. Anderson, Georgina Born, Tim Havens, Dave Hesmondhalgh, Philip Schlesinger, and Ida Willig, and we are pleased that some of them are represented in this volume. While most of the chapters here were presented in an earlier form at our conference, a few have been generously authored by other researchers on our invitation. The editors are especially grateful for those efforts. Finally, thanks are due to IAMCR series co-editors Marjan de Bruin and Claudia Padovani for their considerable work in developing and coordinating this important collaboration with Palgrave Macmillan.

Notes on Contributors

Ana Alacovska is an assistant professor at Copenhagen Business School. Under the auspices of the Danish Council for Independent Research – the Humanities, she is conducting a post-doc study of the production of Scandinavian crime fiction in the Danish publishing industry. She is also the leader of a research project on post-socialist creative labour funded by the Swiss Development Agency. Her doctoral work on the production of travel guidebooks appeared in the *European Journal of Cultural Studies*, *Communication, Culture & Critique* and *The Sociological Review/Sociological Review Monograph*.

C.W. Anderson is an associate professor at the College of Staten Island, CUNY. He is the author of *Rebuilding the News: Metropolitan Journalism in the Digital Age*, and the forthcoming *Journalism and News: What Everyone Needs to Know*, with Len Downie and Michael Schudson. His project takes a historical look at the use of data in news from the 1910s until the present.

Daniel A. Berkowitz is Professor of Journalism and Mass Communication at the University of Iowa, USA. His research involves the study of news cultures, news production and news texts through the lens of media memory, mythical narrative and boundary work. He is the editor of two books in those areas: *Social Meanings of News* and *Cultural Meanings of News*.

Hanne Bruun is Associate Professor and Head of the Research Programme Media and Communication in the Department of Media and Journalism Studies at Aarhus University, Denmark. Her research areas are the aesthetics of television and its genres with a focus on journalism and entertainment, media history, audience studies and production studies. She is the author of seven books (in Danish), the latest being *Danish Television Satire: Entertainment with an Edge* (2011). She has contributed to several books and journals, including *International Journal of Digital Television, European Journal of Communication* and *Nordicom Information*.

Elina Erzikova is Associate Professor of Public Relations in the Department of Journalism at Central Michigan University. She holds a PhD in Mass Communications from the University of Alabama. A former newspaper editor, Erzikova researches the post-Soviet Russian mass media system and the role of power in relationships between media and government.

Astrid Gynnild is Professor of Journalism and Media Studies and Chair of the Journalism Program in the Department of Information Science and Media Studies at the University of Bergen, Norway. Gynnild has authored a number of international articles and books at the crossroads of technology and online journalism. Her recent works focus on visual technologies and innovative dimensions of journalism. Gynnild has generated several grounded theories and is the editor of the multidisciplinary journal *Grounded Theory Review*. She is also co-author of *Grounded Theory: The Philosophy, Method and Work of Barney Glaser*.

David Lee is Lecturer in Cultural Industries and Communication in the School of Media and Communication at the University of Leeds. He is the author of a number of articles and chapters on creative work, cultural policy, copyright and television studies in international journals including the *International Journal of Cultural Policy*, *Cultural Trends*, *Media, Culture & Society*, and *Television & New Media*. He is the co-author of *Culture, Economy and Politics: The Case of New Labour* (along with David Hesmondhalgh, Kate Oakley and Melissa Nisbett), published by Palgrave Macmillan in 2015. Before working in academia, David worked in documentary production at the BBC on series such as *Newsnight, Panorama* and *The Money Programme*.

Frederik Lesage is an assistant professor in the School of Communication at Simon Fraser University (SFU). His research interests involve applying mediation theory to an analysis of how consumer-oriented digital media are designed and used. His research has appeared in international journals including *Leonardo*, *Digital Creativity*, *Journal of Broadcasting* and *Electronic Media* and *Convergence*.

Zhengjia Liu is a PhD graduate from the School of Journalism and Mass Communication at the University of Iowa and works as a marketing communications professional in a multinational high-tech corporation. Her main research interests focus on field and constructionist approaches to the study of social media from a cultural perspective. Some of her recent articles appeared in *Journalism: Theory, Practice and Criticism*, *International Journal of Sports Communication* and *Journal of Magazine and New Media Research*.

Wilson Lowrey is Professor and Chair of the Journalism Department at the University of Alabama. His scholarship focuses on media sociology. He is co-editor of *Changing the News: The Forces Shaping Journalism in Uncertain Times*, and his research has appeared in a number of academic journals, including *Journalism, Journalism & Mass Communication Quarterly, Journalism Studies, Political Communication* and *International Communication Gazette*.

Michael B. Munnik is Lecturer in Social Science Theories and Methods at Cardiff University. He completed his doctorate at the University of Edinburgh, after an MA in Religion in Contemporary Society from King's College London. Prior to undertaking postgraduate study, he worked for eight years as a journalist with the Canadian Broadcasting Corporation in Ottawa, Canada. His research concerns journalist–source relations, Muslims in Britain, and the role of religion in the public sphere.

Chris Paterson is Senior Lecturer in International Communication in the School of Media and Communication at the University of Leeds. He originated and co-edited, with David Domingo, two volumes of *Making Online News* (2007, 2011) and is the founder of the IAMCR working group on media production analysis. He authored *The International Television News Agencies* (2011) and *War Reporters under Threat: The United States and Media Freedom* (2014). His research encompasses international journalism, communication for development, and news production.

Daniel Perrin is Professor of Media Linguistics, Director of the Institute of Applied Media Studies (IAM) of the Zurich University of Applied Sciences, Winterthur; Vice President of the International Association of Applied Linguistics (AILA); and co-editor of the *International Journal of Applied Linguistics* and the De Gruyter Mouton *Handbooks of Applied Linguistics* series. His main areas of research and teaching are text linguistics, media linguistics, methodology of applied linguistics, text production research, and analysis of language use in the media and in professional communication. Daniel worked as a journalist and writing coach before his academic career and is still engaged in training and coaching media and communication professionals.

David M. Ryfe is Professor and Director of the School of Journalism and Mass Communication at the University of Iowa. He has written widely in the areas of public deliberation, political communication, and the history and sociology of news. His most recent book, *Can Journalism Survive?* (2012), represents the most intensive ethnographic study of newsrooms in a generation. His current work examines the growth of online news sites in regions across the United States.

Anamik Saha is a lecturer in the Department of Media and Communications at Goldsmiths, University of London. His research interests are in race and the cultural industries. His work has appeared in journals including *Media, Culture & Society*, *Ethnic and Racial Studies*, and *European Journal of Cultural Studies*. Most recently he has edited a special issue of *Popular Communication* with David Hesmondhalgh on race and ethnicity in cultural production.

Willemien Sanders is an assistant professor at the Institute for Cultural Inquiry (ICON) and the Department of Media and Culture Studies at Utrecht University, The Netherlands. In her thesis, 'Participatory Spaces' (2012), she investigates documentary filmmaking ethics. Her research interests include documentary film, production studies and digital media studies. She is involved in EUscreenXL (www.euscreen.eu) and in SiFTI (www.sifti.no).

Philip Schlesinger is Inaugural Chair in Cultural Policy at the University of Glasgow, Scotland, UK and Deputy Director of CREATe, the UK Research Councils' Centre for Copyright and New Business Models in the Creative Economy. He is researching cultural crisis in Europe and is also working on a study of contemporary British film policy. His most recent, co-authored, books are *The Rise and Fall of the UK Film Council* (2015) and *Curators of Cultural Enterprise* (2015).

Tore Slaatta is a professor in the Department of Media and Communication at the University of Oslo, working on cultural theory, media and art sociology and production studies. He is Director of the NRC project *Art! Power: Orders and Borders in Contemporary Art in Norway* (2012–2015) and engages in research on literature, international publishing and European cultural policies. He translated two books by Pierre Bourdieu into Norwegian in 2007 and was a visiting professor at MSH/CNRS in Paris in 2006.

Ida Willig is Professor of Journalism Studies at Roskilde University, Denmark. Her research interests include journalistic practices, norms and values, media systems, press history and reflexive sociology. Her current projects focus on media pluralism and journalistic quality (using a mixed-methods approach of content analysis, survey and policy study of Danish news media).

Anna Zoellner is Lecturer in Media Industries at the University of Leeds with a professional background in documentary production. Her research interests are the intersection of media industries, media production studies, cultural labour research, and television studies with a methodological interest in ethnography and internationally comparative research. Her work has appeared in a number of edited volumes and journals including *Mass Communication and Society, Journal for the Study of British Cultures* and *Journal of Media Practice*.

Part I
Debates and Transitions

1
Production Research: Continuity and Transformation

Chris Paterson, David Lee, Anamik Saha, and Anna Zoellner

At the heart of this book is the question: how well do we understand the institutions which create our media, our information, and our culture? Rather than seeking to reveal the substantially hidden world of cultural production (as many works cited in this introductory chapter do well), this anthology explores many of the contemporary challenges to understanding the nature of cultural production – considering the research process, rather than research findings. By doing so, we hope to encourage researchers to push the boundaries of production research beyond the traditional (but still very necessary) 'newsroom observation' in order to expand production research across boundaries of genre and medium, to liberally borrow theory and method across previously rigid disciplinary borders, and to confront new challenges which threaten to insulate the creation of media and culture from rigorous independent examination.

Notwithstanding the strong (and justified) continuities in media production studies, research has changed radically since the early formative ethnographic and qualitative studies of the field in the 1970s and 1980s. The growing number of media and communication scholars interested in studying the everyday production of media texts are visible in the growth of related publications, specialized conferences and the establishment of association subgroups such as the International Association of Media and Communication Researchers (IAMCR) working group for Media Production Analysis (established in 1999) and the European Communication Research and Education Association (ECREA) working group Media Industries and Cultural Production (established in 2011).

One cause of an expansion in media production research is the development of the media industries themselves. Research agendas and methodologies have been shaped by recent transformations of the media landscape and production practice, exploring new research questions, sites and methodologies. And as the internal workings of media institutions change beyond the recognition of an earlier generation of researchers, and challenges to understand those internal functions become ever greater, there is a need to review what new knowledge is emerging from production research, what gaps remain, what challenges to production research persist, and to debate how those might be overcome. Our hope is to take an international and interdisciplinary approach to exploring in-depth research into processes of cultural production (whether through classically ethnographic immersion or other means) across a wide range of genres and forms of cultural institution, from funding bodies to television public affairs to newspaper journalism.

Early production studies and the development of a 'field'

Formative research carried out in the 1970s inside US national television news organizations (Gans, 1979; Epstein, 1974; Tuchman, 1978; Altheide, 1976), alongside work undertaken in the UK (Blumler, 1969; Elliott, 1972; Golding and Elliot, 1979), was crucial in establishing ethnographically informed media sociology as a tradition within media and communications research. As Schlesinger argues in this book, media sociology was comprised of a handful of scholars at this period, and this early research was deeply influential for an emerging generation of UK scholars who were also largely focusing on the production of news (Blumler, 1969; Elliott, 1972; Schlesinger, 1978; Golding and Elliot, 1979) as well as research on crime reporting and source relationships (Schlesinger and Tumber, 1994), 'competitor-colleagues' in news production (Tunstall, 1971), television production (Elliot, 1972) and media organizational culture more generally (Burns, 1977).

This work is now sometimes referred to somewhat problematically as the 'first wave' of media sociology (Cottle, 2000; Willig, 2013), with contemporary researchers keen to stress the differences (organizationally, theoretically and methodologically) between this work and contemporary variations undertaken in a different context. There are significant differences. Much of the work cited above focuses on singular news organizations within highly unionized and relatively stable fields of employment. 'Precarity', 'multi-tasking', 'insecurity', and 'self-exploitation', all of which have become staple touchstones for contemporary accounts of media production (Banks, 2007; Gill and Pratt, 2008), are absent from these accounts, which focus on the bureaucratic routines of news organizations (questions of decision-making, news judgements, source relationships) as well as questions of power, influence and ideology. Claims of truth, objectivity and impartiality were deconstructed and critically analysed by this generation of researchers.

Research dealing with media production today must address a field transformed by digital technology as well as the proliferation and fragmentation of creative production roles (Deuze, 2007), a marked shift in the speed of production (what McRobbie (2002a) has termed 'speeded up creative worlds'), and the impact of social media and so-called 'citizen' originated news production (Allan, 2013). As Schlesinger will also suggest in Chapter 2, we increasingly must undertake research in an environment shaped by the global discourse of the 'creative economy' as well as in the context of 'research impact', with the obligations to show relevance that come with research council funding.

While it is important to recognize the significant differences between media production research historically and today, we must also recognize the continuities. Challenges to such research abound and are escalating, ranging from increasingly secretive corporate cultures which see little value in inviting observation of their work, to pressure on scholars to produce more with less – leading to faster and easier modes of research. Full-scale immersive ethnographies are still relatively rare and tend to be undertaken by PhD researchers, due to their resource-intensive nature (however, brief ethnographic immersion has become far more common, as Ryfe maintains in Chapter 3). Access is still a vital issue, due to the ongoing need to deal with and convince gatekeepers to media organizations, although researchers are far more visible now than before in terms of their research profiles and writing being available online.

As noted by Schlesinger (1980) and others, the process of gaining the access to conduct long-term observational research within media organizations is usually challenging, and that access, when granted, can be tenuous. Paterson (2011: xi) observed in the introduction to his partially ethnographic study of (previously almost entirely unresearched) television news agencies, a longstanding obstacle to genuinely ethnographic production research 'is that organizations risk criticism when they permit independent analysis of what they do: what makes sense in the context of their business may look irresponsible or arrogant to people outside of that context.' Suspicion and caution about the purpose of media production research from inside media organizations continues to be a problematic issue for researchers. In Chapter 10, Munnik explores how recent events such as the Jimmy Savile and newspaper phone-hacking scandals in the UK have made access even more difficult than before. At the same time, we have seen an explosion in recent decades in forms of cultural production, making the object of analysis ever harder to identify. Some of the authors in this volume challenge us to expand our conceptions of cultural production along with our methodological repertoire, as with Lesage's examination of software in our final chapter. And there is a continued focus in production research on media power and interactions between journalists, governments, lobbyists and public relations workers as well as consideration of how news is funded and influenced. As much of the work in this anthology demonstrates, questions of power, access and observation remain as vital today as they were in the 1970s and 1980s.

The transformation of the media industries

In the last decades media production has raised the interest of investors and policy-makers for its economic potential, supported by a general turn towards neo-liberalism. Deregulation and the promotion of the 'creative industries'[1] as sources of new revenue have driven policy initiatives – not only in the Western world (see Hesmondhalgh, 2013). The subsequent growth of media organizations followed by centralization and integration created a media ecology consisting of both large multinational media corporations and small-scale, even DIY, media production. Substantial competitive pressure and commodification of media texts characterize this environment and validate the continuity of classic production study questions about the influence of commerce, power and the role of creativity. In addition to such important continuities, industry transformations since the 1990s/2000s have also broadened the subjects of production research and widened the methodological canon of the field, supporting necessary shifts towards multinational, multi-sited and multi-method research to explore these developments. Media production research has spread beyond its traditional focus on news and television production, studying other forms of media and cultural production including popular culture and entertainment in diverse media industries such as music, publishing and new media. Furthermore, the investigation has been extended beyond the work of primarily creative media personnel to include workers 'below the line' (e.g. Mayer, 2011).

Research examining media production as an occupation has expanded rapidly in the last twenty years, stimulated to some degree by the optimistic policy discourse surrounding creative work as well as the growth and the flexibilization of the workforce. Critical cultural labour research explores, amongst other things, the consequences of the casualization of employment, the nature of creativity, and the division of work roles as well as questions of ethics and diversity in media production. A growing body of literature on media work provides in-depth discussions of these matters both from a sociological and cultural studies perspective (e.g. Hesmondhalgh and Baker, 2011; Banks et al., 2013; Johnson et al., 2014). This scholarship provides us with important insights into media producers' experience, yet methodologically such research relies mainly on the traditional interview, and to some degree, observation. Although we do not explicitly focus on labour in this volume, the chapters by Sanders, Perrin and Alacovska suggest alternative approaches to expand our understanding of what media workers do.

Whilst our knowledge of labour conditions continues to grow, production research related to digital technologies is still nascent. The substantial technological developments of recent decades (most notably digitalization), the emergence of the Internet, and the related convergence of texts and media devices, have deeply affected media production. This includes the emergence of new forms of media and communication including, for example, social media, online blogs/vlogs, and interactive virtual books, but it also adds another dimension to the production of 'traditional' media texts. Important work has been undertaken especially within journalism production research as scholars investigated the particularities of online news production (e.g. Paterson and Domingo, 2008; Domingo and Paterson, 2011). Other studies have focused on multiplatform production, interactive media texts and the virtual world of CGI (e.g. Bennett et al., 2012; Sorenson, 2012; Nash, 2012). However, further research is needed to explore the role of technologies in media production including, for example, the influence of grassroots production, participatory and collaborative production, the impact of social media, as well as the use of production software and hardware as suggested in Lesage and Perrin's chapters.

The expansion of media production as a business sector combined with technological development has made transnational media production and distribution more important for media producers. The media are both shaping and are being shaped by economic, political and cultural globalization; and scholarship needs to investigate the international connections, processes and influences of media production. Production research – partially due to its resource-intensive nature and its reliance on case studies – so far tends to focus on single national settings. Particular cultural or geographical sites certainly remain of high importance for media production research, as does domestic production for media producers, but the movement of labour (and therefore skills but also cultural consciousness), finance (including certain forms of subsidies), and goods (especially the easily reproducible, immaterial media texts) across national borders is of great significance for the nature and production processes of media texts.

Research has been carried out especially in the study of international media distribution as well as the global trade and local adaptation of media texts (e.g. Steemers, 2004; Moran, 2006). Increasingly, there is also interest in contemporary transnational collaboration and runaway productions especially in the film industry. Yet, multiple international research sites and comparative research designs, such as discussed in Chapter 6 by Lowrey and Erzikova, are still a rare occurrence. More work is needed to explore the international dimensions of media production in more detail and, in the course of this, to question concepts of national culture and identity.

Cultural studies of production

There has also been a significant shift in theoretical focus within (some) production research. Influential research on contemporary media production has drawn extensively on a range of social theories, in particular those that focus on the shaping of the self within late modernity (McRobbie, 2002b; Ursell, 2000; Gill, 2011). This has led to attention being paid to the subjective experiences of cultural workers, with concepts such as emotional labour (Hochschild, 2003), governmentality (McRobbie, 2002b) and moral economy (Hesmondhalgh, 2011) coming to the fore as tools for understanding media production within a new context.

In addition, a relatively new field of research (particularly in the US) has emerged that draws more explicitly from cultural studies. Cultural studies has generally been seen as interested primarily in texts and audiences, but as Havens (2014) points out there is a history, albeit an unrecognized one, of cultural studies that are more interested in media and cultural production (see Williams, 1973; Frith; 1981; Gitlin, 1983; Negus, 1992; D'Acci, 1994). Nonetheless, in recent times we have seen a renewed interest by cultural studies scholars in media production (predominantly focused on entertainment and popular culture). This new surge of research operates under several names including production studies (Mayer et al., 2009), critical media industry studies (Havens et al., 2009), and creative industries (Hartley, 2005). While they apply different labels, they each can broadly be described as cultural studies of media production.

Cultural studies approaches to media production share three main characteristics. Firstly, they emphasize their basis in critical scholarship – often in distinction to the more descriptive and neutral tone of the organizational sociology that characterizes production of culture studies (Hesmondhalgh, 2010). Thus these accounts are grounded in questions of power; that is, how cultural producers inhabit and exercise it. Secondly, they are interested in the 'cultures of production' (Negus, 1997), or as Meyer et al. (2009: 2) put it, 'production as culture'. Thus the task is 'to understand how people work through professional organizations and informal networks to form communities and shared practices, languages and cultural understandings of the world' (ibid.). Other cultural studies theorists take this further and attempt to draw connections between the social and cultural conditions of production and the text itself (Havens, 2014; Havens et al., 2009; Saha, 2012). Thirdly, cultural studies of production are interested in the micro and the everyday interactions of cultural production. Havens et al. (2009) describe the critical media industry studies approach as 'midlevel fieldwork' – a 'helicopter view' that can track individual agents as they negotiate the terrain of cultural production, in contrast to the broad 'jet-plane view' offered by political economy.

Reflecting its interdisciplinary nature, cultural studies of production incorporate ethnographic research influenced by sociology and anthropology, but also the methods of literary analysis – including oral interviews, memory analyses, and auto-biographical methods as well as textual analyses of industry material like trade magazines that are treated as discourses of media production that constitute the media industries themselves. Havens (2014) observes new studies that are influenced by economic anthropology and cultural economy (du Gay and Pryke, 2002); following the notion of production as culture, these two disciplines offer methods that are directly suited to the task of interpreting and deconstructing the codes, rituals, representations and discourse of cultural production.

Yet despite its engagement with questions of power, some scholars have drawn attention to cultural studies of production's reluctance to deal with normative questions regarding media production. With its empirical emphasis on how cultural work is represented by workers themselves – and how production itself is a culture to be studied – Hesmondhalgh (2013: 56) asks how 'we are ultimately supposed to *evaluate* what is being observed' [our emphasis]. In contrast, Hesmondhalgh's own empirical study with Sarah Baker into cultural production in three media industries (Hesmondhalgh and Baker, 2011) tackles the normative head-on, asking whether creative labour can be considered 'good' or 'bad' work. Hesmondhalgh is working in the cultural industries tradition of critical political economy, but this approach shares strong affinities with cultural studies of production, not least the emphasis on the micro level and the need for empirical work (in contrast to political economy's perceived apathy towards micro studies of media production). Yet, it is due to its strong social theoretical grounding, that cultural industries research is perhaps better equipped to tackle normative questions relating to power, social justice and inequality – particularly in relation to the experiences of the cultural worker as mentioned above.

Indeed, when it comes to advancing media production research, the main contributions of both of these fields is mostly in terms of politics, in drawing attention to what is at stake politically for this field. In terms of methodological advancements, however, neither cultural studies of production or cultural industries research have much to add, other than recognition that 'ethnographic methods can enrich the field of media industries research hugely' (Hesmondhalgh, 2010: 250). Hesmondhalgh, in an essay entitled 'Politics, Theory, and Method in Media Industries Research', highlights the need to foreground 'empirical work (which means an engagement with methodological problems and dilemmas)' (ibid.), yet actual engagement with these issues is light. Cultural studies of production and similar critical empirical studies have much to offer in terms of focusing us on the everyday dynamics of media production in a way that does not shy away from and, in fact, treats seriously the 'messy, informal world of human actions' (Negus, 1997: 84) that characterize the cultural industries. Yet perhaps, this field would benefit from engaging with the methodological advancements and practices (and the problems and dilemmas that arise) in other fields that have had a sustained presence in media production research, such as news and journalism studies.

Keeping up with journalistic change

While researchers in cultural industries and theorists of culture have begun to engage more recently, if enthusiastically, with production research which examines the site and processes of media production, the tradition of production research has long been crucial to understanding news work and the journalistic cultures which play such a prominent role in shaping the public conversation. The pace of change in news production is fast, and the very boundaries which once defined journalism now seem constantly in flux. Usher (2014) and Ryfe (2012) have impressively shown that the tradition of long-term newsroom observation is not over (though Ryfe observes in Chapter 3 how it is in danger).

Several authors in this book revisit the accomplishments of news production research to date and focus their recommendations on gaps in our understanding of a fast-changing contemporary journalism. Reviews of online journalism research (Boczkowski, 2002; Domingo, 2005) suggest that studies in the earlier days of online news tended to concentrate on news content, the nature of the news workers, and on the audience, rather than on production routines and the production context.

Newsroom production ethnography has experienced a resurgence in the past decade. However, as Ryfe observes in his chapter, the long-term researcher exposure, which many writers regard as vital to a genuinely 'ethnographic' understanding, is rare indeed, and few contemporary researchers set out with the ambition of years – much less weeks or months – of observing their research setting. But how little immersive research is too little? Are alternative or complementary methods of investigating the creation of 'news' as, or more, effective than ethnographic processes?

As Paterson has observed elsewhere, without the many early ethnographic investigations of news production (prominent examples are cited earlier in this chapter), our understandings of journalism would be limited to what little we are able to glean from the observation of news content, or from what journalists say they do. Jerolmack and Khan (2014: 178) usefully demonstrate that it is a significant methodological problem that purely interview-based research tends to ignore 'the fact that what people say is often a poor predictor of what they do', and that surveys and interviews too often conflate attitude and behaviour. They respond to the argument that survey and interview research is more generalizable than ethnographic research by asking 'generalizable to what?' given the 'attitudinal fallacy' which they demonstrate. One response in media research is to continually test interview data against observational data, and to let one process inform the other (a central approach in Paterson, 2011). But there is reason to believe this is less than adequate, as was perhaps demonstrated by the spectacle of British tabloid journalists recounting, only when under oath and before Judge Leveson, extraordinary institutional pressure to produce an exploitative and socially toxic journalism which had rarely (if ever) been described in interviews with academic researchers (Leveson, 2012).

Much of the ethnographically informed research into news production of the past decade has usefully shown that utopian myths about revolutionary change in the nature of journalism have been just that, and the still evolving multimedia news production of the Internet age suffers from as many of the constraints as old news production, only with added constraints like twenty-four-hour production cycles and shovelware dependence on public relations and wire services to meet content production targets limiting it further (Paterson and Domingo, 2008). There is ample, though often anecdotal, evidence that news-producing organizations are increasingly closed to researchers, making the discussion of how we are informed (by researchers) about how we are informed (by news media) ever more pressing.

Information is increasing shared through society in new ways, and indeed some argue that new structures of informal information sharing have effectively superseded or made less relevant the traditional hierarchical news media, making clear the need for methodological innovation which moves news production research beyond the boundaries of the traditional newsroom and is better able to grasp the conditions of production of this 'ambient journalism' (Hermida, 2010). One of the most dramatic and fast-paced changes to information acquisition in recent years has been the dramatic growth of new information providers which are social media natives, like *Buzzfeed*. Such organizations command the attention of millions around the world and are likely the main source of journalistic information for many, but research into their highly Web-metric-driven production practices remains rare; Anderson (2011), Usher (2013) and Tandoc (2014) provide important exceptions.

With our focus on shifting the conversation about advancing production research beyond its largely journalistic focus of the past, we refrain from further speculation about how new forms of news might be more effectively investigated and invite the reader to delve into the chapters ahead and to allow these to inspire their own investigations.

The structure of this book

This opening section of the book is designed to provide an overview of challenges confronting production research, and the major debates concerning research into a fast-changing media industry. Following this introductory chapter by the editors, this section includes essays by Philip Schlesinger and by David Ryfe, two of the three principle speakers at the 2013 conference which is the foundation of this book. That one-day conference was simultaneously an International Association of Media and Communication Researchers (IAMCR) pre-conference and an International Communication Association (ICA) post-conference, held at the University of Leeds in June 2013, and it is further described on the Acknowledgements page which precedes this introduction.

Schlesinger's chapter is both an account of an 'ethnographic life', surveying how the field of media production studies has shifted considerably since his formative work in the 1970s (Schlesinger, 1978), as well as a timely reflection on the current structure of UK research funding – in particular, the Research Excellence Framework and the need to demonstrate 'impact' (and the effect that this is having on production studies). In Chapter 3, Ryfe self-reflexively examines the benefits and challenges of finding time to immerse oneself deeply in a media production culture in order to come to thoroughly understand the production setting and the change taking place within it. Chapter authors then address proposals for theoretical innovation and methodological innovation, in turn.

In the second part of the book, we have grouped chapters with a focus on how theory could more usefully inform and shape research into cultural production. Authors offer novel approaches to revealing the hidden nature of media and cultural production through engagement with alternative theoretical paradigms and through methodological innovation, and explore many – though certainly not all – emerging challenges to production research. In Part II, both Ida Willig (Chapter 4) and Tore Slaatta (Chapter 7) revisit the influential work of French sociologist Pierre Bourdieu in production studies. Willig, whose own ethnographic research on Danish journalism drew extensively from Bourdieu, provides a useful overview of the advantages of a field theory approach to understanding production and a useful catalogue of research which has been shaped by this approach.

In Chapter 5, veteran US journalism researcher Dan Berkowitz and co-author Zhengjia Liu discuss the advantages and trade-offs inherent in analysing media production through the texts it produces. In Chapter 6, Wilson Lowrey and Elina Erzikova contribute to the expanding field of news ecology research, considering the concept of 'population' as a way of thinking through the external and internal dynamics that shape media collectives in news ecosystems. The use of the term 'population' is intended to draw attention to the inner guiding logic that leads a media collective to act a particular way in the face of outside change. Drawing from a comparative study of two sets of media populations in the US and Russia, the aim is to gain a keener understanding of the dynamics between internal and external forces when trying to evaluate the changes and continuities of media production over time, suggesting a solution to the lack of historical specificity and a theorization of time that too often characterizes production research. In Chapter 7, Slaatta calls for the reincorporation of field theory and field analysis into production research, and a new programme that brings macro-level studies of production fields (involving quantitative research) alongside ethnographic studies of micro practices, a dual approach that Bourdieu himself advocated.

In Part III, authors shift the focus toward methodological innovation in production research, although several of their arguments resonate with those made in the preceding section, making clear the impossibility of separating research from theory. Astrid Gynnild begins the section, in Chapter 8, by revisiting the significance of grounded theory for her own ethnographic studies of journalism, arguing that it is a vital but often misunderstood tool for conceptualizing and undertaking research into media production environments. In Chapter 9, Hanne Bruun analyses the particularities of qualitative research interviews in media production research and discusses their implications for research questions and design. In Chapter 10, Michael Munnik examines the dilemma of ever decreasing access to newsrooms, with particular reference to British media organizations made anxious by public discussion of their roles in various scandals. His answer was to trade on his own professional capital to pry open those doors, echoing Paterson and Zoellner's (2010) survey of production researchers, suggesting the value of professional experience in gaining research access. In Chapter 11, Swiss researcher Daniel Perrin illustrates how progression analysis that includes 'computer-based workplace tracking' can help with making backstage production processes accessible for analysis.

Finally, in Part IV of the book we shift the focus 'beyond the newsroom' (while acknowledging that prior authors were not exclusively focused on news). In Chapter 12, Ana Alacovska argues for greater recognition of genre, and the genre-knowledge and perceptions of media producers in particular, as an active factor in production analyses. Willemien Sanders proposes, in Chapter 13, a method to better study the largely under-researched non-professional participants in media production, in particular, contributors in documentary programmes. And Frederik Lesage finally reminds us that cultural production extends to the computer software which most of us engage with daily, in Chapter 14. He uses the photo-editing software Adobe Photoshop as a case study, considering how classificatory orders within the field of software both enable and constrain creative practitioners. In his epilogue, C.W. Anderson offers the reader a final overview of these collected chapters and his own insights on 'advancing media production research'.

Whether the object of analysis is documentary production, software production, or news production, the editors have sought in this volume to bring together the latest thinking about the underlying theories and methods of exploration which promise to contribute to a richer analysis of all forms of information and cultural production. Our 'shared reality' (Berger and Luckman, 1966; Tuchman, 1978) is shaped by the production practices of media professionals and a wide range of other cultural producers, and it is impossible to comprehend the nature of that manufactured reality without getting to the heart of the manufacturing process and the shared culture of the manufacturers. Indeed, media scholars increasingly suggest that the mediatization of society affects all spheres of social life (Hjarvard, 2013), and all spheres of social life increasingly conform to a media logic. And it is in this context that we remarkably seem to know less and less about the conditions of media production, as rigorous production research allows.

This book is an effort to open up discussion of approaches which show promise in increasing our understanding of why our information and cultural space is the way it is. It is also an effort to unite scholars from disciplines which have not always communicated well with each other, despite a mutual focus on communication. In this book and in the conference which inspired it, scholars have joined together from journalism studies, cultural studies, and critical political economy/cultural industries research traditions. Our aim has been to create a dialogue between these approaches, underlining the value of an interdisciplinary and transnational approach to understanding how media and cultural production operates. Finally, we remind the reader that this collection of chapters springs (almost entirely) from one symposia (see the preceding Acknowledgements page for detail) and represents the editors' selection of presentations best suited to this collection. We have no ambition of describing the vast range of approaches to media production research, nor indeed to adequately describe the extent of innovation seeking to 'advance' our understanding and maintain a flow of data from the site of media production in the face of emerging obstacles. But it is in that context that we do hope this collection spurs a continuing conversation about advancing research into the production of culture and offers ideas and inspiration to the next generation of media production researchers.

Note

1. See, for example, the 'Creative Industries Mapping Document' created by the British Creative Industries Task Force in 1998 as one of the first systematic attempts to define and measure the economic value of the creative industries.

References

Allan, S. (2013) *Citizen Witnessing: Revisioning Journalism in Times of Crisis* (Malden, MA: John Wiley & Sons).
Altheide, D. (1976) *Creating Reality: How TV News Distorts Events* (Beverly Hills: Sage Publications).
Anderson, C. (2011) 'Between creative and quantified audiences: Web metrics and changing patterns of newswork in local US newsrooms.' *Journalism* 12(5), 550–566.
Banks, M. (2007) *The Politics of Cultural Work* (Basingstoke: Palgrave Macmillan).
Banks, M., Gill, R., and Taylor, S. (eds) (2013) *Theorizing Cultural Work: Labour, Continuity and Change in the Cultural and Creative Industries* (London: Routledge).
Bennett, J., Strange, N., Kerr, P. and Medrado, A. (2012) *Multiplatforming Public Service Broadcasting: The Economic and Cultural Role of UK Digital and TV Independents* (London: Royal Holloway, University of London).
Berger, P. L. and Luckman, T. (1966) *The Social Construction of Reality: A Treatise in the Sociology of Knowledge* (Garden City, NY: Anchor Books).
Blumler, J. G. (1969) 'Producers' attitudes towards television coverage of an election campaign: A case study' in P. Halmos (ed.), *The Sociology of Mass-Media Communicators* (*Sociological Review Monograph Series, Monograph 13*) (Keele: University of Keele).
Boczkowski, P. J. (2002). 'The development and use of online newspapers: What research tells us and what we might want to know' in L. A. Lievrouw and S. Livingstone (eds), *Handbook of New Media* (pp. 270–286) (London: Sage).
Boczkowski, P. J. (2004). Digitizing the News: Innovation in Online Newspapers (Cambridge, MA: MIT Press).
Burns, T. (1977) *The BBC: Public Institution and Private World*. London: Macmillan.
Cottle, S. (2000) 'New(s) times: Towards a "second wave" of news ethnography.' *European Journal of Communication Research* 25(1): 19–41.
D'acci, J. (1994) *Defining Women: Television and the Case of Cagney & Lacey* [online]. University of North Carolina Press.
Deuze, M. (2004) 'What is Multimedia Journalism?' *Journalism Studies* 5(2), 139–152.
Deuze, M. (2007) *Media Work* (Cambridge: Polity Press).
Domingo, D. (2005) The difficult shift from utopia to realism in the Internet era. A decade of online journalism research: theories, methodologies, results and challenges. Paper presented at the First European Communication Conference. Amsterdam. Retrieved from: http://www.racocatala.cat/dutopia/docs/domingo_amsterdam2005.pdf
Domingo, D. and Paterson, C. (eds) (2011) *Making Online News – Volume 2: Newsroom Ethnographies in the Second Decade of Internet Journalism* (New York: Peter Lang).

du Gay, P. and Pryke, M. (eds) (2002) *Cultural Economy: Cultural Analysis and Commercial Life* [online] (London; Thousand Oaks, CA; New Delhi: Sage.)

Elliott, P. (1972) *The Making of a Television Series: A Case Study in the Sociology of Culture* (London: Constable).

Epstein, E. (1974) *News from Nowhere* (New York: Vintage Books).

Frith, S. (1981) *Sound Effects: Youth, Leisure and the Politics of Rock* (London: Constable).

Gans, H. (1979) *Deciding What's News: A Study of CBS Evening News, NBC Nightly News, Newsweek, and Time* (New York: Pantheon).

Geertz, C. (1973) *Interpretation of Cultures* (New York: Basic Books).

Gill, R. (2011) 'Life is a pitch: Managing the self in new media work' in M. Deuze (ed.), *Managing Media Work* (pp. 249–262) (London: Sage).

Gill, R. and Pratt, A. (2008) 'In the social factory? Immaterial labour, precariousness and cultural work.' *Theory, Culture & Society*, 25(7–8), 1–30.

Gitlin, T. (1983) *Inside Prime Time* (New York: Pantheon Books).

Golding, P. and Elliott, P. (1979) *Making the News* (London: Longman).

Hartley, J. (ed.) (2005) *Creative Industries*. (Malden; Oxford; Victoria: Wiley-Blackwell).

Havens, T. (2014) 'Media industry sociology: Mainstream, critical, and cultural perspectives' in S. Waisbord (ed.), *Media Sociology: A Reappraisal* (pp. 98–113) (Cambridge; Malden, MA: Polity Press).

Havens, T., Lotz, A. D., and Tinic, S. (2009) 'Critical media industry studies: A research approach.' *Communication, Culture & Critique* 2(2), 234–253.

Hermida, A. (2010) 'From TV to Twitter: How ambient news became ambient journalism.' *Media/Culture Journal* 13(2).

Hesmondhalgh, D. (2009) 'Politics, theory and method in media industries research' in J. Holt and A. Perren (eds), *Media Industries: History, Theory, Method* [online] (Malden, MA; Oxford: Blackwell Publishing).

Hesmondhalgh, D. (2010) 'Media industry studies, media production studies' in J. Curran (ed.), *Media and Society* (pp. 145–163) (London; New York: Bloomsbury).

Hesmondhalgh, D. (2013) *The Cultural Industries*, 3rd ed. (London: Sage).

Hesmondhalgh, D. and Baker, S. (2011) *Creative Labour: Media Work in Three Cultural Industries* (London: Routledge).

Hjarvard, S. (2013) *The Mediatization of Culture and Society* (New York: Routledge).

Hochschild, A. R. (2003) *The Managed Heart: Commercialization of Human Feeling, with a New Afterword* (University of California Press).

Jerolmack, C. and Khan, S. (2014) 'Talk is cheap: Ethnography and the attitudinal fallacy.' *Sociological Methods & Research* 43(2), 178–209.

Johnson, D., Kompare, D., and Santo, A. (eds) (2014) *Making Media Work: Cultures of Management in the Entertainment Industries* (New York; London: New York University Press).

Kopper, G., Kolthoff, A., and Czepek, A. (2000) 'Online journalism: A report on current and continuing research and major questions in the international discussion.' *Journalism* Studies, 2(1), 499–512.

Leveson, L. J. B. H. L. (2012) An Inquiry into the Culture, Practices and Ethics of the Press: Executive Summary and Recommendations [Leveson Report]. The Stationery Office.

Mayer, V. (2011) *Below the Line: Producers and Production Studies in the New Television Economy* (Durham: Duke University Press).

Mayer, V., Banks, M. J., and Caldwell, J. T. (eds) (2009) *Production Studies: Cultural Studies of Media Industries* (London: Routledge).

McRobbie, A. (2002a) 'Clubs to companies: Notes on the decline of political culture in speeded up creative worlds.' *Cultural Studies, 16*(4), 516–531.

McRobbie, A. (2002b) 'From Holloway to Hollywood: happiness at work in the new cultural economy' in P. du Gay and M. Pryke (eds) *Cultural Economy* (pp. 87–114) (London: SAGE).

Moran, A., with Malbon, J. (2006) *Understanding the Global TV Format* (Bristol; Portland: Intellect).

Nash, K. (2012) 'Modes of interactivity: Analysing the webdoc.' *Media, Culture & Society 34*(2), 195–210.

Negus, K. (1992) *Producing Pop* (London: Edward Arnold).

Negus, K. (1997) 'The production of culture' in P. du Gay (ed.) *Production of Culture/Cultures of Production* (pp. 67–118) (London; Thousand Oaks, CA: Sage, in association with the Open University).

Paterson, C. (2011) *The International Television News Agencies: The World from London* (New York: Peter Lang).

Paterson, C. and Domingo, D. (2008) *Making Online News: The Ethnography of New Media Production* (New York: Peter Lang).

Paterson, C. and Zoellner, A. (2010) 'The efficacy of professional experience in the ethnographic investigation of production.' *Journal of Media Practice 11*(2), 97–109.

Ryfe, D. M. (2012). *Can Journalism Survive: An Inside Look at American Newsrooms* (Malden, MA; Cambridge: Polity Press).

Saha, A. (2012) 'Beards, scarves, halal meat, terrorists, forced marriage: television industries and the production of "race".' *Media, Culture & Society 34*(4), 424–438.

Schlesinger, P. (1978) *Putting 'Reality' Together: BBC News* (London: Constable).

Schlesinger, P. (1980) 'Between sociology and journalism' in H. Christian (ed.), *Sociology of Journalism and the Press* (pp. 341–369) (Keele: Univ. of Keele).

Schlesinger, P. and Tumber, H. (1994) *Reporting Crime: The Media Politics of Criminal Justice* (Oxford: Clarendon Press).

Sørensen, I. (2012) 'Crowdsourcing and outsourcing: The impact of online funding and distribution on the documentary film industry in the UK.' *Media, Culture & Society 34*(6), 726–743.

Steemers, J. (2004) *Selling Television: British Television in the Global Marketplace* (London: BFI).

Tandoc, E. C. (2014) 'Journalism is twerking? How web analytics is changing the process of gatekeeping.' *New Media & Society 16*(4), 559–575.

Tuchman, G. (1978) *Making News: A study in the Social Construction of Reality* (London: The Free Press).

Tunstall, J. (1971) *Journalists at Work: Specialist Correspondents, Their News Organizations, News Sources, and Competitor-Colleagues* (London: Constable).

Ursell, G. (2000) 'Television production: Issues of exploitation, commodification and subjectivity in UK television labour markets.' *Media, Culture & Society 22*(6), 805–825.

Usher, N. (2013) 'Al Jazeera English online: Understanding web metrics and news production when a quantified audience is not a commodified audience.' *Digital Journalism, 1*(3), 335–351.

Usher, N. (2014) *Making News at the New York Times* (Ann Arbor: University of Michigan Press).

Williams, R. (1973) 'Base and superstructure in Marxist cultural theory.' *New Left Review*, 82, 3–16.

Willig, I. (2013) 'Newsroom ethnography in a field perspective.' *Journalism 14*(3), 372–387.

2
On the Vagaries of Production Research

Philip Schlesinger

The editors of this volume have asked me to undertake a brief stock-taking: to reflect on my experience of undertaking production research of various kinds in the media and cultural fields since the early 1970s. I shall begin by discussing my earliest research and then – covering intervening decades – consider examples of other projects pertinent to the concerns of this book, as well as changes in how the role of the researcher has been conceived and enacted. This essay is intended to be exploratory rather than comprehensive – a first pass at an argument. If this text seems to be unduly self-referential, my apologies, but that goes with the territory I have been asked to traverse.

A beginning

My first deep – and enduring – professional formation was in ethnographic sociology, when I undertook a long-term study of journalism – between 1971 and 1976 – at the BBC, initially for my doctorate and then with a follow-up period for my book, *Putting 'Reality' Together* (Schlesinger, 1978). That volume was about the daily round of BBC journalism, the beliefs and practices that sustained it, the ways in which news production was controlled and enabled, and the pressures that its producers faced. I then regarded that study – and still do – as an exercise in the sociology of knowledge, and that has been a keystone for subsequent work.[1] To judge by continuing citations and occasional correspondence from students, my first work still has some life left in it (if only to be critiqued), despite momentous changes in the media and communications landscape and the refocusing of academic research since the 1970s.

When I began my project, the then tiny cohort of British media sociologists was deeply influenced both by key examples of fieldwork inside US network broadcasting organizations and, at the same time, rapidly developing an indigenous tradition of its own.[2] Not all production studies undertaken at that time focused on journalism. Although the news was undoubtedly the central object of study, there was also novel observational work on current affairs, documentary, and film production.[3]

What began originally as a markedly Anglo-American venture, driven by a desire to demystify the socially central definitional powers of network news and to unpick its legitimations – notably occupational claims to objectivity and impartiality – has subsequently multiplied adherents, significantly shifted its objects of study, and greatly widened its geographical reach, as this volume amply testifies.

I am intrigued by the curious view that the so-called 'first wave' of media ethnographies eventually became an orthodox trammel on research, requiring a 'second wave' in order to think matters through afresh. It is self-evident that news production has greatly changed in the digital age, when the boundaries of journalism have become increasingly unsettled and contested, as has the institutional form of newspapers and broadcasting. There is now more complexity due to innovations resulting from the introduction of digital technologies, and obvious disruption of established patterns of temporality and the production cycles that went with these. So it goes without saying that a new approach is required to analyse the world as we now find it.

The work that I undertook, along with others at the time, was certainly conducted under more stable conditions in a more easily decipherable media environment than today's. Once its particularity is recognized, and the prevailing conditions that gave it anchorage identified, it is hard to see why these should be regarded as imposing an obstacle to successor work, or why the insights garnered should be discarded, rather than providing a basis for a critical reworking and, where there is still analytical purchase, adaptation to present circumstance. Indeed, making a broader case for a revival of media sociology in general, Howard Tumber (2014: 75) has recently argued that any contemporary

> revision of sociological definitions and frameworks for media analysis should also consider existing continuities in the way that news organizations operate and interact with other institutions such as private companies, governments and lobbies. In the requirement to include the use of new technologies, actors, and the configuration of roles, media researchers should not forget that there are several continuities in the way that news production is funded, influenced and validated.

For sure, the conditions of media production, distribution and consumption have changed radically as we live in the moment of mobile connectivity, user-generated content and social media. Such transformations do pose new challenges for research, not least in terms of how to address technological developments, changed political and economic contexts, and new organizational and occupational forms (Waisbord, 2014). That said, in the field of journalism, for instance, carefully weighed continuities with previous research are evident in some current studies, with suitable adjustments made to scope and method without therefore needing to argue for a radical break (Puijk, 2008; Willig, 2013). In this vein, for instance, I would argue that a focus on contemporary management strategies devised to address the impact of digitization on the newspaper is perfectly complementary to the continuing need to understand present-day processes of news production (Schlesinger and Doyle, 2015).[4]

But the issue is more fundamental than a matter of adapting research methods to new conditions or the complexity that results from the transformative effects of technological change. The acid test concerns the questions that we think are worth posing. Media production research is but one quite specialized line of inquiry in media research in general. Then, as now, 'first wave' concerns were of a piece with those of others working in the field. Researchers wanted to examine the nature of media power – how decision-making was mediated through organizations – to demystify claims to professionalism and objectivity made by journalists, to show how the market for news was structured and what its outcomes were. While some of the best-known work was conducted in public service or regulated organizations, questions concerning ownership and control, political and other influence, social conflicts and the reproduction of consensual ideologies were all part of the wider agenda in which production studies were conducted. The list is far from exhaustive. Have these kinds of issue suddenly become irrelevant? If we take just one key issue – the exercise of power and its control – the answer is a resounding no. Plainly, this is a continuing concern from a range of perspectives, and still at the heart of much contemporary media research (Castells, 2009; Davis, 2007; Freedman, 2014).

Beyond how research is framed, a different question that we need to address anew concerns the role of the academic researcher. In the UK, at least, the conditions under which we undertake research have begun to change quite radically. Writing this essay in 2015, it is striking how expectations about the public role played by academic researchers are being profoundly redefined. In Britain, often the precursor in these matters, the present sea change has been driven by systems of official accountability that are reshaping academic norms. The Research Excellence Framework (REF), installed at the UK government's behest by the various higher education Funding Councils, the results of which were reported at the end of 2014, has begun to implant a culture in which thinking of the 'impact' of research 'beyond academia' is now part and parcel of our working practices and career structures. This focus is not by any means totally new. But what is different is that it is becoming a general condition, beyond being a requirement restricted to those who have had to design their 'pathways to impact' when applying for a Research Council grant.

In the UK certainly, but also elsewhere, the present imperatives have propelled us into demonstrating publicly that we undertake 'knowledge exchange' with those that we research, and to show that we can exact some extra-academic impact by accounting for the value of our research. Taken together, such approaches are transforming the normative foundations of academic work. And they make considerable demands on our reflexivity as we negotiate funding and, if successful, how we seek to pursue the work that we really wish to undertake.

At one level, imparting what we have discovered to wider publics is quite unexceptionable and indeed desirable. And trying to influence or transform a debate or a condition is a laudable aspiration. It is what you would expect of any intellectual or scientific endeavour. However, I am opposed to the coercive aspects of this new regime and think we need to defend the maximum autonomy feasible. There is a moral and political difference between opting to be a citizen-academic and being compelled to be one. In short, it is important to be alert to the undoubtedly perverse effects of the present commanding heights approach to managing the norms and values of academic research. The logic is that of accounting; the cover story is that we are all to become public intellectuals.

Those who can readily recall how expectations have shifted within the lifespan of a career, or just part of one, even when working in institutions that have been far from privileged, do have a role to play. One easy response, of course, is to quit the scene in disgust amidst well-publicized recriminations. Another is to try to develop resilient cultures, which sustain the continuing value and importance of the academic freedom to think, to produce, and to pursue a project that matters. These ideals have always been qualified in practice, and much depends on where you work, the resources available, and the openness of the local regime. But even if more honoured in the breach than the observance, the value of academic freedom and its supporting norms have a crucial constitutive role in imagining what it is to be an academic, providing both ideological armour and a point of contrast with the imperatives of the system as presently constituted. Increasingly, therefore, the challenge is to identify what is positive in the new research order and to make it our own in ways of our own devising, as it cannot be avoided.[5]

While the idea of some engagement in the wider policy process was hardly alien when I undertook my first research, I cannot but be struck by the distance travelled as we have finally entered REF-land to receive the new tablets of stone. My study of the BBC was in many respects typical of a truly different moment, as I consciously eschewed the discourse of improvement for that of critique, in ways that I now consider rather naïve, as I quickly discovered that critique has its own force and may propel you to where you do not expect to be. In an article written at that time reflecting on my fieldwork, I underlined the difference between my approach and that of Elihu Katz who, along with others at that moment, was working in the Lazarsfeldian tradition of contributing to policy formation at the BBC (Schlesinger, 1980).

In retrospect, it is clear that I did not anticipate some consequences of my research. They were not great, but they were certainly professionally significant for me. First, my analysis of the BBC's coverage of the violent conflict in Northern Ireland – then a highly contentious topic – was taken up by the campaign against censorship in broadcasting. Second, after an initially cool reception, my book became part of the common sense of a new generation of journalists at the BBC. Following a decent interval, for instance, I was invited to contribute to an internal review of industrial news and current affairs reporting. Third, I found that I had acquired the aura of expertise, which led to some broadcast interviews and appearances and occasional journalism. None of this – as it would be now – was part of a calculus about the impact of research; it just happened.

The distinction between 'critical' and 'administrative' approaches outlined by Lazarsfeld (1941), still a live reference point at the time, was certainly not absolute among media researchers in the 1970s and early 1980s – and remains pertinent today. For instance, academics in the field (myself included) did engage in debate with broadcasters, regulators, and politicians about matters of public policy when the first such encounters began to be increasingly common.[6] Some contributed research to parliamentary enquiries into the ownership and regulation of the press. By the early 1980s, left-orientated cultural policy advice and cultural industries consultancy had become fashionable and quite established. So, too, had conducting broadcasting research intended to be credible to the industry from outside the academy as well as at arm's length from the broadcasters' own research departments.[7] By then, however, the 'first wave' of production studies had largely passed into history.

Some later work

In retrospect, I am struck by the extraordinary privilege of being able to conduct a solo ethnography. In what has been a busy career, the opportunity to do so again has so far not arisen. One – very recent – attempt to gain access for an ethnography of a performing arts institution of world class met with an eventual no, as, after a lengthy interrogation by a fist of executives and then a request to read my work, they finally took fright at the risk of letting me in. There's one for the chapbook of refusals.

There is doubtless a broader lesson here and an imperfect generalization. As your career progresses, if it does, and life makes ever more complex demands on your time, pursuing a long-form solo ethnography becomes ever more difficult, unless you manage to secure a fellowship to finance time out, or take leave. My most common practice – paralleled by that of colleagues and contemporaries – has long involved a well-defined division of labour in research teams in line with the funding economy's rules of the game. A principal investigator (PI), co-investigator(s) (CI), and postdoctoral research associate(s) (PDRA) are the personnel that now make up most British teams. Seniority, as I know too well, takes one increasingly towards project management and often blocks your working on the most interesting aspects of front-line research. In countervailing mode, whatever the difficulty, I have made it a rule to undertake interviews and, where possible, to pursue some distinctive line of observation in any major fieldwork project that I have led.

Production research on culture and media commonly involves several methods. The most privileged, of course, is observation – the researcher being present in the settings to be investigated. Where feasible, this is generally coupled with interviewing and also the gathering of documentation and other artifacts that conduce to the further understanding of the production process and the constitutive social relations in play. Since my first work on the BBC, funded by the Social Science Research Council, all the research discussed here has been funded by either the Arts and Humanities Research Council (AHRC) or the Economic and Social Research Council (ESRC) and has been collaborative in the ways outlined. Sometimes, happily, it has involved a genuinely ethnographic dimension – access to a setting and repeated exposure to internal discourse and action.

We do need to be cautious what we claim here. Sociologist Paul Atkinson, in a recent distillation of his decades of practice and reflection, proposed that ethnography 'involves some degree of direct participation and observation [that] constitutes a radically distinctive way of understanding social activity in situ' (Atkinson, 2015: 3–4). That presupposes some significant exposure to a given setting or settings. In part, this is about time spent in a particular way; but it is also signally about what insights such access may afford that are simply unavailable in any other way.

To indicate both continuity and change in the trajectory of my work, I shall next briefly discuss two studies involving teamwork. These contrast greatly with my work on the BBC, which focused principally on the internal workings of the news operation of a single organization, then as now, enormously central to British life. Of course, although the wider political and economic contexts were crucial to making that account comprehensible, most analysis was of what Tom Burns (1977), in his penetrating work, aptly called the private world of a public institution.

The two cases in question were conducted in well-defined milieux. They also investigated the relations between specific institutions and organizations and various networks of actors in full pursuit of their diverse interests. In this, they reflect a given stage in the further development of production studies whose particularity has perhaps not been fully recognized and discussed. Much 'second wave' analysis has been a response to technology-generated complexity in the media field. Well before this, however, immanent developments were occurring in the field, reflected in the projects next discussed. Each involved a division of labour, along the lines indicated, that combined observation, interviewing, the collection of documentation, and analyses of media output.

Reporting Crime (Schlesinger and Tumber, 1994) was a study of the media politics of crime journalism.[8] With most research undertaken in London, it analysed diverse interactions between policy-makers, pressure groups, criminal justice professionals, and specialist reporters in shaping crime news; fieldwork was mainly conducted between 1986 and 1988, with some later follow-ups. The players were the police in several major cities, the Home Office (then the sole UK government department dealing with criminal justice), legal and civil liberty bodies, media organizations, and numerous others, all integral to the process of shaping the production of news because of how their fields of activity intersected.

By stepping out of the workings of any particular organization and its production of news, this work deliberately eschewed media-centrism: it insisted on the importance of sources' relations to journalists and focused on how they used the various resources at their disposal in pursuit of their media strategies.[9] The resulting relational perspective on transactions between media and sources, for some time at least, proved to be quite influential in informing subsequent research. Without our then knowing it, this approach to 'promotional culture' (Wernick, 1991) in some respects anticipated the more complex world of content production beyond institutional journalism that now characterizes the Internet age, in which the role of sources continues to be a matter of debate (Franklin and Carlson, 2011). Some of this research was disseminated by way of presentations and accessible articles to non-academic audiences, and evidence was also given to the Home Office's Working Group on the Fear of Crime, which reported in 1989.

Open Scotland? (Schlesinger, Miller and Dinan, 2001) had a more expressly interventionist aim. It investigated the initial post-devolution moment, when a new political communication system was being set up in Edinburgh. It drew substantially on theories of nationalism and also built on the rethinking of media-centrism already alluded to.[10] In this respect, the study depicted the interaction between journalists, spin doctors and lobbyists whose communication strategies were addressed to the new parliament; fieldwork was conducted between 1999 and 2000.[11] This was a formative moment in Scotland, and the new parliament and government and the political space afforded have been a precondition for the still unresolved debate over independence v. devolution that has followed and has impacted hugely on British politics.

We undertook some observational research, in my own case inside the expert panel that was drafting the rules for media coverage of the new body, including parliamentary TV, which was a meeting point and locus for negotiation for officials and competing media interests. It was a ringside seat at the writing of one part of the material constitution. As much as showing how different actors were readying either to cover politics, manage government communications, or lobby for specific interests, this was also a study of the collective production of a new space.

Open Scotland? investigated the construction of the new political communication system in its initial phase and provided a critique of some early failures to live up to new ideals. It achieved some thoughtful coverage in both the UK and Scottish press. The study was a platform for the research team's evidence to the Scottish Parliament, notably about how lobbying might be regulated and conducted in a more transparent fashion. One unexpected consequence was an invitation by the Presiding Officer of the Scottish Parliament for me to lead a confidential audit of the new legislature's communication strategies. Advice was being sought on how best to proceed at a time when, after various early scandals, the Scottish Parliament's reputation was faring particularly badly. *Open Scotland?*, then, analysed a foundational moment and made a contribution to debate in the public domain, as well as leading to some private influence. At a personal level, this work reflected my own civic engagement in, and commitment to Scotland, which continues.[12]

Some current work

The third project that I wish to discuss has involved a sequence of studies of diverse but interconnected aspects of the so-called creative economy, which is still a work in progress. With fieldwork located both in London and Scotland, in some respects this research has been framed by post-devolution changes in the UK's political geography since 1999 and the strains imposed on the British state by an increasingly outmoded constitution.

Should this work classify as a production study? It should, if we shift attention from media and cultural production proper to some of its preconditions. The focus in this work has been the production of the know-how embodied in organizations set up to intervene in the creative economy. Such investigations, once again, fall under the sociology of knowledge.

Rather than being a single piece of work on the model of the three projects already discussed, however, this line of inquiry has taken the serial form of distinct studies that have involved different collaborations and kinds of fieldwork. Nonetheless, these have built on a longer-term guiding interest, shaped by shifting opportunities both in funding and in the access afforded by various bodies and actors. Once again, at times, this work has involved me – and my collaborators – in engagement beyond the academy, as the opportunity to influence policy debate or industry thinking has arisen.

In retrospect, I now see that what has become a personal programme of work began quite routinely in 2003 with an invitation to run a specialist seminar on the creative industries for the ESRC and the Office of Science and Technology, a government body; a further such meeting was requested in 2005.[13] These events involved bringing together policy-makers, industry figures, and academics with an interest, on the first occasion, in the disruptive role of digital technologies and, on the second, in the exploitation of intellectual property – issues that are both staple policy concerns. The role in which I was cast (already extremely familiar) was that of brokerage and reportage.

The official interest piqued my own and led in the first instance to asking why the creative industries had become such a focus of policy. That led, by degrees, to a study of creative industries policy-making, with a focus on the BBC as well as the leading film agency at that time, the UK Film Council (UKFC).[14] The idea was to see whether top-down policy-making in the UK government, and the then frenetic production of creativity discourse, had worked its way through two quite different bodies seen as linchpins of the creative economy: the BBC, both a major media production house and central cultural institution, and the UKFC, a key new intermediary for film policy (Magor and Schlesinger, 2009; Schlesinger, 2007; Schlesinger, 2010). This work re-ignited my earlier interest in the role of policy intellectuals, resulting in a study of creative economy ideas brokers, underpinned by a series of interviews (Schlesinger, 2009).[15]

Over more than a decade, this run of research has been interspersed with regular policy-orientated interventions. One of these involved devising a series of seminars at the behest of the Scottish Arts Council and the Scottish Executive (later, the Scottish Government) in 2007. These events were intended to offer a systematic take on the state of Scotland's creative industries in order to inform the process of setting up Creative Scotland, the new lead national agency for the arts and creative industries ultimately established in 2010. The project concluded with a paper for, and briefing of, the pro tem board of the new body.[16]

Since then, much of my empirical research has focused one way or another on related themes, including fieldwork on creative work and copyright (Schlesinger and Waelde, 2010; Waelde and Schlesinger, 2009). Most recently, it has involved two further organizational studies. Each of these projects addressed the question of how cultural intermediaries operate within the framework of creative industries policies. The studies also considered the distinct institutional landscapes within which creative economy support bodies operate in the UK and Scotland. These projects have been conceived relationally. This has involved considering how each agency has been connected with its clientele, its political masters and funders, and a range of enterprises of diverse scales, as well as the broader currents of fashionable thought about what constitutes relevant know-how for intervening in, and building, a competitive creative economy.

The first, *The Rise and Fall of the UK Film Council* (Doyle, Schlesinger, Boyle and Kelly, 2015), investigated the decade-long life of Britain's lead film agency, which was set up to ensure the 'sustainability' of Britain's film industry.[17] Both the creation and destruction of the UKFC raised far-reaching questions about the rationality of film policy, which has been passed like a parcel between the political parties. It also queried the realism of official aspirations for the UK film industry on the global stage. In many ways, film policy, with its constant oscillation between cultural and economic goals, has been the model for the wider cross-party creative industries policies now in place. As an institutional invention – dismantled in a mere decade – the UKFC belongs in a near century-long history of intervention in the film sector by all governments. It is clear that the longevity of any agency is quite an achievement. Inevitably, there was a political dimension: created by a British Labour government in 2000, the decision to close the UKFC in 2010 was taken by Conservative ministers (in a coalition government with the Liberal Democrats).

This work was based on interviews with most key dramatis personae, supported by such internal documentation as could be unearthed. My prior research on the UKFC, undertaken when it was still a going concern, helped frame a new agenda after its demise, also providing a baseline for comparison with interviews conducted previously. Thus far, the research has been relayed to key industry figures; while arguing with some interpretations, they have not doubted the credibility of the findings. Whether the lessons for taking a longer-term view of film support will be taken up in policy-making circles (a faint hope) remains to be seen.

The second study of this pair, *Curators of Cultural Enterprise*, which exceptionally afforded almost unqualified access for research, was based on ethnographic teamwork in 2013–2014 (Schlesinger, Selfe and Munro, 2015a, b). It focused on a small Scottish agency called Cultural Enterprise Office (CEO), a provider of business support to cultural microbusinesses, which are mostly precarious enterprises. The research team was able to observe routine office activity, attend meetings between creative clients and CEO advisers, discuss strategy with the board and executives, and have access to the organization's database. But, rather like the UKFC, although much smaller, CEO also proved to be vulnerable to the capricious winds of change. The departure, while we were writing up our analysis, of CEO's chair of the board, and then its director, meant that this research occurred under sometimes quite volatile conditions, requiring considerable delicacy and finely honed ethical judgements about confidentiality. These two leading figures left for reasons to do with overall creative economy policy in Scotland and the organization's adverse funding settlement.

Of all the research discussed so far, *Curators of Cultural Enterprise* was unquestionably a product of the new research order, being designated a 'creative economy knowledge exchange' project in an AHRC programme.

This did not affect the principal aim, which was to undertake in-depth research into the work of a cultural intermediary.[18] But it did create at least two major complications.

First, we had to learn how to manage the regular presentation of work in progress to the staff of CEO, as sometimes this held up a challenging mirror to their practices and beliefs; the reactions, positive and negative, shaped the next phase of fieldwork. In this connection, and in keeping with the usual need to seek legitimacy during fieldwork, the role of academic analyst as opposed to the more usual one of consultant needed to be explained, as did the time cycle of even a relatively quick-fire project (funded for one year) such as this. Consultants are paid to work for the client, which limits the extent to which they can detach themselves from their brief. Academics, with a source of funding independent of the body being studied – even where knowledge exchange is central to the remit – have scope to raise fundamental questions about their objects of study. Crucially, then, there is a structural difference in how the roles may be conceived and performed.

Secondly, another key practical issue is how to manage the considerable effort involved in effective knowledge exchange, given its impact on the time budget of empirical research. Preparation for meetings, the running of formally structured feedback sessions, and the incorporation of what is freshly discovered through discussion into the main research process, all take time and demand attention. Our project was not adequately funded to take account of this extra commitment, and we had to seek other resources to extend it. As this kind of approach to research grows in importance, funders will need to recognize that they are asking for more, and pay for it.

Concluding thoughts

Writing this essay in the UK at the start of a new phase of the REF, it is hard to ignore the fact that achieving 'impact' for one's research beyond academia will be the order of the day. Fortune may smile on those few British academics undertaking production studies under the new dispensation. Characteristically, such work involves interaction with cultural and media organizations, policy communities, and those engaged in creative labour. Production researchers selected by their institutions to write 'impact case studies' might well have a story to tell about how their research has affected the extra-academic world. The empirical warp and weft of such studies puts them in the right place for that kind of treatment.

The cultural change faced by all researchers – desired by the creators of the new system – is the requirement to design 'impact' into the research process from the very start. As it happens, we really cannot know, in advance, how such an approach will work out. There is certainly no interest in our recounting negative impacts, such as a rejection of advice, or the collapse of a body that you are researching, or failing to have any discernible effect on practices because that wasn't the name of the game. In short, telling a good story is not guaranteed, but those undertaking production studies are at least better placed to do so than many others.

As the wider cultural economy has undergone profound transformations in respect of production, distribution, and consumption, the once singular tradition of media production research – now dignified, or discarded, as the 'first wave' – has rightly needed to be rethought. So, for instance, diverse forms of media work that might earlier have been compartmentalized have become an integral part of wider analyses of cultural labour (Deuze, 2007; Hesmondhalgh and Baker, 2011). In arriving at this point, however, much academic research now has to negotiate with a creative economy discourse that has a global purchase as an embedded belief-system for policy-makers and the gamut of experts (academics included) that constitute the relevant epistemic communities. It has become a major focus for the UK Research Councils, which have funded a number of knowledge exchange 'hubs', research centres, and programmes to address the linked themes of the creative economy, digitization, cultural value and intellectual property.

This framing of the field, so evidently driven by the political imperative of supporting the national economy in the context of global competition, has engendered two basic responses in the academic world, which I shall simplify as follows. On the one hand, there are the endorsers, who work enthusiastically within the terms of the discourse, treating the creative economy as real. They take their place among the major developers of its lexicon and pursue the further institutionalization of research on the topic – which has become a major topic for textbook treatment and teaching, not least at postgraduate level.

And then there are the dissenters, who are inclined to deconstruct and disaggregate the constitutive parts of the creative economy into a range of cultural practices, critique the discourse as mystifying, and stand back from the policy imperatives, which for them are objects of analysis rather than articles of faith. The price is to be largely ignored outside academic debate and sometimes within it. Of course, in reality the line-up is more complex.[19] Critics pitching for support need to marshal their tropes adeptly to cross the threshold of credibility.

So far as access goes, along with my various colleagues on the projects discussed, I have been very fortunate in securing permission to interview, observe and gather documentation for a wide range of studies. This has not been effortless by any means, but closed doors have been the exception. Along with such obvious factors for engaging in successful fieldwork as the researcher's reputation and capacity for rapport and trustworthiness, in today's no-hiding-place cyberspace our easily accessible profiles are increasingly important in establishing the bona fides sought by those who control access. That said, personal connections, or helpful brokers who know those who need to be known, still seem to be indispensible to opening doors and crossing thresholds, and they will remain crucially important for those conducting future production studies.

Acknowledgement

As this essay draws on reflections provoked by my most recent research, I gratefully acknowledge the support of the UK Arts and Humanities Research Council for 'The UK Film Council: A study of film policy in transition' (AH/J000457X/1) and 'Supporting creative business: Cultural Enterprise Office and its clients' (AH/K002570/1) as well as the UK Economic and Social Research Council for 'Multi-platform media and the digital challenge: Strategy, distribution and policy' (ES/J011606/1).

Notes

This chapter picks up from and greatly enlarges on aspects of my presentation at the 'Advancing Media Production Research' conference, University of Leeds, 24 June 2013.

1. Karl Mannheim's work on intellectuals was used in analysing the BBC's doctrine of impartiality, and the wide influence of Peter Berger and Thomas Luckmann's social constructionism is evident from titles of works on news published at the time.
2. Epstein (1973), Altheide (1976), Tuchman (1978), and Gans (1979) were all key points of reference from across the pond. Back home, Tunstall (1971), Blumler (1969), Halloran, Elliott and Murdock (1970), and Golding and Elliott (1979) were important contemporary influences.
3. See Elliott (1972); Tracey (1978); Alvarado and Stewart (1985); Silverstone (1985).
4. This argument derives from a project on multiplatform media and the digital challenge, with Gillian Doyle PI, Philip Schlesinger CI, and Katherine Champion PDRA.

5. This is a complex topic and takes me well beyond the confines of this essay. I have touched on it elsewhere in Schlesinger (2013) and Schlesinger, Selfe and Munro (2015b). In approaches taken to the REF, and its long-running predecessor, the Research Assessment Exercise (RAE), there has always been a tension between true believers and sceptics, even among the administrators of the system. The sceptics have included both vocal opponents and quiet subversives. Whether scope for academic freedom will be further eclipsed or marginalized in any given place depends on people's contracts, institutional tradition, collegiality and the work regime in play. Those who know the history of the stages by which we have arrived at where we are now do need to mentor new generations of researchers both to cope with present demands and simultaneously to help them recognize that the obligation to conform to performance criteria does not means that the real is the ideal.
6. The Broadcasting Symposia at the University of Manchester, urbanely conducted by George Wedell, now largely lost to memory, were an important forum at the time.
7. I am thinking here of several media academics' contributions to the Third Royal Commission on the Press, which reported in 1977; the setting up of Comedia, both as a publisher and a consultancy, in 1978, whose founder, Charles Landry, later became a guru of the creative economy; and of the policy research in 1983 on cultural industries for the Greater London Council by Nicholas Garnham. The setting up of the Broadcasting Research Unit in the early 1980s, under Michael Tracey, housed at the British Film Institute, was a significant forerunner of later developments in centres and institutes both within and outside academia. Cultural policy analysis – as distinct from cultural studies – developed shortly thereafter (Bennett, 2007) and it has played into creative economy thinking.
8. Howard Tumber was research fellow, Graham Murdock CI, and Alison Anderson RA.
9. Pierre Bourdieu's work, flexibly adapted, influenced how the various fields and actors in this study were conceptualized as did a critique of Stuart Hall's approach to 'primary definition'.
10. Among many others, the work of Karl Deutsch, Ernest Gellner, Benedict Anderson, and Tom Nairn was influential.
11. David Miller was CI and William Dinan RA.
12. Committee work has been the default route. From 1997–2004, I was appointed to the Board of Scottish Screen, the national moving image agency, and was also a Trustee of TRC Media (originally the Research Centre for Television and Interactivity), a charitable body involved in developing independent TV producers' businesses, from 1998–2008. In 2004, I was appointed to the UK communications regulator Ofcom's Advisory Committee for Scotland (ACS), which I then chaired from 2009–2014, with an ex officio seat on Ofcom's Nations Committee. I still sit on the ACS, as member for Scotland of Ofcom's Content Board, which has a UK-wide regulatory remit. Of course, what is learned in such contexts deeply affects your understanding of the inner life of institutions and has a major influence on your thinking.
13. Richard Paterson co-directed these seminars with me.
14. Simon Frith and Richard Paterson were CIs, with Pille Petersoo, then Maggie Magor as PDRAs, and Lynne Hibberd as linked PhD.

15. Inter alia, my earlier work had discussed intellectuals and political violence as well as the Cold War (Schlesinger, 1991).
16. Raymond Boyle, Maggie Magor, and Lynne Hibberd also worked on this project. The briefing given to the board fell on deaf ears, but that's another story.
17. Gillian Doyle was PI, Raymond Boyle and Philip Schlesinger CIs, and Lisa Kelly PDRA.
18. There is a wider issue here: the framing and provenance of research funding by no means determines all the outcomes. How to manage the gap between framing and finding is a key skill needed in the new research order, but it is certainly not a new one. Melanie Selfe was CI and Ealasaid Munro PDRA.
19. I am aware of the irony of my own position, as a sceptical deputy director of the RCUK Centre for Copyright and New Business Models in the Creative Economy.

References

Altheide, D. L. (1976) *Creating Reality: How TV News Distorts Events* (Beverly Hills: Sage Publications).

Alvarado, M. and Stewart, J. (1985) *Made for Television: Euston Films Ltd.* (London: British Film Institute).

Atkinson, P. (2015) *For Ethnography* (London: Sage Publications).

Bennett, T. (2007) *Critical Trajectories: Culture, Society, Intellectuals* (Malden, MA: Blackwell Publishing).

Blumler, J. G. (1969) 'Producers' attitudes towards television coverage of an election campaign: A case study' in P. Halmos (ed.), *The Sociology of Mass-Media Communicators (The Sociological Review Series, Monograph 13)* (pp. 85–115) (Keele: University of Keele).

Burns, T. (1977) *The BBC: Public Institution and Private World* (London: Macmillan).

Castells, M. (2009) *Communication Power* (Oxford: Oxford University Press).

Davis, A. (2007) *The Mediation of Power: A Critical Introduction* (London and New York: Routledge).

Deuze, M. (2007) *Media Work* (Cambridge: Polity Press).

Doyle, G., Schlesinger, P., Boyle, R., and Kelly, L. W. (2015) *The Rise and Fall of the UK Film Council* (Edinburgh: Edinburgh University Press).

Elliott, P. (1972) *The Making of a Television Series: A Case Study in the Sociology of Culture* (London: Constable).

Epstein, E. J. (1973) *News from Nowhere: Television and the News* (New York: Random House).

Franklin, B. and Carlson, M. (eds) (2011) *Journalists, Sources and Credibility: New Perspectives* (London and New York: Routledge).

Freedman, D. (2014) *The Contradictions of Media Power* (London: Bloomsbury).

Gans, H. J. (1979) *Deciding What's News: A Study of CBS Evening News, NBC Nightly News, Newsweek, and Time* (New York: Pantheon).

Golding, P. and Elliott, P. (1979) *Making the News* (London: Longman).

Halloran, J. D., Elliott, P., and Murdock, G. (1970) *Demonstrations and Communication: A Case Study* (Harmondsworth: Penguin).

Hesmondhalgh, D. and Baker, S. (2011) *Creative Labour: Media Work in Three Cultural Industries* (London: Routledge).

Lazarsfeld, P. (1941) 'Remarks on administrative and critical communications research.' *Studies in Philosophy and Social Science IX*(1), 3–20.

Magor, M. and Schlesinger, P. (2009) '"For this relief much thanks." Taxation, film policy and the UK government.' *Screen 50*(3), 299–317.

Puijk, R. (2008) 'Ethnographic media production research in a digital environment.' in C. Paterson and D. Domingo (eds), *Making Online News: The Ethnography of New Media Production* (pp. 29–41) (New York: Peter Lang).

Schlesinger, P. (1978) *Putting 'Reality' Together: BBC News* (London: Constable).

Schlesinger, P. (1980) 'Between sociology and journalism' in H. Christian (ed.), *The Sociology of Journalism and the Press* (The Sociological Review Series, Monograph 29) (pp. 341–369) (Keele: University of Keele).

Schlesinger, P. (1991) *Media, State and Nation: Political Violence and Collective Identities* (London: Sage).

Schlesinger, P. (2007) 'Creativity: From discourse to doctrine.' *Screen 48*(3), 377–387.

Schlesinger, P. (2009) 'Creativity and the experts. New Labour, think tanks, and the policy process.' *International Journal of Press/Politics 14*(3), 3–20.

Schlesinger, P. (2010) '"The most creative organization in the world"? The BBC, "creativity" and managerial style.' *International Journal of Cultural Policy 16*(3), 271–285.

Schlesinger, P. (2013) 'Expertise, the academy and the governance of cultural policy.' *Media, Culture & Society 35*(1), 27–35.

Schlesinger, P. and Doyle, G. (2015) 'From organizational crisis to multi-platform salvation? Creative destruction and the recomposition of news media.' *Journalism: Theory, Practice and Criticism 16*(3), 305–323.

Schlesinger, P., Miller, D., and Dinan, W. (2001) *Open Scotland? Journalists, Spin Doctors and Lobbyists* (Edinburgh: Polygon).

Schlesinger, P., Selfe, M., and Munro, E. (2015a) *Curators of Cultural Enterprise: A Critical Analysis of a Creative Business Intermediary* (London: Palgrave Macmillan).

Schlesinger, P., Selfe, M., and Munro, E. (2015b) 'Inside a cultural agency: Team ethnography and knowledge exchange.' *Journal of Arts Management, Law and Society 45*(2): 66–83.

Schlesinger, P. and Tumber, H. (1994) *Reporting Crime: The Media Politics of Criminal Justice* (Oxford: Oxford University Press).

Schlesinger, P. and Waelde, C. (2010) 'Copyright and cultural work: An exploration.' *Innovation – The European Journal of Social Science Research 25*(1), 11–28.

Silverstone, R. (1985) *Framing Science: The Making of a Television Documentary* (London: British Film Institute).

Tracey, M. (1978) *The Production of Political Television* (London: Routledge and Kegan Paul).

Tuchman, G. (1978) *Making News: A Study in the Construction of Reality* (New York: The Free Press).

Tumber, H. (2014) 'Back to the future? The sociology of news and journalism from black and white to the digital age' in S. Waisbord (ed.), *Media Sociology: A Reappraisal* (pp. 63–78) (Cambridge: Polity).

Tunstall, J. (1971) *Journalists at Work: Specialist Correspondents, their News organizations, News Sources, and Competitor-Colleagues* (London: Constable).
Waelde, C. and Schlesinger, P. (2009) 'Music and dance: Beyond copyright text?' *SCRIPT-ed* 8(3), 257–291.
Waisbord, S. (2014) 'Introduction: Reappraising media sociology', in S. Waisbord (ed.), *Media Sociology: A Reappraisal* (pp. 1–21) (Cambridge: Polity).
Wernick, A. (1991) *Promotional Culture: Advertising, Ideology and Symbolic Expression* (London: Sage).
Willig, I. (2013) 'Newsroom ethnography in a field perspective.' *Journalism: Theory, Practice and Criticism* 14(3), 373–387.

3
The Importance of Time in Media Production Research
David M. Ryfe

In a review of my book (Ryfe, 2012), David Domingo (2014) begins by noting that it 'could well be the last of newsroom ethnographies as we know them' (p. 115). Why the last? Because, he writes, 'spending months among journalists to understand their practices, their values, and their aspirations will not soon be enough to analyze the evolution of journalism.' Domingo clearly wishes to say that studying *journalists* is no longer enough if one wants to understand the evolution of *journalism*. Fair enough. But when I initially read the sentence, my eyes fixed on its first two words, 'spending months'. I didn't spend months, I thought to myself. I spent *years*. In fact, I spent approximately two-and-a-half years, stretched over five total years, in newsrooms. In that time, I followed reporters around and sat in on their meetings. I went to lunch with them. I hung around their cubicles to 'shoot the bull'. I even reported and wrote stories myself. As I reflected on this time, which represented a big chunk of time in my life, I thought that Domingo could have ended the sentence with those first two words and still have been correct. My ethnography of news may be the last of its kind because few researchers will have *time* to spend years in the field, hanging out with journalists (or any news producer), talking with them, observing their practices and engaging in their rituals.

This is the theme of my essay, then: time. I wish to address the following questions. Why will it be more difficult to spend the time to do significant ethnographic studies of media production? Why is spending this time necessary? What will be lost if researchers either can't or won't take the time? What can be done about the current trends? Ethnographies of media production are of course about space – getting to a location and inhabiting that place with others. But they are also about time and, as I think back on my own ethnographic research, I realize that, of the two, time has been the more important.

A political economy of time

The word 'ethnography' conjures images of anthropologists spending years living among natives, watching and perhaps even participating in the local culture. I know of few, if any, studies of media production that fit this image. In my own subfield of news production, studies done during its 'golden age' in the 1970s come closest. Between 1970 and 1980, no fewer than 14 significant ethnographic studies of newsrooms were conducted, mostly in the US and UK. The most famous and influential of these studies, at least in the United States, were Gaye Tuchman's *Making News* (1978) and Herbert Gans' *Deciding What's News* (1979). Tuchman describes her method in a first chapter on 'News as Frame'. 'The data' for this study, she writes, 'were gathered by participant observation and interviews over a period of ten years' (p. 9). In those ten years (1966–1976), she visited four sites. At site one, she observed events in the newsroom at least one day a week during 1966–1967, and then 'intermittently' for another two years. Over a six-month period in 1967–1968, she conducted research nearly every day at site two. She then interviewed reporters at site three during much of 1975 and conducted another six months of fieldwork in 1975–1976. Tuchman doesn't give us a count, but conservatively she likely spent one-and-a-half to two years in newsrooms over a stretch of ten years. Gans tells a similar methodological story (1979: xii–xiii). Between 1965–1969, he spent at least three to four months in each of four newsrooms (two television shows and two national magazines) for a total of twelve months of fieldwork. He then devoted a few years to writing two drafts of a book, neither of which he published! After several years, he decided to go back to the project and in 1975, spent another month in newsrooms to collect additional data. In each case, the authors spent large chunks of time in newsrooms stretching over many years. However, even they are nothing like the immersive experience of anthropologists, who often spend years at a time in the field.

After 1980, a virtual 'moratorium', as Cook (1998: 238) puts it, seems to have been put on the ethnographic study of news production. Schlesinger's (1987) study of the BBC was the major work published in the 1980s (but based on fieldwork conducted in the mid-1970s). A few studies appeared in the 1990s, most notably Pedelty's (1995) examination of foreign correspondents and Jacobs' (2000) study of race and media in Los Angeles. But they were far fewer in number than in the 'golden age', and together they had less impact on the field. In recent years, ethnography has enjoyed a renaissance in media studies (e.g. Cottle, 2009).

At least in journalism studies, however, the new work has moved even further from the classic ethnographic experience. Boczkowski's (2004) analysis of digital newsrooms was probably the earliest of the recent efforts. He spent roughly a year in three digital newsrooms. This is a period of time comparable to Gans' effort, but it is packed into three (1997–1999) rather than ten years. Born's (2011) update of Schlesinger's study of the BBC is perhaps the richest of the lot. She spent parts of several years conducting fieldwork. Anderson's (2013) work on the Philadelphia news ecosystem consisted of about seven months during one year (2008) in the field. The most recent book to come out, Usher's (2014) examination of the *New York Times*, is based on five months of research conducted in 2010.

Except for the rare exception, it appears that scholars are spending less and less time in the field spread over fewer and fewer years. My interpretation of Domingo, in other words, seems right. Moving forward, we are likely to see few multi-year ethnographic studies of production. The most thorough major news production studies typically now involve many months of fieldwork spread over a year's time.

We might stop here for a moment and ask why this is the case. Why is it that researchers are spending less and less time in the field? Part of the reason, I think, has to do with changes in the environment of news production. It may be harder than during the 'golden age' of news ethnography, for instance, to gain access to newsrooms. As Paterson (2011: xi) observes, most newsrooms operate within commercial institutions. Competitive pressures alone incline them to secrecy and risk aversion – like the risk of opening their doors to an ethnographer. Usher describes months of 'hammer[ing] out an agreement' with *New York Times* lawyers before she could get into the newsroom. This agreement included her willingness to 'focus...away from delicate subjects like sourcing' and a right for the newspaper to review the finished product. My experience in regional newspapers was not quite as daunting. I never met a company lawyer, for instance. But like Usher I did have to cultivate relationships with editors. For the first newsroom in my study, it took months, several lunches (some including faculty in my department who had worked with the editor in the past and could vouch for my trustworthiness) and many emails to set everything up. And then the editor took a job at another newspaper! So I had to wait until the new editor was hired, wait some more for him to get settled, and then go through the entire process again. Multiply this experience three times and it easily took a year or more just to establish access to the sites included in my study.

In some ways, the logistical issues only get more difficult when news production moves out of traditional venues. As an example, currently I am conducting a study of online-only news sites in several regions of the United States. Many of these sites are small, run by one or two people. More than a few do not have an office. Sometimes they are units of other organizations, as with a news site housed within a regional transportation agency. Often, they do not even consider what they do to be 'news production'. Traditional newsrooms may be difficult to access today, but at least they have offices. A researcher knows whom to contact; that person has a phone number with voicemail or, even better, an assistant who can take a message. When I call or email, they recognize my inquiry because they identify themselves as producers of news. I can take none of this for granted in my recent research on online news sites. Sometimes, the only way to reach the people who manage these sites is a 'contact us' button on the bottom of the homepage. Other times, it is difficult to know whom to contact at all. When a news site is housed within a transportation agency, do I contact the person who manages the site or the person who heads the agency? It can take weeks and months to get a reply from these sites, and then the reply is often 'we are not a news site.' Even when I do make contact, it can take more weeks and months to explain to the Institutional Review Board on my campus why I am collecting data from these people when they clearly are *not* journalists.

If journalism is more complicated, it is also more disrupted. This is truer in the United States than elsewhere, but journalism across the Western world has felt some degree of change (e.g. Kuhn and Nielsen, 2013; Levy and Nielsen, 2010; Nielsen, 2014). It was one thing for producers at *CBS News* to grant Gans access when the organization was at its height of prestige and power. It is quite another to grant permission when the organization faces a crisis. I am paraphrasing, but for my newspaper newsroom study, one of the editors with whom I talked said, essentially, 'We are fighting for our lives here, and we don't need someone watching over our shoulder as we do.' He declined my request for access. I have not tried to gain entry into newsrooms for a few years, and I have less knowledge of the climate in other parts of the world, but I can't help but think that the difficulty of gaining access tracks, more or less, with the economic fortunes of these companies. Of course, online news sites do not have the same sense of impending doom. However, their financial situation is often as tenuous, if not more, than that of mainstream newsrooms. They are therefore reluctant, rightly so perhaps, to grant access to a researcher who may only get in the way.

Compared to the past, then, the environment of news production may be more difficult. This goes some way toward explaining why we are likely to see fewer significant ethnographic studies. But it is only part of the reason, and to my mind not the most important. That distinction goes to the political economy of academic research.

The following is mostly an American story. However, while the academy is organized differently in other societies, similar trends are apparent, at least across Western Europe. Moreover, the academic market increasingly is international in scope. PhDs will often search for jobs across Europe and the United States. This lends academic culture a measure of uniformity that it perhaps did not have in the past.

In 1995, just over half of instructors at American four-year universities were in the tenure system (either tenure track or tenured). By 2011, they accounted for, on average, only one-third of instructors on campus (e.g. MLA, 2014). These numbers indicate that tenure-track jobs, that is, academic jobs that have a significant research component, are getting scarcer. In other countries, the details are a bit different. In the United Kingdom, for instance, the concept of tenure generally does not exist. Instead, most instructors are 'at will' employees, and there is often a clearer separation between teachers and researchers. Still, in the UK, as in the US, the number of research positions, or positions with research as a significant part of their duties, is dwindling (e.g. Universities UK, 2012). The same is true more or less across Western Europe.

Strangely enough, this trend has not led to fewer people vying for these jobs. In fact, a report of the Council of Graduate Schools (Gonzales et al., 2013) finds that in the decade between 2002 and 2012, the number of applications to American graduate schools increased by 4.5%, and the number of people holding doctoral degrees increased by a similar percentage. Again, the details differ cross-nationally, but the same long-term trends are evident. In Canada, for example, the number of students enrolled in PhD programs has grown four-fold since 1980 (e.g. AAUC, 2011: 10).

These facts set up a basic supply/demand problem: there are more qualified applicants for research-intensive positions than there are research-intensive jobs. An unsurprising result follows. The publishing requirements for obtaining a tenure-track position (in the United States) or an equivalent position (elsewhere) have increased, as has the quantity of research necessary to gain tenure. In communication-related fields, it is not uncommon for successful applicants for such jobs to have two, three or more journal articles published – and perhaps even a book – at the time of application. Once hired, the productivity demands do not relent. Young professors are told that when it comes to the quantity of research required for them to gain tenure, there are no explicit guidelines. However, in the United States, a rule of thumb has circulated for at least as long as I have been in this business. To succeed in the American tenure process, an assistant professor in the communication disciplines *should have published roughly two journal articles per year and one book every five years*. Meaning that when assistant professors come up for tenure, they will have produced the equivalent of twelve journal articles and one book, and have made good progress on a second book. This particular rule of thumb may not apply elsewhere, but the publishing demands are equal, or nearly equal, to the American context.

I do not know if anthropologists face these productivity demands. I suspect not. However, within communication-related fields, they certainly exist, which puts a great deal of pressure on those who prefer ethnographic approaches to research. For graduate students, pursuing ethnographic research means they risk not completing their degrees in a timely manner. A dissertation that revolves around significant ethnographic data collection can take as many as seven to nine years to complete. Moreover, after this time, students likely will not have produced enough journal articles to gain a tenure-track job. After all, they will have been in the field while others in their cohort are publishing. And if they happen to complete their degree and obtain a tenure-track job, they will have difficulty acquiring tenure because they are spending so much time collecting data rather than churning out articles.

This is the root, I think, of the astonishment that greets me – especially among graduate students – when I describe exactly how long I spent collecting data in newsrooms. You did what? they ask. For how long? The political economy of the academic tenure process makes such work unlikely, if not impossible.

It is now time for a caveat. I am not claiming that there will never be another ethnography of news production based on years rather than months of field research. There is always the chance that a researcher will throw caution to the wind and simply *do it*. But this is my point. 'Doing it' entails precisely throwing caution to the wind, because the political economy of the academy tends to reward productivity over time. It is the rare graduate student or young researcher who will take such a risk.

Why time is vital

Why is spending more rather than less time important for the ethnographic study of news? There are a number of reasons, I think, which I place under the general labels of logistics and theory.

Anderson (2013: appendix) provides an excellent discussion of the logistical issues raised by 'network ethnography' (e.g. Howard, 2002); that is, ethnography in new digital contexts. To conduct his study of the Philadelphia news ecosystem, Anderson first had to create a series of network maps. He then had to identify significant clusters within these maps and within these clusters key news organizations. Since he was more interested in the network than in the sites themselves, Anderson had to find a way to position himself *between* these organizations. This meant following the assemblage of people and information as they swept across the network. In his appendix on methods issues, he isn't quite clear on how one follows an assemblage, but in the text it appears to entail a process of constant movement: moving from one journalist to the next, one news story to another, as the network mobilizes to produce news. Anderson could never stay in one place for long, for fear of missing the dynamic of the system.

The logistical issues presented by the physical space of a conventional newsroom are tame in comparison. Still, there are problems to be solved. Even conventional newsrooms look and feel different than in the past. They have experienced vast layoffs. They also have created entirely new areas of news production, with new types of journalists, new practices, and new processes. It can be difficult to get one's bearings in this environment, especially for academics that may have little direct experience of newsrooms. As I say in my book, I had never set foot in a newsroom before my first day of fieldwork. Everything was new and different and disorienting. I spent a week or two just mapping out who sat where. The most basic questions took time to answer, like where should I sit? With all the layoffs in newsrooms, there were many options. I could find a seat just about anywhere in the newsroom. Did I want to sit next to the government folks? In the Cops 'n' Courts pod? I tried out various places and finally decided to sit as close as I could to the city editor. It took me some time to realize that the city editor was the nerve centre of the newsroom. Eventually, anything that ended up on the front page of the newspaper or the local section went through his desk. So I sat near him.

Another logistical issue has to do with gaining access to everyday interactions. Newsrooms are no longer noisy places where reporters openly talk with one another. In fact, for much of the time researchers can find themselves staring at the backs of reporters' heads as they type into a computer. Still, some conversations do occur. In my research, it took me a while to realize that they were often an extension of email interactions. Eventually, I asked for a company email account in every newsroom I visited and got it.

The logistical issues of doing ethnography in a news environment are difficult. They take time to solve. They may even take a good deal of time to surface. However, they are crucial. Making a mistake in placing oneself in a newsroom, or failing to observe key interactions, poses a threat to the entire project. It would be as if a public opinion researcher failed to ask important questions in his or her poll, or textual analysts failed to consider a robust sample of texts. When we read such studies, their deficits are clear. The same is true of ethnographic research that relies on a small sample of observations. When researchers elect to spend only a few weeks or months observing, they risk missing important dimensions of the news culture.

This point leads me to conceptual issues. Ethnography is an effort to say something intelligent about a culture. This is a complicated term, culture; but in my own work, here is how I have come to think about it. In the first instance, journalists do not confront 'technology' or 'economics' or any of the other things people identify as disruptive to the industry. Rather, in the first instance, they confront one another. Much like farmers staring at a broken fence, they stand side by side in contemplation of their dilemma, and they try to make some sense of it all. 'What is happening?' 'Why is it happening?' 'Maybe we should do this.' 'Why in the HELL would I do that?' 'I have no idea what you are asking me to do.' Culture is the stuff they borrow from to do this sense making. Scholars have used a number of analogies to describe this 'stuff'. They call it a 'web' or a 'code', a 'toolkit' or a set of 'recipes'. Essentially, what they mean is that culture lies in language and practices and things, and, from the perspective of cultural natives, it is associated or linked together in more or less sensible, this is to say, meaningful, ways. It is this 'stuff' that journalists reach for as they to understand what it is they are facing and make proposals for what it is they might do.

Within this perspective, interaction is more important than action, because it is in interaction that people mobilize culture to justify what they do to others. One may glean aspects of these justifications from interview transcripts, focus groups or textual analysis. But there is nothing like observing them first-hand, as they happen in real time. I interviewed nearly one hundred reporters for my study and what they told me was interesting. It was not always reliable, but it was interesting. I learned more about journalistic culture, however, in moments of interaction. One day, for example, I followed a twenty-year veteran's last day in the newsroom. He had quit and taken a job as the public information officer for a government agency. Along with spending his day saying goodbye to folks, he spent it justifying to himself and to others why this was the right choice. These interactions provided an extraordinary window into the culture of journalism. I recall other such moments, as when I happened to be talking to a cops reporter and his phone rang. It was the marketing department downstairs trying to sell him a subscription to the newspaper. He told the person twice that she had reached the newsroom. She finally got it on the third attempt. This reporter then proceeded to tell the story over and over again to others in the newsroom as an example of just how inept the business side of the newspaper had become. There were also awkward moments, as when a group of reporters sat around a conference table trying to figure out what they would put on their business cards when the title 'reporter' was taken away from them (as the editor was promising would happen very soon). And tense moments, as when the editor in one newsroom called an impromptu all-hands meeting in the middle of the newsroom, read the names of twenty people being laid off and then added his name at the end. Listen to reporters talk to one another in the aftermath of a bombshell like that and you will learn much of what you need to know about the culture of journalism today. Each of these moments opens a window into the culture. None would have been available to me had I not been on site, sometimes for no other than reason than to hang around.

Participation can be especially beneficial when trying to get into the rhythm of associations made within a culture. When I entered my first newsroom, everyone knew I was an academic, which meant they refused to engage with me beyond politely answering my questions. Then I began working as an 'intern'. Two days per week for six months I came into the newsroom and reported directly to the city editor. He gave me reporting assignments, the first of which involved a local court case. That first day, not only had I never written a news story, but I had never been in a courthouse. Nonetheless, I dutifully went, and the inevitable happened: I got a significant fact wrong in my story. After getting chewed out by the city editor the next morning, I slunk back to my desk. I felt about five inches tall. Yet, all day, reporters dropped by with big smiles on their faces. 'I heard you made a mistake in your story!' They then proceeded to tell me of their first mistake. Much as with Geertz and his Balinese cockfight (Geertz, 1973), the newsroom opened up to me afterward. People volunteered information. They shared stories and ideas. They invited me to lunch. I was, if only a little bit and for a brief time, allowed into the tribe. This never would have happened if I had not taken the time.

In short, time allows a researcher to make mistakes. In my own research, I made lots of them. Things I thought were true going in later turned out to be untrue. Lines of thought I developed at time zero turned into dead ends by the third time. On more than a few occasions, I found myself excitedly scribbling down new ideas in my notebook, only to scratch them out later due to a lack of evidence. Why was it so difficult? Partly, it is due to the fact that culture rarely presents itself squarely, and it doesn't stand still. For example, in interviews, participants often made declarative statements about how things worked, which I dutifully wrote down, but which turned out, in practice (that is, in their interactions), to be wrong. All of us, even long-time participants, apprehend culture sideways. We catch it in glances and glimpses. It manifests in strips of interaction. The more of these strips an ethnographer collects, the greater the likelihood that he or she will say something interesting, and even compelling, about a particular community.

Another way to say this is that explanation develops iteratively, over time, as data and concepts come together to create a picture of what is happening in a setting and why. Immersion is required to let this process unfold. Over the course of five years, I engaged in an iterative process of failure. Lots of things I tried turned out to be untrue, but I wouldn't have known this if I had not taken the time to let the data accumulate. The old maxim that we learn best from our mistakes is a maxim for a reason. Without time to make mistakes I might have made the ultimate mistake of misunderstanding the culture.

Moving forward

Mine has been an appeal to advance the study of media production by slowing it down. We may need better concepts and more finely tuned methods, but mostly we need more time. This may make the reader frustrated, as I have also argued that the primary impediments to taking this time are structural. They lie in the political economy of the academy, over which researchers have little control, and in the environment of news production, over which they have even less. You may be saying to yourself, 'Of course more time is better than less. But how am I to accomplish that!?' I wish I could provide a grand answer to this question, but I cannot. From my perch in the discipline of communication, absent a fundamental change, it seems that the productivity requirements for tenure-track (and equivalent) faculty are likely to continue to rise. Reversing this trend, or even slowing it down, will not come easily or quickly. Doing so is certainly out of the hands of pre-tenured faculty.

For this reason, I advise researchers who are early in their careers to adopt a strategy of local incursion rather than wholesale war. I use my own experience as an example. The productivity demands of the modern academy were already in place during the pre-tenure phase of my career. I could do nothing to change these facts. I could, however, engage my department chair with my research plan. Once I convinced him of the project's worthiness, he worked with me to create a teaching schedule that fit my needs. For instance, one year I taught more classes in fall semester and fewer in the spring. Combined with the summer, this gave me six months of relatively uninterrupted time to do participant-observation in the newsroom. Once I convinced my chair of the project's worth, he was able to defend the research plan to senior faculty in my department when it came time to do yearly reviews, and then again at the college level when my third-year review came up. It turns out that many people on campus are concerned about the productivity mill that academic research has become and, given the option, would like to err on the side of quality rather than quantity. With a great deal of conversation, my project – and the amount of research it generated – became acceptable at all levels of the review process.

I can imagine other researchers following this strategy. However, it is not without risks – or trade-offs. A primary risk is that a department head may leave, or a new administrator may arrive, just as a researcher is readying his or her case for promotion. If agreements have not been made in writing, such changes can put an application at risk. This is a risk individual researchers will have to weigh for themselves. A primary trade-off, at least in my experience, has to do with one's career trajectory. Put bluntly, this strategy may make it difficult for an academic to obtain a position at a more prestigious university. In the modern academy, prestige is often associated with productivity. Academic staff are given more time to produce research at these universities. In exchange, they are asked to produce more of it. Ironically, for this reason, researchers at the most prestigious institutions often do not produce the best ethnographic work. Instead, these ethnographies come from individuals working at institutions where the productivity requirements are not quite so pressing. This was certainly true of my experience. On leaving graduate school, I interviewed for tenure-track jobs at no fewer than a dozen institutions. Almost without fail, the more prestigious institutions were looking to hire someone who engaged in a narrow band of research, and who would burrow in to that subfield by producing a great quantity of research. I wasn't a 'good fit' for such jobs – the exact code words used by search committees on more than one occasion as they explained why they had gone in a different direction.

This is certainly a trade-off! I wouldn't want to claim that it is, or will be, faced by every ethnographer. I would say, however, that it is a serious consideration, a pressure if you will, on young academics struggling to start their careers. If they have a choice between doing ethnographic work or some other, most will make the rational choice and adopt research agendas that promise career rewards. If they choose to do ethnographic work, they will minimize the risk by doing less fieldwork than a researcher might have done in the past. As the pressures mount, we should expect to see fewer and fewer significant ethnographic studies of news production, if by significant we mean work based on extensive time in the field. Obviously, to me, the risks and trade-offs associated with this work were worth it. I hope others will see it the same way.

There are certainly other ways of studying the culture of journalism. One may examine texts or discourse, as just two examples. However, there is a reason that ethnography is the classic approach to the study culture. There simply is nothing like immersion to provide a deep understanding of a culture. Immersion requires time. I encourage young scholars, in particular, to take as much of it as they can.

References

Anderson, C. W. (2013) *Rebuilding the News: Metropolitan Journalism in the Digital Age* (Philadelphia: Temple University Press).

Association of Universities and Colleges in Canada (2011) *Trends in Higher Education, Vol. 1* (Ottawa: Ontario).

Boczkowski, P. (2004) *Digitizing the News: Innovation in Online Newspapers* (Cambridge, MA: MIT Press).

Cook, T. (1998) *Governing with the News: The News Media as an Institution* (Chicago: University of Chicago Press).

Cottle, S. (2009) 'New(s) times: Towards a "second wave" of news ethnography' in A. Hansen (ed.), *Mass Communication Research Methods* (pp. 366–386) (London: Sage).

Domingo, D. (2014) *Can Journalism Survive? An Inside Look in American Newsrooms* [Book Review]. *Digital Journalism* 2(1), 115–123.

Gans, H. (1979) *Deciding What's News: A Study of CBS Evening News, NBC Nightly News, Newsweek, and Time* (NY: Pantheon Books).

Geertz, C. (1973) *The Interpretation of Cultures* (NY: Basic Books).

Gonzales, L., Allum, J. R., and Sowell, R. S. (2013) *Graduate enrollment and degrees: 2002–2012* (Washington, DC: Council on Graduate Schools).

Howard, P. (2002) 'Network ethnography and the hypermedia organization: New media, new organizations, new methods.' *New Media & Society* 4(4), 550–574.

Jacobs, R. (2000) *Race, Media, and the Crisis of Civil Society: From Watts to Rodney King* (NY: Cambridge University Press).

Kuhn, R. and Nielsen, R. (eds) (2013) *Political Journalism in Transition: Western Europe in a Comparative Perspective* (Oxford: Reuters Institute for the Study of Journalism).

Levy, D. and Nielsen, R. (eds) (2010) *The Changing Business Model of Journalism and Its Implications for Democracy* (Oxford: Reuters Institute for the Study of Journalism).

MLA (2014) 'Our PhD employment problem, part 2' [blog]. Accessed at: http://mlaresearch.commons.mla.org/2014/03/11/our-phd-employment-problem-part-2/.

Nielsen, R. (eds) (2014) *The Uncertain Future of Local Journalism: The Decline of Newspapers and the Rise of Digital Media* (Oxford: Reuters Institute for the Study of Journalism).

Paterson, C. (2011) *The International Television News Agencies* (Oxford: Peter Lang).

Pedelty, M. (1995) *War Stories: The Culture of Foreign Correspondents* (NY: Routledge).

Ryfe, D. (2012) *Can Journalism Survive? An Inside Look in American Newsrooms* (London: Polity Press).

Schlesinger, P. (1987) *Putting 'Reality' Together: BBC News* (NY: Methuen).

Tuchman, G. (1978) *Making News: A Study in the Construction of Reality* (NY: Free Press).

Universities UK (2012) *Futures for Higher Education: Analysing Trends* (London: UK).

Usher, N. (2014) *Making News at the New York Times* (Ann Arbor: The University of Michigan Press).

Part II
Theory and Research

4
Field Theory and Media Production: A Bridge-Building Strategy
Ida Willig

Field theory and media studies

Pierre Bourdieu's book *On Television* (1998a), which was published in French in 1996, was an essayistic and critical analysis of the French journalistic field, of the power of journalism and journalists and of the professional ideology guiding the journalistic field, such as a constant drive for 'scoops'. Before that, Bourdieu had not been addressing media production specifically but had worked with more general questions of cultural production and power. *The Field of Cultural production: Essays on Art and Literature* (Bourdieu, 1993) and later *The Rules of Art* (Bourdieu, 1996) present empirical research and essays on art and literature forming a field analysis of the inner workings of small-scale art production; and the seminal work, *Distinction: A Social Critique of the Judgment of Taste* (Bourdieu, 2003), is a mapping of the social space of cultural consumption, proposing a critique of the notion of 'taste' and its (naturalized) relation to power. Other work – for instance, *Homo Academicus* (Bourdieu, 1988), an analysis of the academic field in France – is also important to media production studies as it unfolds and operationalizes the concepts of field, habitus and capital in the context of cultural production.

It was not until late in Pierre Bourdieu's career that he engaged directly with studies of media and media production in the little book *On Television* (Bourdieu 1998). *On Television* might be criticized for being a hasty and somewhat polemic analysis of journalism, but below the seemingly essayistic style of writing runs the consistent, elaborate social theory of reflexive sociology. In this book, Bourdieu uses journalism as an example to present the key concepts of field theory (see Schultz,

2007; Willig, 2012; Bourdieu, 2005; Champagne, 1993, 2005; Marlière, 1998). *Fields* are semi-autonomous microcosms defined, at the same time, by their own game rules and by their relations to (and the game rules of) other fields in the overall social space. In this view, journalism is a hierarchical social space defined by the internal structure of the field (for instance, dominant norms and values, specific logics of practice, etc.) but also by the relation to other fields such as the political field (for instance, the parliamentary system, the relationship between politicians and journalists, etc.). *Capitals* are the forms of both material and immaterial capital that have an effect in the field in question. Most research distinguishes between economic, cultural, and social capital, and the notion of *symbolic* capital describes the form of capital having a specific effect in a given field; theoretically this would be 'journalistic capital' in the journalistic field and 'literary capital' in the field of literature. *Habitus* is also a key concept describing the dispositions of agents in a field, synthesizing the history, experiences, and lived life of an individual as an embodied 'sense of the game'. *Doxa* describes the unquestionable rules of the game in a field and, close to this, the concept of *illusio* describes the necessary belief in the game.

If Pierre Bourdieu can be criticized for not having operationalized field theory in relation to media studies and media production, this is not the case for other media scholars working with reflexive sociology. In 1998, the same year that *On Television* was published in English, Rodney Benson published the article 'Field Theory in a Comparative Context: A New Paradigm for Media Studies' (1999). Drawing on the collective work of Bourdieu's research group, Bourdieu's own writings on fields, habitus, and capital, as well as individual contributions from Patrick Champagne, Benson discusses field theory as a possible new paradigm for media research in a comparative context and highlights three original contributions. Firstly, that field theory addresses the meso level of media analysis and thus 'bridges macro-societal and micro-organizational approaches' (Benson, 1999: 479), which traditionally have been separated in many empirical studies. Secondly, field theory also bridges the analytical questions of media production and media reception as a homology, and 'mutual adjustment' between production and reception is a key assumption of field theory. Thirdly, Benson emphasizes that reflexive sociology focuses on historical change and on the interplay between different fields in this context (1999). Although Benson argues in the context of news media and media studies in general, we can draw on the same arguments when discussing media production studies. Whether the object of analysis is the production of television drama, Bollywood films, reality shows, or news content, field theory is useful for bridging micro and macro in media production studies, for analytically connecting media production with media reception, and for thinking in terms of historical change.

In 2003, Nick Couldry continued the discussion about the contribution from field theory for media studies (2003). The main argument is that we should take inspiration from Bourdieu's early reflexive sociology on symbolic systems in developing a theory of media as central social institutions with meta-capital:

> Media, it is proposed, have meta-capital over the rules of play, and the definition of capital (especially symbolic capital) that operate within a wide range of contemporary fields of production. This level of explanation needs to be added to specific accounts of the detailed workings of the media. (Couldry, 2003: 653)

In the quote above, Couldry argues that the rules of play of the journalistic field are not only internal rules of play, so to speak, but more transcending rules of play that have an effect in other fields of production – we might think of science or politics. This leads Couldry to suggest research that is not only preoccupied with the symbolic power of media internally in the journalistic field but the symbolic power of media in the production processes of other fields: 'We need to study the categories (in a Durkheimian sense) through which an increasingly pervasive "mediatization" of public and private life may be becoming normalized, even legitimated' (Couldry, 2003: 670). In relation to the advancement of media production studies, Couldry's suggestion to study the symbolic power of media could suggest a focus on media power understood as 'the concentration of symbolic power in media institutions' (Couldry, 2001: 155) and more generally on media consumption (Couldry et al., 2007).

In 2004, Benson followed up his earlier contribution on the uses of field theory in relation to media studies in the article 'Bringing the Sociology of Media Back In' (2004). Based on a critique of political science for treating news media as independent variables – not taking into account the cultural, social, and economic features of journalism differing from country to country – Benson suggests a number of hypotheses about the relation between journalistic field and news content and 'how variable characteristics of media systems shape news discourse' (Benson, 2004: 275). The suggestion to study how various structural features of media fields or systems influence content is not only relevant for the study of news media. The question of how media systems, understood broadly as the various cultural, social, and economic characteristics of a specific national or transnational field, shape various media production fields and influence the media content is equally relevant for studying the music industry, film making, etc.

In the same year, 2004, Dan Hallin and Pablo Mancini published *Comparative Media Systems*, where they proposed a theory of three Western media systems characterized by various structural settings such as the political parallelism of the press, the professionalization and independence of journalists, the degree and type of public media support, etc. (Hallin and Mancini, 2004). Where Couldry (2003) suggested further research on the symbolic power of media and Benson suggested further research on how media systems influence content, Hallin and Mancini emphasized the structural settings of various media systems as a research object in its own right. Some of the questions relevant to ask in future media production studies include what is the history of a media production field? What are the dominant interests of the field? What is the autonomy of the field in relation to other fields? What is the relation of the field vis-à-vis the (national) field of power, etc.?

In 2006, David Hesmondhalgh set out to 'evaluate Bourdieu's analysis of cultural production in terms of its effectiveness for understanding contemporary media production' (2006: 211). One of his critiques, based on a reading of Bourdieu's writings on art and literature, is that Bourdieu has focused on media consumption, and the work on media production is concentrated on small-scale production, not large-scale production (e.g. the multinational entertainment industry). Over the years, other media scholars have worked with the framework of field theory and thus contributed to advance media production studies (Born, 2010), and many of these will be addressed in the literature review that follows later in the chapter.

Summing up the theoretical contributions discussing Bourdieu with relevance for advancing media production studies, Benson has suggested more *comparative research* (1999) and in line with this, Hallin and Mancini have forwarded the theory of comparative media systems, emphasizing the *structural settings* of media production (2004). Benson also calls for more research on how media systems shape *media content* (2004) and Couldry, arguing that media have a meta-capital, suggests more research on the *symbolic power of media* (2003) and media consumption (2001). Also, Hesmondhalgh has contributed to the discussion on how field theory can advance our understanding of media production and suggested that future studies focus on *large-scale production* rather than small-scale production (2006). The chapter will end by discussing examples of media production studies in relation to the suggestions for advancement reviewed above. But first, the following section will discuss some of the difficulties of defining 'media production studies' in a field perspective.

How to define media production studies in a field perspective

As we have seen above, one of the key characteristics of field theory is that it transcends or bridges analytical borders that are often present in traditional approaches of media studies – as cultural production is closely linked to cultural consumption, macro is closely linked to micro, etc. (Wacquant, 1989; Bourdieu and Wacquant, 1992; Bourdieu, 2000). Furthermore, Bourdieu is, first and foremost, an open-minded empiricist who lets the research question decide the methodology used, which has led him and his research team to use and develop a wide range of empirical methods – from anthropological fieldwork (Bourdieu, 1998b) to statistical correspondence analysis (Bourdieu, 2003), text studies (Bourdieu, 1993), and interviews (Bourdieu et al., 1999).

This broad, consistent and relational analytical framework of field theory, as well as the openness towards empirical methods, makes it difficult to make a clearly cut definition of a 'media production study' within the framework of reflexive sociology. On the one hand, there is the question of which studies to include from a theoretical perspective. A strict theoretical reading would only include studies that worked directly in line from and in accordance with the analytical framework introduced by Bourdieu, or working specifically to develop the analytical framework. A more pragmatic theoretical reading would include studies where field theory holds a dominant position but is used in combination with other theories and analytical concepts. On the other hand, there is the question of which studies to include from a methodological perspective when deciding what a media production study in a field perspective might be. Here a strict understanding of 'media production studies' might only include studies aiming to produce knowledge of the media production practices by studying the media production *process* itself; for instance, ethnographic studies, policy studies, interview studies and observations of media production processes. A more pragmatic methodological approach to 'media production studies' would be to include studies also aiming at producing knowledge of media production practices but doing so by studying media *products*, understood as media texts in the broadest sense of the word (i.e. news, films, online chat, photos for social media, etc.). This would follow the suggestion of Benson to study how the media system influences media products (2004). Also, studies of the *structural settings* of media production (for instance, studies of media policies, media subsidies, media economy, etc.) could reasonably be included in a definition of media production studies within the framework of field theory, as these empirical questions address the core concept of field. This would follow the field-inspired approach of Hallin and Mancini (2004) and the early suggestions of Benson (1999). Likewise, studies of different forms of 'mediatization' produced by different media production fields could also be included in a pragmatic understanding of 'media production studies', and thus follow the suggestion of Couldry (2003) to research the *symbolic power* of the media. Finally, Hesmondhalgh's (2006) call for research on *large-scale production* would naturally fit under the umbrella of media production studies.

Studies of media production in a field perspective

This section will review examples of media production studies from a field perspective, drawing on a pragmatic understanding including contributions where field theory is the main (but not necessarily the only) theory and where 'media production studies' is understood as studies of processes, content, and settings, producing knowledge about different fields of media production and about the symbolic power of media. That said, there are still examples of research that resist any easy categorization or fall out of the definition but can be said to contribute to researchers who wants to advance media production studies inspired by field theory. One example is the empirically rich investigation of film and video production in Los Angeles, *Production Culture: Industrial Reflexivity and Critical Practice in Film and Television* (Caldwell, 2008), which – in terms of research questions, methodological approach, relational thinking and a preoccupation with the relationship between cultures of production and production of culture – in many ways could have been an investigation conducted within the framework of field theory – but is not.

Theoretical contributions

Looking at the literature on how field theory can contribute to media studies and, more specifically, to advancing media production studies, there are several theoretical contributions discussing field theory as a social theory (Swartz, 2002, 2003, 2008, 2014), theoretical contributions dealing with the overall question of cultural production (e.g. Gartman, 2011; Gartman, 2007; Fowler, 2012) and more specific theoretical contributions in relation to specific (sub)fields of cultural production – for instance, pop music (Kropf, 2012), journalism and critical engagement (Markham, 2014), Arab journalists as cultural intermediaries (Mellor, 2008), the rules of the game in the journalistic field (Marlière, 1998), American media discourse (Rohlinger, 2007), online interaction (Julien, 2015), literature (Boschetti, 2006), cultural economy theorizing (Hinde and Dixon, 2007), and the sociology of music (Prior, 2011). Also the concept of capital, or rather the different forms of capital, has been discussed theoretically with relevance for media production studies (e.g. Bolin, 2012; Driessens, 2013; Hess, 2013).

Media production practices

A range of studies have used field theory to produce knowledge on media production practices, using methods such as participant observations, surveys and interviews. Ethnographic field studies serve as the empirical background for analysing punk as a (sub)field of cultural production, in the article 'Friends Don't Let Friends Listen to Corporate Rock' (Moore, 2007) and for analysing contemporary Western popular music songwriting (McIntyre, 2008). A study based on observations and interviews investigates how journalists in American newspaper organizations adapt video for news presentation (Bock, 2011), and, using in-depth interviews, a Turkish study looks at the production and discourses around the Turkish production front of *Eurovision Song Contest* in a field perspective (Akin, 2013). Ethnographic methods have also been used in a study of Danish online journalists discussing the practice of routinizing breaking news (Hartley, 2011) and a new role perception that is more audience-driven and source-detached (Møller Hartley, 2013). Another Danish study has looked at exclusivity as an orthodox news value of Danish journalists (Schultz, 2007) and developed an analytical framework for studying newsroom ethnography in a field perspective (Willig, 2012).

The survey has also been used as a methodological tool for constructing and analysing fields of media production. A very ambitious and rigorous illustration of this is Jan Fredrik Hovden's use of correspondence analysis to sketch a model of the Norwegian journalistic field (Hovden, 2008, 2012, 2014). Another Scandinavian survey study drawing on field theory is 'Lonely at the Top: Gendered Media Elites in Sweden' (Djerf-Pierre, 2005), analysing gender in Swedish media elites, and field theory is also the backdrop for studying journalism students in the Scandinavian countries (Hovden et al., 2009; Bjørnsen et al., 2007). In Germany, 500 interviews with journalists were the empirical base for presenting a typology of role perceptions inspired by field theory (Meyen and Riesmeyer, 2012), and a survey of 206 online editors in the US (Tandoc, 2014) concluded that they used web analytics according to their understanding of the competition in the journalistic field and of the audience. In the US, field theory was the inspiration for a survey study showing a shift in the dominant capital among journalists publishing online from objectivity to transparency-orientation (Hellmueller et al., 2012), and in Austria, surveys were used to investigate working conditions and career strategies of journalists working in news media (Hummel et al., 2012).

In-depth interviews are also used in many studies of media production practice inspired by field theory. A recent study drawing on interviews with 'filmers' conceptualizes the phenomenon of music fans filming concerts on mobile devices and uploading the footage to YouTube as 'small-scale broadcasting' and as a way of gaining recognition and cultural capital (Colburn, 2014). In Russia, interviews with journalists showed a distinction between older and younger journalists (Erzikova and Lowrey, 2012).

The structure of media production fields

Another line of empirical studies emphasizes the structural settings of different media production fields. Examples include studies of the UK custom publishing field (Haeusermann, 2013), the tattoo world (Kosut, 2013), the collective bio of journalists in the German Democratic Republic (Meyen and Fiedler, 2012), the fashion fields (Rocamora, 2002), young female journalists in the Austrian union of journalists (Prandner, 2013), definitions of quality in the Israeli television drama field (Lavie, 2015), and how manga were introduced in the US publishing field (Brienza, 2009).

Based on interviews in the UK film and television industry, Randle et al. (2014) analyse the social composition and internal distinctions of workers in the industry. In the UK, field theory has also been the inspiration for looking at contemporary British art in the 1990s (Grenfell and Hardy, 2003). A study on the US journalistic field, 'Reporting and the Transformations of the Journalistic Field: US News Media, 1890–2000' (Krause, 2011), investigates the rise of the ideal of public service.

Bridging media production and media consumption

Another thread in the research literature is field-inspired studies bridging media production and consumption with the symbolic power of media.

A study of radio consumption in France argues that the theory of cultural production should be developed, criticizing terms such as 'the public' and more specifically the Bourdieusian field of large scale production' (Glevarec and Pinet, 2008). A study of the media coverage of the French 2005 riots suggests that the arrival of 'audience-participants' into the journalistic field poses new challenges to field theory (Russell, 2007). In Australia, three qualitative case studies of local journalism, drawing on interviews with editors, journalists, sales people, readers, non-readers and other sources, lead to the suggestion of a 'local habitus' (Hess and Waller, 2014; see also Hess, 2014).

Interviews with Asian immigrant women in South Korea show that their media use and reading strategies are 'omnivorous' and help them acquire 'the host culture capital' as well as maintaining 'the home cultural capital' (Yoon et al., 2011). 'Cultural omnivores', describing segments that enjoy both 'high' and 'popular' cultural goods, are also the subject matter of an article on consumption patterns in South Africa (Snowball et al., 2009) and a German study of the pop-music field (Kropf, 2012). Also based on Bourdieu, a theoretical essay proposes that journalism should be regarded as 'a structure of public communication which is mutually enacted by journalists and audiences alike' (Raetzsch, 2014: 65).

Bridging media system and media content

A number of research contributions use reflexive sociology as an analytical framework for studying media content. An example of a content analysis analysing media production practices is the article 'Playing the Media Game: The Relative Invisibility of Coal Industry Interests in Media Reporting of Coal as a Climate Change Issue in Australia' (Bacon and Nash, 2012). Here reflexive sociology has inspired the researchers to 'embrace the issue of visibility and invisibility of agents and their positions in the field' (p. 243). Another example of how content analysis can be used to develop theories and findings about media production practices is the longitudinal case study over six years of how CNN includes iReporters and which positions are being assigned to participatory journalists and CNN journalists (Hellmueller and Li, 2014).

There are also examples of comparative content studies drawing on field theory and media system theory, such as the comparison of offline and online newspapers in the US, Denmark and France (Benson et al., 2012) and the study of newspapers in the US and France (Benson, 2005). A study of generalized and specialized subfields of cultural journalism based on a content analysis of Finnish dailies proposes the notion of 'aesthetic tourism' to describe the practices enabling journalists to transition from an elitist to a pluralistic cultural journalism (Jaakkola, 2012). A Korean study was inspired by *On Television* to explore the processes of 'monitoring and imitation' in newsrooms and used content study of thirteen news websites to explore how tracking of competitor websites was used in the editorial process (Lim, 2012).

An explorative study of the relationship between role perception and role enactment of journalists was conducted by comparing survey data with content analysis (Tandoc et al., 2012), concluding that the relationship between what journalists ideally see as their role and how they actually practice journalism should be questioned rather than presumed. In Australia, an analysis of the media discourse of the prime minister in television political interviews proposed that 'political subjectivity' can be seen as a negotiation between the political and the journalistic field (Craig, 2013). New media have also been studied with inspiration from Bourdieu, such as a Belgian study of conversation patterns on Twitter during election times (D'heer and Verdegem, 2014) and a study of bloggers' media criticism, arguing that the practices on new platforms appear to live up to traditional journalistic norms, thus suggesting a stable field (Vos et al., 2011).

Conclusion

This chapter set out to review the literature on media production inspired by field theory. Drawing on contributions on various topics, such as journalism, art, popular music, literature, online communities, punk, etc., it is argued that a strict reading of media production studies as studies using participant observation, interviews and other methods used to look at the production process itself would rule out interesting research contributions. Not least, studies of media texts and media discourses can – when analysed within the framework of field theory – help us understand practices of media producers as well as the structures of the media production field in question. Also, reception studies, and not least digital platforms, where users are often also producers, can contribute to our understanding of media production.

I have not been able to acknowledge all of the media production research done within a Bourdieusian perspective; neither has it been possible to discuss the research contributions in great detail. However, the reading offers a few concluding remarks across the many different contributions. Firstly, field theory is helpful when designing production studies. Much can and has been said about the balance between inductive and deductive approaches to fieldwork. Used with care, field theory can provide helpful analytical lenses through which media production can be studied systematically and in accordance with an overarching social theory, without closing down for the unexpected insight, which is one of the great rewards of studying media production practices and one of the best arguments for doing, for instance, participant observational studies. Field theory is also helpful in the analytical phase of the production research. Not least because reflexive sociology offers many concepts within the theoretical framework, it is possible to look at empirical findings from different angles, investigating them in light of the different theoretical concepts and relating them to other empirical findings within a consistent theoretical framework. Last, but not least, as can be seen from many of the studies reviewed in this chapter, one of the most prominent benefits of field theory in relation to media production studies is its explanatory power. Empirical findings can be put into an explanatory framework and thus lifted from the particular to the general. This is most likely because field theory is a social theory and not a theory concerning a specific medium or a specific form of cultural production.

To conclude, by addressing the topic of this book – the advancement of media production studies – the research done in the past two decades shows that field theory is more than a 'promising analytical framework' (Willig, 2012) for media production studies, whether they are based on observation studies, surveys, interviews, content studies or a mixed methods approach. Field theory has proven to be an original, productive analytical framework, potentially bridging the gap between social theory and empirical media studies, reconciling macro with micro, content with context, and production with consumption.

References

Akin, A. (2013) 'Turkey, the Middle East & the media – "The reality is not as it seems from Turkey": Imaginations about the Eurovision song contest from its production fields.' *International Journal of Communication 7*, 19.

Bacon, W. and Nash, C. (2012) 'Playing the media game'. *Journalism Studies 13*(2), 243–248.

Benson, R. (1999) 'Field theory in a comparative context: A new paradigm for media studies.' *Theory and Society 28*(3), 463–498.

Benson, R. (2004) 'Bringing the sociology of media back in.' *Political Communication 21*(3), 275–292.

Benson, R. (2005) 'Mapping field variation: Journalism in France and the United States' in R. Benson and E. Neveu (eds), *Bourdieu and the Journalistic Field* (pp. 85–112) (Cambridge: Polity Press).

Benson, R. et al. (2012) 'Media systems online and off: Comparing the form of news in the United States, Denmark, and France.' *Journal of Communication* 62(1), 21–38.

Bjørnsen, G., Hovden, J. F. and Ottosen, R. (2007) 'Journalists in the making.' *Journalism Practice* 1(3), 383–403.

Bock, M. A. (2011) 'Newspaper journalism and video: Motion, sound, and new narratives.' *New Media & Society* 14(4), 600–616.

Bolin, G. (2012) 'The forms of value: Problems of convertibility in field theory.' *TripleC* 10(1), 33–41.

Born, G. (2010) 'The social and the aesthetic: For a post-Bourdieuian theory of cultural production.' *Cultural Sociology* 4(2), 171–208.

Boschetti, A. (2006) 'Bourdieu's work on literature: Contexts, stakes and perspectives.' *Theory, Culture & Society* 23(6), 135–155.

Bourdieu, P. (1988) *Homo Academicus* (Cambridge: Polity Press).

Bourdieu, P. (1993) *The Field of Cultural Production: Essays on Art and Litterature* (Cambridge: Polity Press).

Bourdieu, P. (1996) *The Rules of Art: Genesis and Structure of the Literary Field* (Stanford California: Stanford University Press).

Bourdieu, P. (1998a) *On Television* (New York: The New Free Press).

Bourdieu, P. (1998b) *Practical Reason: On the Theory of Action* (Cambridge: Polity Press).

Bourdieu, P. (2000) *Pascalian Meditations* (Cambridge: Polity Press).

Bourdieu, P. (2003) *Distinction: A Social Critique of the Judgement of Taste* (London: Routledge).

Bourdieu, P. (2005) 'The political field, the social science field, and journalistic field' in R. Benson and E. Neveu (eds), *Bourdieu and the Journalistic Field* (pp. 29–47) (Cambridge: Polity Press).

Bourdieu, P. and Wacquant, L. J. D. (1992) *An Invitation to Reflexive Sociology* (Chicago: University of Chicago Press).

Bourdieu, P. et al. (1999) *The Weight of the World. Social Suffering in Contemporary Society* (Cambridge: Polity Press).

Brienza, C. E. (2009) 'Books, not comics: Publishing fields, globalization, and Japanese manga in the United States.' *Publishing Research Quarterly* 25(2), 101–117.

Caldwell, J. T. (2008) *Production Culture Production Culture: Industrial Reflexivity and Critical Practice in Film and Television* (Durham: Duke University Press).

Champagne, P. (1993) 'The view from the state' in P. Bourdieu et al. (eds), *The Weight of the World* (pp. 213–221) (Cambridge: Polity Press).

Champagne, P. (2005) 'The "double dependency": The journalistic field between politics and markets' in R. Benson and E. Neveu (eds), *Bourdieu and the Journalistic Field* (pp. 48–82) (Cambridge: Polity Press).

Colburn, S. (2014) 'Filming concerts for YouTube: Seeking recognition in the pursuit of cultural capital.' *Popular Music and Society* 38(March), 59–72.

Couldry, N. (2001) 'The hidden injuries of media power.' *Journal of Consumer Culture* 1(2), 155–177.

Couldry, N. (2003) 'Media meta-capital: Extending the range of Bourdieu's field theory.' *Theory and Society* 32(5/6), 653–677.

Couldry, N., Livingstone, S., and Markham, T. (2007) *Media Consumption and Public Engagement* (Basingstoke: Palgrave Macmillan).

Craig, G. (2013) 'How does a prime minister speak? Kevin Rudd's discourse, habitus, and negotiation of the journalistic and political fields.' *Journal of Language and Politics* 12(4), 485–507.

D'heer, E. and Verdegem, P. (2014) 'Conversations about the elections on Twitter: Towards a structural understanding of Twitter's relation with the political and the media field.' *European Journal of Communication* 29(6), 720–734.

Djerf-Pierre, M. (2005) 'Lonely at the top: Gendered media elites in Sweden.' *Journalism* 6(3), 265–290.

Driessens, O. (2013) 'Celebrity capital: Redefining celebrity using field theory.' *Theory and Society* 42(5), 543–560.

Erzikova, E. and Lowrey, W. (2012) 'Managed mediocrity?' *Journalism Practice* 6(3), 264–279.

Fowler, B. (2012) 'Pierre Bourdieu, social transformation and 1960s British drama.' *Theory, Culture & Society* 29(3), 3–24.

Gartman, D. (2007) 'The strength of weak programs in cultural sociology: A critique of Alexander's critique of Bourdieu.' *Theory and Society* 36(5), 381–413.

Gartman, D. (2011) 'Bourdieu and Adorno: Converging theories of culture and inequality.' *Theory and Society* 41(1), 41–72.

Glevarec, H. and Pinet, M. (2008) 'From liberalization to fragmentation: A sociology of French radio audiences since the 1990s and the consequences for cultural industries theory.' *Media, Culture & Society* 30(2), 215–238.

Grenfell, M. and Hardy, C. (2003) 'Field manoeuvres: Bourdieu and the young British artists.' *Space and Culture* 6(1), 19–34.

Haeusermann, T. (2013) 'Custom publishing in the UK: Rise of a silent giant.' *Publishing Research Quarterly* 29(2), 99–109.

Hallin, D. C. and Mancini, P. (2004) *Comparing Media Systems: Three Models of Media and Politics* (Cambridge: Cambridge University Press).

Hartley, J. M. (2011) 'Routinizing breaking news: Categories and hierarchies in Danish online newsrooms' in D. Domingo and C. Paterson (eds), *Making Online News, Vol. 2* (pp. 73–86) (Oxford, New York: Peter Lang Publishing).

Hellmueller, L. and Li, Y. (2014) 'Contest over content.' *Journalism Practice* [published online]. DOI: 10.1080/17512786.2014.987553.

Hellmueller, L., Vos, T. P., and Poepsel, M. A. (2013) 'Shifting journalistic capital?' *Journalism Studies* 14(3), 287–304.

Hesmondhalgh, D. (2006) 'Bourdieu, the media and cultural production.' *Media, Culture & Society* 28(2), 211–231.

Hess, K.(2013) 'Tertius tactics: "Mediated social capital" as a resource of power for traditional commercial news media.' *Communication Theory* 23(2), 112–130.

Hess, K. and Waller, L. (2014) 'River flows and profit flows.' *Journalism Studies* [published online]. DOI: 10.1080/1461670X.2014.981099.

Hinde, S. and Dixon, J. (2007) 'Reinstating Pierre Bourdieu's contribution to cultural economy theorizing.' *Journal of Sociology* 43(1994), 401–420.

Hovden, J. F. (2008) *Profane and Sacred: A Study of the Norwegian Journalistic Field*, doctoral thesis, University of Bergen, Norway.

Hovden, J. F. (2012) 'A journalistic cosmology: A sketch of some social and mental structures of the norwegian journalistic field.' *Nordicom Review* 33(2), 57–76.

Hovden, J. F. (2014) 'To intervene or be neutral, to investigate or entertain? National and intranational factors in the formation of Nordic journalism students' role perceptions.' *Journalism Practice* 8(5), 646–659.

Hovden, J. F. et al. (2009) 'The Nordic journalists of tomorrow.' *Nordicom Review* 30(1), 149–165.

Hummel, R., Kirchhoff, S., and Prandner, D. (2012) '"We used to be queens and now we are slaves": Working conditions and career strategies in the journalistic field.' *Journalism Practice* 6(5–6), 722–731.

Jaakkola, M. (2012) 'Promoting aesthetic tourism.' *Journalism Practice* 6(4), 482–496.

Julien, C. (2015) 'Bourdieu, social capital and online interaction.' *Sociology* 49(2), 356–373.

Kosut, M. (2013). 'The artification of tattoo: Transformations within a cultural field.' *Cultural Sociology* 8(2), 142–158.

Krause, M. (2011) 'Reporting and the transformations of the journalistic field: US news media, 1890–2000.' *Media, Culture & Society* 33(1), 89–104.

Kropf, J. (2012) 'Der symbolische Wert der Popmusik. Zur Genese und Struktur des popmusikalischen Feldes.' *Berliner Journal für Soziologie* 22(2), 267–292.

Lavie, N. (2015) 'Israeli drama: Constructing the Israeli "quality" television series as an art form.' *Media, Culture & Society* 37(1), 19–34.

Lim, J. (2012) 'Power relations among popular news websites for posting headlines through monitoring and imitation.' *New Media & Society* 15(7), 1112–1131.

Markham, T. (2014) 'Journalism and critical engagement: Naiveté, embarrassment, and intelligibility.' *Communication and Critical/Cultural Studies* 11(2): 158–174.

Marlière, P. (1998) 'The rules of the journalistic field: Pierre Bourdieu's contribution to the sociology of the media.' *European Journal of Communication* 13(2), 219–234.

McIntyre, P. (2008) 'Creativity and cultural production: A study of contemporary Western popular music songwriting.' *Creativity Research Journal* 20(1), 40–52.

Mellor, N. (2008) 'Arab journalists as cultural intermediaries.' *International Journal of Press/Politics* 13(4), 465–483.

Meyen, M. and Fiedler, A. (2012) 'Journalists in the German Democratic Republic (Gdr).' *Journalism Studies* 14(3), 321–335.

Meyen, M. and Riesmeyer, C. (2012) 'Service providers, sentinels, and traders.' *Journalism Studies* 13(3), 386–401.

Moore, R. (2007) 'Friends don't let friends listen to corporate rock: Punk as a field of cultural production.' *Journal of Contemporary Ethnography* 36(4), 438–474.

Møller Hartley, J. (2013) 'The online journalist between ideals and audiences.' *Journalism Practice* 7(5), 572–587.

Prandner, D. (2013) 'Young female journalists in Austria's journalists' union: Part of the working poor?' *Catalan Journal of Communication & Cultural Studies* 5(1), 69–81.

Prior, N. (2011) 'Critique and renewal in the sociology of music: Bourdieu and beyond.' *Cultural Sociology* 5, 121–138.

Raetzsch, C. (2015) 'Innovation through practice.' *Journalism Practice* 9(1), 65–77.

Randle, K., Forson, C. and Calveley, M. (2014) 'Towards a Bourdieusian analysis of the social composition of the UK film and television workforce.' *Work, Employment & Society* [published online]. DOI: 10.1177/0950017014542498.

Rocamora, A. (2002) 'Fields of fashion.' *Journal of Consumer Culture* 2(3), 341–362.

Rohlinger, D. A. (2007) 'American media and deliberative democratic processes.' *Sociological Theory* 25(2), 122–148.

Russell, A. (2007) 'Digital communication networks and the journalistic field: The 2005 French riots.' *Critical Studies in Media Communication* 24(4), 285–302.

Schultz, I. (2007) 'The journalistic gut feeling.' *Journalism Practice* 1(2), 190–207.

Snowball, J. D., Jamal, M., and Willis, K. G. (2009) 'Cultural consumption patterns in South Africa: An investigation of the theory of cultural omnivores.' *Social Indicators Research* 97(3), 467–483.

Swartz, D. L. (2002) 'In memoriam: Pierre Bourdieu 1930–2002.' *Theory and Society* (31), 533–547.

Swartz, D. L. (2003) 'Drawing inspiration from Bourdieu's sociology of symbolic power.' *Theory and Society* 32(5), 519–528.

Swartz, D. L. (2008) 'Bringing Bourdieu's master concepts into organizational analysis.' *Theory and Society* 37(1), 45–52.

Swartz, D. L. (2014) 'Theorizing fields.' *Theory and Society* 43(6), 675–682.

Tandoc, E. C. (2014) 'Why web analytics click.' *Journalism Studies* [published online]. DOI: 10.1080/1461670X.2014.946309.

Tandoc, E. C., Hellmueller, L., and Vos, T. P. (2012) 'Mind the gap.' *Journalism Practice* 7(5): 539–554.

Vos, T. P., Craft, S., and Ashley, S. (2011) 'New media, old criticism: Bloggers' press criticism and the journalistic field.' *Journalism* 13(7), 850–868.

Wacquant, L. J. D. (1989) 'Towards a reflexive sociology: A workshop with Pierre Bourdieu.' *Sociological Theory* 7(1), 26–63.

Willig, I. (2012) 'Newsroom ethnography in a field perspective.' *Journalism* [published online]. DOI: 10.1177/1464884912442638.

Yoon, T.-I., Kim, K.-H. and Eom, H.-J. (2011) 'The border-crossing of habitus: Media consumption, motives, and reading strategies among Asian immigrant women in South Korea.' *Media, Culture & Society* 33(3), 415–431.

5
Studying News Production: From Process to Meanings

Daniel A. Berkowitz and Zhengjia Liu

With a history going back to at least the 1950s, long-term research in media production environments remains challenging. Much of the research on news production has come from a sociological direction that examines the *process* of production. By choosing this route, research has tended to focus on interactions among journalists at the small group and organizational levels. This vein of research mainly emphasizes the limitations and constraints on what might become the news product.

Methodologically, long-term study within production environments poses two key challenges. First, institutional review boards (or ethics panels) have become significantly more demanding in the measures required to assure both maximum privacy and minimum risk for the people being studied. A second challenge is that increasing pressures for faculty productivity toward tenure and promotion make the time demands of long-term research unfeasible (a problem Ryfe explores in Chapter 3 of this volume). In all, long-term on-site research has become a difficult undertaking, most easily accomplished by either graduate students or by senior scholars who live near appropriate research sites.

For scholars wanting to study media production, yet who are unable to clear these two hurdles, text-based culturally oriented research becomes a valuable tool, especially when informed by concepts gleaned from on-site studies. An added advantage is that an emphasis on media texts can focus on questions about *meanings* of journalism to journalists and *meanings* of journalism within its societal context. This approach moves the level of study from organizational work toward macro-cultural aspects that consider journalism more broadly as a professional phenomenon. However, researchers should keep in mind that relying on journalistic texts alone brings a trade-off with the grounded context that comes from observing production interactions directly.

This chapter will first discuss a framework for exploring production research systematically, followed by an overview of professional, sociological and cultural approaches to studying production and the trade-offs that each brings. Then field theory is introduced as a big-picture means of studying media texts through three lenses: mythical narratives, collective memory and ideographs. Finally, the chapter reconsiders the advantages and challenges of studying media production through its artifacts: the texts.

Locating media production questions and methods

To consider what can be gained by moving from ethnographic work to the study of news texts, research needs to be dissected by four basic aspects: topic, focus of research, level of analysis, and paradigm. At the most basic point, the *topic of study* explores a case study for conceptual exploration. On its own, though, the topic of study essentially remains descriptive. The *focus of the research* begins moving forward from the topic, identifying the importance of that topic to the exploration that follows: producers, audience or product. For the purposes of this chapter, the focus will always be the producer, even though data might come from media texts. *Level of analysis* is key, considering the kind of social aggregation related to the study focus: individuals, small groups, organizations, professions or institutions. However, the *unit of analysis* at which data is collected is less crucial than the level of analysis at which inferences are made.

Understanding a researcher's *paradigm* – the assumptions that guide the research – is also important, if also somewhat latent to observe. For example, researchers studying the same aspect of media production from normative/professional, positivist/behavioural, constructivist/cultural or critical/ideological paradigms would see their work through different lenses that would impact guiding theory, research questions, data collection, and data analysis/interpretation.

It should be clear that methodological choices are unavoidably linked to topic, research focus, level of analysis and paradigm. For example, observational research can be studied and analysed through a behavioural lens and quantitative data; qualitative data could be interpreted from more of a constructivist position. Ultimately, the *purpose of the research* – description, prediction, explanation, understanding – follows from the choices that have been made in the four previous points. By reflecting on the purpose, the role of theory can also be better understood. New media phenomena, for example, might benefit from basic descriptive research (Kim and Weaver, 2002; Wimmer and Dominick, 2006), while questions related to more long-standing areas such as mythical narratives in the news can contribute by broadening understanding of the meanings of news production.

Sociological approaches to studying news production

At the most basic level, news production can be studied from a professional vantage point that addresses normative or descriptive questions (Siebert, Peterson and Schramm, 1956). By normative questions, we refer to efforts that judge whether production has conformed to a specific set of ideals, principles or standards. By descriptive questions, we mean story-telling and anecdotes about what takes place. A key problem with a professional vantage point is that it provides answers and assessments that are inherent to the belief system of the observer. While this vantage point helps a reader see *what* goes on in a media production environment, it is not as helpful for understanding *why* these events are going on or *why* media production efforts have made one choice rather than another, other than to assert that it was the right thing to do.

That is where a *sociological* vantage point is of value, offering insights that help explain social forces that have shaped media production decisions and constrained the choices because of social expectations and organizational resource limitations. This is the direction where most of the long-term production research has taken place. Other chapters in this volume present an overview of this sociological vein of work.

Long-term research within production environments confronts researchers with a variety of contemporary challenges. Many of the classic studies were related to dissertations, a time when the researcher is least encumbered. The time between beginning the research and the appearance of publications was significant. Many of the studies – especially the comparative ones – were conducted in major metropolitan areas, which are not accessible to every scholar. And, centrally, most of these studies focused on production of news, especially the processes and constraints involved. Questions about newsroom culture and its meanings were less often addressed by these ethnographies, although some studies did discuss the role of culture in different terms.

We now turn to examine how the questions a researcher asks interface with the research method used, making a case for the utility of studying news texts for understanding cultural elements of news.

Toward cultural meanings of news

In order to discuss news from a text-oriented *cultural meanings* perspective, the concept of 'cultural' must first be defined and discussion located within that definition. Three definitions of the term are in common use (Berkowitz, 2011: xv–xvi).

The first meaning – the one we focus on – is more or less an anthropological answer that depicts a culture as built on shared and lived meanings. As Coman and Rothenbuhler (2005: 1) explain, this approach emerged as a hybrid between anthropology of modern societies and the cultural turn in media studies to engage in symbolic construction of reality, especially those symbolic structures related to myth, narrative, representation and ritual in everyday life (p. 3). These dimensions lend themselves well to the study of texts rather than process, because that is what they best illustrate. In all, there exists a strong rationale for viewing culture as meaning, and for turning to texts to view those meanings, although a few newsroom studies have also adopted the perspective (e.g. Ehrlich, 1995; Schultz, 2007).

A second use of the term 'cultural' refers to the British cultural studies tradition that emphasizes ideology, hegemony and power (e.g. Hall, 1982). This meaning considers who is powerful and who is dominated by that power. It further conveys the idea that those power relationships are embedded and transmitted through media messages. This work is most often accomplished through textual studies but has also been suggested occasionally for newsroom observation studies to address 'questions of economy, culture, power, politics, etc.' (Willig, 2013: 375). For purposes of this chapter, though, this meaning of culture is not as close a fit.

A third use of 'cultural' really refers to global studies, especially research that compares media texts across two or more countries. A challenge for this kind of work is to convey cultural meanings of a country and its political, economic and media systems. This, again, becomes a good area of exploration for textual studies that want to compare how a similar occurrence was depicted between differing news production settings. For example, Nossek and Berkowitz (2006) compared the news texts of US and Israeli media that both covered the same terrorist bombing yet told different stories that represented national narratives of the US (The Wild West) and Israel (The Holocaust). Berkowitz and Eko (2007) compared the news narratives of US and French news media coverage of the Mohammad cartoon controversy in a way that reflected both differences in the meaning of nationalism and the meaning of journalism itself. These examples could be considered 'doubly cultural' by simultaneously considering cultures of news production alongside of contrasting cultures of a society.

Approaching news texts from a cultural perspective

Field theory provides a helpful theoretical perspective to understand cultural meanings embedded in news texts (Schultz, 2007; Vos, Craft and Ashley, 2012; Willig, 2013). *Field* is the concept proposed by Bourdieu (1973, 1986, 2005; Bourdieu and Johnson, 1993) to conceptualize social relation space, including competitive hierarchies of economic, cultural and social capitals. Because journalists are members of their professional institutions and members of the society they live within, as insiders, they may be able to 'feel' the 'right' things to do their professional work but may not be able to consciously realize the exact criteria. Similarly, as members of their society, audiences may be able to 'feel' whether journalists have done 'right' to produce news but may not be able to consciously realize the exact criteria of 'right'. As the connection between journalists and audiences, media texts reflect journalists' unspoken criteria of 'right' in news production, resonating with audiences' taken-for-granted expectation of 'good' journalism. (For further discussion of field theory, see Chapter 4 by Willig in this volume.)

With the knowledge of journalism as a professional field, media research can see unspoken, taken-for-granted presuppositions in news production. Three conceptual dimensions – mythical narratives, collective memory and ideographic labels – can be effectively applied to the study of media texts to help understand dimensions of media production as a reproduction of cultural meanings.

Mythical narratives: repeated cultural studies

One thing that cultural scholars can read from media texts is repeated storylines, which can be discussed as mythical narratives from a cultural perspective. Here, myth refers to an enduring story type that contains predictable plots, recognizable characters, widely held significant values and accepted morals (Berkowitz and Nossek, 2001; Bird and Dardenne, 1988; Lule, 2001; Smith, 1997).

Seven mythical templates have commonly been used by journalists to craft news stories: the victim, the scapegoat, the hero, the good mother, the trickster, the other world and the flood (Lule, 2001). Each of these myths contains standard characters, essential plotlines and core values of a culture. Yet, there really is no 'official list' of narratives – this is one of those know-them-when-you-see-them kinds of cultural elements. As Bird (2005: 226) criticized, arguing for a standard set of templates 'pays scant attention to the differences in time and place that produce particular cultural moments and narratives.' Her larger point is that journalists do not create myth on their own, instead serving as 'the brokers for the stories a culture is already telling' (p. 227). Therefore, storylines in media texts retell a society's enduring legacy and reinforce its significant cultural values.

For example, the 'hero' is a common narrative in many societies. Such a story usually is about an individual who undertakes self-sacrifice in order to right some crucial wrong or to protect society from some looming evil (Kitch and Hume, 2007). Heroes can take a variety of forms of varying magnitudes, from a fireman who rescues a small child out of a burning building to a platoon of soldiers who secure a victory after a long-odds battle against a brutal attempted-conqueror. At the Virginia Tech shootings (the murder of 32 people at a US university in 2007), for example, the hero in news stories was a professor who survived the Holocaust only to die while protecting his students from an armed gunman on an otherwise placid campus (Berkowitz, 2010). Exactly who is considered eligible for the hero designation, though, comes from the culture that retells the story. For instance, when the Chinese neo-liberal media covered his death, Steve Jobs was portrayed as a hero who sowed hope, opportunity and money to Chinese high-technology elites. Essentially, the hero narrative reinforced enduring cultural themes – technological progress, consumerism and nationalism – in post-reform Chinese society (Liu and Berkowitz, 2014).

In each of the cases just discussed, journalists told a narrative that was most culturally resonant for themselves, their colleagues and their audiences. The importance of the adaptation of mythical narratives to the construction of news is that it helps make news look 'culturally correct' while also streamlining a journalist's work efforts by providing a basic storyline, story themes, and likely story characters. In other words, drawing on mythical narrative helps news appear not as a construction but as 'the way it is', with appropriate cultural values, story outcomes and social actors. In essence, culture itself has created the news as the journalist becomes society's story-telling bard.

Collective memory: the reconstructed past for the present

Collective memory helps define news and gives it perspective and historical connections. It suggests that recollections of the past guide interpretations of the present (Kitch and Hume, 2007; Meyers, 2011; Zelizer, 2011). However, the past is not necessarily applied as context for an emerging story but rather as a means of comparison that provides a point of reference to shape the meaning of a current occurrence within the realm of possible cultural meanings.

For instance, in 2008, Barack Obama came to American voters as a young and inexperienced presidential candidate, an African American from a single-parent home who grew up in Hawaii – he didn't match the usual presidential mould. However, drawing on collective memory made Obama more tangible and familiar (Berkowitz and Raaii, 2010). In news of Obama's presidential campaign, reporters compared him to Abraham Lincoln, his public speaking ability and age to John F. Kennedy, and the financial crisis facing the nation to that facing Franklin D. Roosevelt. By doing so, he could be imagined as appropriately presidential. Once Obama was victorious in his presidential bid, news of his inauguration could go one step further and cast his story in the shadow of Martin Luther King Jr. Likewise, when covering the 2003 re-entry disintegration of the space shuttle Columbia, journalists drew on collective memory of the 1986 space shuttle Challenger launch disaster to conduct interviews and craft stories, even though the two incidents involved vastly different circumstances (Edy and Daradanova, 2011).

Collective memory shows that when covering something new and unexpected, a journalist can turn back to similar events of the past to see how this kind of story has gone before. Doing so provides a template of probable actors and news sources, as well as key story themes and cultural narratives. Drawing on memory of the past, however, does not assure that news coverage will exactly match what has just taken place, but it does provide a high likelihood that a story will be familiar and ring true. The journalist then will be able to assemble a story from time-honoured 'parts', while news audiences will be more eager to accept the story that has been presented, since what they consume better aligns with what they know and expect.

The ideograph: a label with constructed cultural meanings

On the surface, the words of any language carry meanings that can be agreed upon and inserted into a dictionary. At a deeper level, though, words can be seen as conveying a whole ideology. That is, some words or phrases mean much more than they appear to, what is called an *ideograph* (McGee, 1980). Some common ideographs include liberty, property, freedom of speech, religion, and equality. Each of these ideographic labels carries vague meanings at first glance, yet in each case that meaning is ideological, whether in agreement with or in opposition to. For instance, Zheng (2008) found that in discussion of Chinese media, two terms – liberalism and democracy – were often interchanged without question. Such confusion resonated with the neo-liberal ideology in Chinese society.

Further, although an ideograph shapes cultural construction of news, it would be reductionist to think of this construction from a media-centric perspective. Rather, ideographs lie in the centre of a society and are interactively shaped by popular culture, public officials, news media (broadly construed), and society overall. Likewise, ideographs shape meanings in each segment, so that the process becomes two-way and dynamic with ideographic meanings shifting like sand dunes over time.

Ideographs can be conceptually placed between officials, the public, and news media in a diamond-shaped relationship that incorporates meanings echoed by a myriad of popular culture forms such as film, television, fiction, social media, and blogs, among others. Further, news media need to be construed broadly in this model as the borders of news blur with popular culture forms. In a media-saturated environment, news comes from blogs, Facebook, and a variety of talk show hosts who bring news into their monologues. News talk programmes blur the definition of news even more, as pundits from the political left and right bandy about ideographs that form the centre of their sparring. Ideographs bring the potential for a wider sense of constructed cultural meanings over time since they hinge on a single word or phrase rather than an overall cultural narrative.

Conclusion

This chapter began by raising three concerns about long-term research in media production environments. First, the general thrust of this kind of research tends to be limited to examinations of process within a sociological framework. For example, when studying the production of news in the newsroom, the *process* of daily news work is most visible. This includes both what journalists do and how they interact as the day's process unfolds. Second, given the emphasis on process, questions tend to be limited to news selection, resource constraints, time constraints, source interactions or work routines. Third, long-term research tends to be logistically challenging. At the beginning, ethics committee clearance from the institution may often take months. Finding time to conduct long-term research can be difficult for academic staff members – many of the classic studies were actually done when the authors were graduate students working on their dissertations. Location may also be a limiting factor if the researcher is not physically close to the necessary research sites. Finally, access may be a problem, as media competition becomes tighter and research findings become more critical of what is observed.

Given the demands and constraints of long-term research in media production environments, this chapter has argued for the value of studying *texts* – the artifacts of journalistic production. On one hand, the logistics of such research become simpler. Human subject clearance is not required. The time to gather data is shorter, with greater flexibility about when data can be collected and how it may be stored. Data analysis applying qualitative methods will be no more demanding in terms of time and materials when compared to data drawn from observation and interviews. On the other hand, text-based research allows culturally oriented research questions to be asked that deal with meanings embedded into text by production by journalists through the society in which they work. These meanings can be drawn out by interrogating media texts to see patterns of themes that regularly appear in the news. Field theory becomes an overarching interpretive lens for examining these artifacts of production as a game with its own cultural set of rules and boundaries. Within that lens, mythical narratives (and their archetypal characters) cast events into familiar stories and values. Collective memory looks to the past for guiding understanding of the present. The ideograph connects key words and phrases to dynamic, ideological meanings.

As a research approach, qualitative examination of media texts still requires the usual caveats. As an interpretive, constructivist approach, this methodology is only as good as its interpretive lens and the researcher who applies it. Another important concern is data collection. A newsroom observer ideally makes strategic choices about where the observer should be located in the production site. A researcher studying texts likewise makes strategic choices about which texts over which time periods are most appropriate to study, scrutinizing whether the chosen texts adequately inform about cultural meanings. In drawing conclusions, the textually based scholar needs to carefully consider what the findings represent and how findings can be meaningfully transferred to help understand other contexts and artifacts of media production.

Beyond all of these considerations, the researcher needs to reflect on the suitability of the method for the questions being asked. For example, media texts are useful for understanding cultural meanings coming from both society and from production. Other questions are a poorer fit, however. For example, texts cannot go very deeply into understanding producer intent, work routines or workplace constraints. Looking farther outward, the study of texts carries minimum utility for understanding effects on media audiences.

In all, long-term research in media production environments can provide rich understandings but is logistically challenging and best suited for certain questions about that environment. This chapter has shown some ways that textually based studies offer a good counterpoint to immersion in production environments, while being more manageable to execute, yet still addressing many of a researcher's questions and the theoretical paradigms in which these questions are embedded.

References

Berkowitz, D. and Eko, L. (2007) 'Blasphemy as sacred rite/right: 'The Mohammed cartoons affair' and maintenance of journalistic ideology.' *Journalism Studies* 8(5), 779–797.

Berkowitz, D. and Nossek, H. (2001) 'Myths and news narratives: Towards a comparative perspective of news.' *Ecquid Novi* 22(1), 41–56.

Berkowitz, D. and Raaii, S. (2010) 'Conjuring Abraham, Martin and John: Memory and news of the Obama presidential campaign.' *Memory Studies* 3(4), 364–387.

Berkowitz, D. (2010) 'The ironic hero of Virginia Tech: Healing trauma through collective memory of the Holocaust.' *Journalism: Theory, Practice & Criticism* 11(6), 643–659.

Berkowitz, D. (2011) *Cultural Meanings of News: A Text-Reader* (Thousand Oaks, CA: Sage Publications).

Bird, S. E. and Dardenne, R. W. (1988) 'Myth, chronicle and story: Exploring the narrative qualities of news' in D. Berkowitz (ed.), *Social Meanings of News: A Text-Reader* (pp. 333–350) (Thousand Oaks, CA: SAGE).

Bird, S. E. (2005) 'CJ's revenge: A case study of news as cultural narrative' in E. W. Rothenbuhler and M. Coman (eds), *Media Anthropology* (pp. 220–228) (Thousand Oaks, CA: Sage).

Bourdieu, P. and Johnson, P. (1993) *The Field of Cultural Production: Essays on Art and Literature* (New York: Columbia University Press).

Bourdieu, P. (1973) 'Cultural reproduction and social reproduction' in R. K. Brown (ed.), *Knowledge, Education and Cultural Change* (pp. 56–86) (London: Tavistock).

Bourdieu, P. (1986) 'The forms of capital' in J. G. Richardson (ed.), *Handbook for Theory and Research for the Sociology of Education* (pp. 241–258) (New York: Greenwood).

Bourdieu, P. (2005) 'The political field, the social science field, and the journalistic field' in R. Benson and E. Neveu (eds), *Bourdieu and the Journalistic Field* (pp. 29–47) (Cambridge, MA: Polity Press).

Coman, M., and Rothenbuhler, E. W. (2005) 'The promise of media anthropology' in E. W. Rothenbuhler and M. Coman (eds), *Media Anthropology* (pp. 1–11) (Thousand Oaks, CA: Sage).

Edy, J. A. and Daradanova, M. (2011) 'Reporting through the lens of the past: From Challenger to Columbia' in D. Berkowitz (ed.), *Cultural Meanings of News: A Text-Reader* (pp. 305–320) (Los Angeles, CA: Sage).

Ehrlich, M. C. (1995) 'The competitive ethos in television newswork.' *Critical Studies in Mass Communication* 12(2), 196–212.

Hall, S. (1982) 'The rediscovery of "ideology": Return of the repressed in media studies' in M. Gurevitch, T. Bennett, J. Curran, and J. Woollacott, *Culture, Society and the Media* (pp. 56–90) (London: Methuen).

Kim, S. T. and Weaver, D. (2002) 'Communication research about the internet: A thematic meta-analysis.' *New Media & Society* 4(4), 518–538.

Kitch, C. and Hume, J. (2007) *Journalism in a Culture of Grief* (New York: Routledge).

Liu, Z. and Berkowitz, D. (2014) '"Where is our Steve Jobs?" A case study of consumerism and neo-liberal media in China.' *Journalism: Theory, Practice and Criticism* 15(8), 1006–1022.

Lule, J. (2001) *Daily News, Eternal Stories* (New York: The Guilford Press).

McGee, M. (1980) 'The "ideograph": A link between rhetoric and ideology.' *Quarterly Journal of Speech* 66(1), 1–16.

Meyers, O. (2011) 'Memory in journalism and the memory of journalism: Israeli journalists and the constructed legacy of *Haolam Hazeh*' in D. Berkowitz (ed.), *Cultural Meanings of News: A Text-Reader* (pp. 321–336) (Los Angeles, CA: Sage).

Nossek, H. and Berkowitz, D. (2006) 'Telling "our" story through news of terrorism: Mythical newswork as journalistic practice in crisis.' *Journalism Studies* 7(5), 691–707.

Schultz, I. (2007) 'The journalistic gut feeling.' *Journalism Practice* 1(2), 190–207.

Siebert, F. S., Peterson, T., and Schramm, W. (1956) *Four Theories of the Press* (Urbana, IL: University of Illinois Press).

Smith, R. R. (1997) 'Mythic elements in television news' in D. Berkowitz (ed.) *Cultural Meanings of News: A Text-Reader* (pp. 325–333) (Los Angeles, CA: Sage).

Vos, T. P., Craft, S., and Ashley, S. (2012) 'New media, old criticism: Bloggers' press criticism and the journalistic field.' *Journalism* 13(7), 850–868.

Willig, I. (2013) 'Newsroom ethnography in a field perspective.' *Journalism: Theory, Practice & Criticism* 14(3), 372–387.

Wimmer, R. D. and Dominick, J. R. (2006) *Mass Media Research: An Introduction* (8th ed.) (Belmont, CA: Wadsworth Publishing).

Zelizer, B. (2011) 'Cannibalizing memory in the global flow of news' in M. Neiger, O. Meyers, and E. Zandberg (eds), *On Media Memory: Collective Memory in a New Media Age* (pp. 27–36) (Basingstoke: Palgrave Macmillan).

Zheng, Y. (2008) *Technological Empowerment: The Internet, State, and Society in China* (Stanford, CA: Stanford University Press).

6
News Media Ecosystems and Population Dynamics: A Cross-Cultural Analysis

Wilson Lowrey and Elina Erzikova

Much of the classic sociological research on news production was conducted at the level of the news organization (e.g. Epstein, 1973; Tuchman, 1978; Tunstall, 1971). However, for some time, scholars have also recognized that news organizations are porous, and news is influenced by the organization's environment (e.g. Carroll and Hannan, 1995; Tichenor, Olien and Donohue, 1980). In the early to mid-1900s, Robert Park of the Chicago School of Sociology mapped urban ecologies, studying the relationship between news media readership, community complexity, and community integration (Janowitz, 1967; Park, 1922). Research on the role of news media in complex ecosystems continued with Tichenor, Olien and Donohue (e.g. 1980), Jeffres and colleagues (e.g. 2000); Kim and Ball-Rokeach (2006); and McLeod and colleagues (e.g. 1999), among others. Within the last few years, studies of changing urban news ecosystems and ecologies in the midst of economic, technological and cultural disruption have been common (e.g. Anderson, 2013; Chicago Community Trust, 2011; Robinson, 2011).

However, recently, a different conceptualization of news ecology has gained prominence – one that assumes influences from the external environment and also focuses on influences from within the *collective* environment of similar media outlets. This collective context of similar types helps explain what seems an inexplicable reluctance by news media to change in the face of a disruptive environment – a reluctance documented in ethnographies of news production over the last decade (see Lowrey, 2012). A media collective is a semi-autonomous space that consists of similar kinds of media entities (and sometimes, depending on conceptualization, other entities that are interdependent with media). Collectives have their own internal logic. They are influenced by external political, social, and economic environments, but they *refract* the impact of these environments. The collective's internal logic shapes media producers' responses to the external environment.

Scholars have used a variety of spatial metaphors to describe collectives – notably, 'fields', 'populations', and 'jurisdictional areas', and each is part of a distinct theoretical approach, though there is conceptual overlap among them (Abbott, 1988; Benson & Neveu, 2005; Carroll and Hannan, 2000; Lowrey, 2012; Weber, 2013). In this paper, we adopt the concept of the 'population', which stems from organization ecology, a theoretical and empirical approach that explains how environments influence organizations' viability and changes over time. A population is made up of similar, interacting organizations, dependent on similar niche resources (Carroll and Hannan, 2000; Lowrey, 2012).

The organization ecology approach can advance media production research in several ways:

(1) It helps to explain media production behaviour that is not instrumentally rational – that is, when decision-makers 'fail' to respond to external changes. Media decision-makers may respond more directly to the internal logic, taken-for-granted processes, and commonly shared practices that have developed within the population than they do to external changes.
(2) The approach offers an explanatory mechanism for tendencies to institutionalize over time – an important tendency regardless of the current fascination in media production research with change and disruption. As populations emerge and mature, the need for a media outlet to establish its legitimacy within the context of the population increases, while immediate responses by media to change in the external environment (such as changing markets) decrease. New media outlets that seek entrance to a maturing population must demonstrate accord with dominant forms and practices in order to be taken seriously by other similar media and by organizations that provide informational and financial resources – official sources, advertisers, etc. (Baum, 2001; Baum and Shipilov, 2006).
(3) It provides a number of ways for media production researchers to introduce time and history into the analysis: (a) as a population institutionalizes over time, the level of institutionalization influences decisions by emerging media outlets as they seek to appear legitimate enough to gain entry to a population; (b) the longer a media form exists within a population, the more 'path dependent'

it is on its past behaviour within the population, stunting change; and (c) competencies and routines are passed down over time in a community from 'parent' organization to new 'offspring' ventures started by former employees – a sort of 'organizational DNA' that encourages continuity and homogeneity in a community (Aldrich and Ruef, 2007).

Of course, media are influenced by their changing external environment as well. So, the juxtaposition of these dual environments – the collective and the external – suggests several important questions: What evidence is there of interaction between influences from the collective population and influences from the external environment? Under what conditions are media more or less likely to respond to population dynamics as opposed to external conditions in their immediate communities? What immediate conditions in the communities may affect the ways media 'flock together' into populations and begin to institutionalize?

This chapter first provides background and detail about organization ecology as well as its 'new institutional' theoretical context. We then offer findings from a qualitative study of news ecologies in four cities – two in the US and two in Russia – in order to demonstrate the new kinds of questions that can be asked and answered by adopting an organization ecology perspective. Finally, we speculate on the meaning of these findings as well as possible future uses and limitations of the organization ecology approach.

Organization ecology, 'mezzo level' approaches, and institutionalism

While scholarship on media production has often focused on disruption and volatility in the current environment, some researchers have begun to focus also on stasis and homogeneity. There has been an interest in mimicry across media operations, encouraged by 'scopic' characteristics of online media (Boczkowski, 2010). Also, political communication scholars have adopted a 'new institutional' approach, focusing on journalists' need to maintain accord with stable institutional environments such as political, government and corporate institutions (Cook, 2005; Lowrey, 2012; Ryfe, 2006). According to the institutional approach, media producers follow routines that are in accord with institutional environments, 'crowd[ing] out alternative ways of practicing journalism – even if these alternatives might respond more efficiently to exogenous pressures' (Ryfe, 2006: 140). Stasis and non-reactance can persist during disruptive times. Benson (2006) notes that journalists may respond to 'mezzo level' factors rather than to the external environment:

> Once formed, fields or institutions tend to be governed by largely implicit 'rules' or 'principles of action', producing a degree of internal homogeneity... and thus 'what happens in it cannot be understood by looking only at external factors' [Bourdieu, 1993: 39] (Benson, 2006: 188).

'New institutional' scholarship has focused on a number of influences on media that do not derive from the external environment: for example, mimicry of other media, 'loose coupling' (or buffering) between the external environment and news outlets' own collectives of similar outlets, and 'path dependence' (i.e. the constraint of past decisions and investments on current and future decisions).

The organization ecology approach has historical roots in early urban ecology research (such as Robert Park's work), but it is also grounded in assumptions from new institutionalism (Mohr, 2005): for example, assumptions of mimicry, of buffering from the external environment, and of a collective with a guiding internal logic – in this case, a 'population'. Like other sociological approaches to explaining organizational behaviour, organization ecology assumes variation in forms and practices, and change in the environment, as well as competition over resource niches. However, it also assumes a collective context in which, once a niche is found, individual organizations are shaped over time by the internal dynamics of their population of similar media types, and only indirectly by external factors (Aldrich and Ruef, 2007; Baum, 2001; Baum and Singh, 1994; Hannan, Polos and Carroll, 2007; Lowrey, 2012; Weber, 2013). This approach assumes an institutionalizing process whereby variations in organizational forms and practices are selected and retained, and an initial scramble for a financial foothold in the environment gives way eventually to economic security and a quest for public legitimacy. Financial, instrumental concerns dominate early in a population's lifespan, but the pursuit of institutional legitimacy becomes increasingly important for both surviving (older) organizations within the population and later entrants to a maturing population (DiMaggio and Powell, 1983; Thornton, Ocasio and Lounsbury, 2012).

Organization ecology provides a helpful way to conceptualize analysis of media production within the context of history and time. For example, the theory lays out mechanisms for population development over time. Typically, 'pioneers' for a potential population emerge, helping to develop best practices and gaining followings. Often pioneers fail, but they help clear a path, offer lessons, and shape the direction for future ventures, aiding the chances that a population will develop. New entrants to a developing population tend to seek accord with forms and practices that have become accepted and legitimated over time, leading to isomorphism (sameness) (Carroll and Hannan, 2000). High density of the population and rate of foundings (new entrants) – which typically take place during the midlife of a population – outwardly signal legitimacy and stability. This attracts new entrants to a population until eventually growing competition diminishes resources and thus the population's carrying capacity (Aldrich and Ruef, 2007; Baum, 2001; Carroll and Hannan, 2000).

The organization ecology approach in use

To demonstrate this conceptual approach within a media production research context, we offer findings from an empirical study of media outlets in four communities: two in the US and two in Russia. We asked the following questions: (1) What evidence is there of media population development in city case studies? What evidence of mimicry? What evidence of pursuit of legitimacy? (2) What evidence is there of interaction between the characteristics of the proximate urban media ecosystem and the development of populations of media types within these cities?

Some context for the study: Data were gathered from local print and online media producers in two US cities in 2010–2011, and two Russian cities in 2009–2011. In each country, a 'Larger City' and a 'Smaller City' were chosen for study.[1] The impact of two predictive variables – community size/complexity and type of media system (US vs. Russian) – was assessed. We expected that the degree of complexity and pluralism in the urban community environment could affect the dynamics of population formation – for example, affecting niche availability and patterns of mimicry and isomorphism within the urban areas. We also expected that a comparison of two media systems would allow us to assess political-economic differences and their impact on community media. Do principles of population formation that operate in a relatively liberal US system also hold in a more top-down, centralized Russian media system?

The first question asked what evidence there is of media population development in city case studies, what evidence of mimicry, and what evidence of pursuit of legitimacy.

US cities

A first step in the formation of populations is dense communication across similar entities and development of shared, widely understood ways to gain a foothold in a productive niche. There was evidence of these dynamics among media within Larger City in the US, and some of these efforts were supported by the city's main daily paper, which despite its diminished stature and resources was still perceived as a reputable leader by many other media in the city. The daily tried to aggregate the city's blogs and neighbourhood news sites, and also played a leadership role in a series of informal 'meet-ups' between working and laid-off journalists, fostering discussions of possible entrepreneurial startups. Populations are initiated by pioneers (Aldrich and Ruef, 2007), and two particular entrepreneurs demonstrated leadership at the meet-ups, gaining reputations for their online news start-ups. One was a seasoned journalist in a northern area of the city that offered a promising niche, as the area was poorly covered by diminished legacy media, and the other was a young entrepreneur who started an aggregation site for online hyperlocal media. Both gained local followings and public legitimacy. According to a hyperlocal journalist, the north-region journalist was an 'inspiration' for hyperlocal journalists in the city who sought sustainability: 'He's really driven, and he's been pretty successful.' The north-region journalist offered regular advice at the meet-ups and began mentoring a journalist who started a news site for African Americans. Area bloggers and hyperlocal site operators viewed the young aggregator as a motivating 'idealist', working to create online community among the area's citizen journalists. Several of the city's legacy media managers mentioned him as well, and their outlets followed him on social media.

Perhaps the best evidence of a growing 'collective' at the local level was seen among crime-coverage websites. Several respondents said crime coverage was a relatively open niche after the daily paper reduced coverage, merging its city and county crime beats. One female blogger, a former crime victim, played a pioneering role, providing several other budding crime sites with advice and with information she gleaned from the police department. Several TV stations in the area had bloggers that focused on crime, and one of the neighbourhood crime bloggers said he 'was in pretty regular contact with them.' A second neighbourhood crime blog 'organized marches on the city', and two of the other bloggers had participated in these.

The organization ecology model predicts an increased institutional orientation and a stronger pursuit of legitimacy over time, as opposed to concern over immediate market environment. A number of Larger

City media operators evidenced this shift. The African American journalist indicated that his site's status had increased, as public information officers began to recognize his site as legitimate: 'Finally, I didn't have to spend time telling them about the site.' The aggregating blogger said his site's legitimacy had risen since beginning a collaboration with a local public TV station: 'Within about three weeks we had press passes to the Olympic Whitewater trials, and then three weeks later we were in the risers next to CNN and ABC News at the Obama rally.' He said he had become 'more hesitant to produce content that was fluff.'

In Smaller City, there is little evidence that emerging media collaborated, and there were no clear local media pioneers. Yet media operators in Smaller City were more likely than those in Larger City to point to media beyond the city, at the national level, as inspirational models. The publisher for the older alternative weekly said he originally modelled the publication after a successful alternative paper in Chicago, but he then found his city was not ready for this type of paper. The operator of a prominent independent news site that purports to focus on 'positive news' regularly attends national workshops on hyperlocal news and blogging, and he is a founding member of a professional association for hyperlocal journalists that began two years ago. The content director of the daily paper's companion citywide website said copycat behaviour was rampant among major online media: 'It's a real herd mentality' (see Lowrey, 2012).

Russian cities

As would be expected, there are a number of major differences between Russian and US city news ecosystems. One is the low level of media variation in Russian cities. There were relatively few blogs, independent websites, and specialized publications, especially in Smaller City. A second major difference is the low level of autonomy, as autonomy is needed for media producers to develop a media collective/population. Media depended on economic and information subsidies from local governments, and media operators had a high level of deference to officials and business-owning oligarchs. Smaller City papers were more dependent than were media in Larger City, which had more dynamic markets and its oil company revenue.

This dependence weakened initiative to pursue media models and trends (within the city or beyond), thus undermining collective action among media. The media-state model in Russia can be seen as partly 'clientelist' (e.g. Roudakova, 2008), a system in which political and economic leaders provide resources and protection in exchange for the media's deference (Stokes, 2007). In clientelist systems, informal, personal connections and arbitrary authority undermine the belief that one can plan and shape one's media product (Collins and Makowski, 2008) – a belief that is critical to population development. Economic tough times in these cities and poor pay for journalists encouraged clientelism. Journalists also make money by writing stories for rival publications. This resulted in an informal 'market' for news stories that actually encouraged a weak, latent form of occupational collectivity of journalists across rival news organizations. As one reporter said: 'Today I help my friend, tomorrow he will help me. It does not matter whether our papers compete.' However, in general, clientelist tendencies, the arbitrariness of official favour, and journalists' desperate financial need for this favour encouraged individualism and fragmentation, and common goals across media were rare.

However, a lack of 'bottom-up' mimicry and modelling across media does not mean an absence of sameness. While the 'isomorphism' in evidence among US media was mostly a result of mimicry ('mimetic isomorphism' [DiMaggio and Powell, 1983]), isomorphism among these Russian papers – particularly in the more dependent Smaller City – was evidence of 'coercive isomorphism', a homogeneity that derives from a common dependence on a superordinate, such as a corporate owner or a government (DiMaggio and Powell, 1983).

In sum, US findings provided evidence of the importance of available niches for emerging media, of the importance of pioneer media, of the possibility of population growth at the local level, and of a growing institutional orientation over time. In contrast, Russian findings showed that population growth is subject to political-economic and cultural variation, and that population emergence requires autonomy by media decision-makers – an autonomy they did not have. Findings also suggested that media sameness is forced from above in some systems.

The second question asked what evidence there is of an interaction between the nature of 'locational' media ecosystems and population development.

US cities

A tendency to 'adopt' national media models for population development but then 'adapt' them to the market and culture of the local community was evident in both US cities, but especially in Smaller City. The publisher for an older alternative weekly in Smaller City said he originally modelled the publication after a successful alternative paper in Chicago, but he found that his city was not ready for this type of paper.

Similarly, two different 'rich niche' neighbourhood papers modelled their publications on those the publishers saw in other cities; however, they modified and tailored them to local readers and advertisers, playing down 'high society' coverage in favour of little league sports and home showings. The publisher of a newer, upscale city magazine said he leaned toward a national-level 'luxury magazine' model, but he thought this form clashed with preferences of local readers and advertisers (see also Lowrey, 2012). He achieved a rough fit with the luxury magazine model that was flexible enough to target local characteristics and distinguish the magazine from local competitors. These results suggest that community size and market size may influence mimicry and population development. Perhaps the mimicry necessary for population development needs to start first in larger cities, before spreading across communities, where it can be adapted to local conditions. Literature on entrepreneurship suggests as much, as new ventures are more likely to emerge successfully if their environment is familiar (Shane, 2008).

The newer, upscale city magazine in Smaller City was also a good example of another mechanism for population development: propagation of routines and practices by 'genetic offspring' (Baum and Singh, 1994). The publisher and several key staff members worked for the traditional city magazine, but they left and started their own publication. The magazine's style was shaped by perceptions of what their former employer was and was not doing. Similarly, a number of online media entrepreneurs in both cities had worked for the main city dailies. Each mentioned advantages conferred on them by the parent paper's legitimacy and network contacts.

Russian cities

In Russian cities, resource availability is tightly controlled, though this varies somewhat across cities, whereas in US cities, resources and markets are more fluid, and media entrepreneurial efforts that can spark populations are much more common. Community conditions in Larger City in Russia are somewhat more like conditions in US cities: the city generated revenue, and so it was less dependent on the national government for resources. Media in the city were more pluralistic and diverse, with more diverse advertising sources; however, the influence of both the government and powerful private companies within the 'oligopoly' were still strong. At the time this chapter was written, media in Larger City could criticize the Kremlin – as a vice-editor said, 'The Kremlin is not our advertiser.' But they still hesitated to criticize local authorities that paid millions of rubles annually to place ads.

Leaders in Smaller City's 'recipient' government were more dependent on state resources and therefore felt a stronger need to demonstrate competence to Moscow. According to interview respondents, Smaller City's local government felt a keen need for the sort of public legitimacy that a lapdog press cannot bring; they therefore encouraged local media to take public officials to task on certain pre-approved, mild problem areas (i.e. to practice a 'preventive journalism'). The media then published government promises to fix the problem. As a result, the local government looks good to the public and to Moscow for responding to public needs via a news outlet that appears more legitimate. The news media benefit by appearing legitimate to the public. Media that cooperate are more likely to gain government funding and information subsidies. Encouraged by government coercion, these 'preventive journalism' practices spread – some evidence of coercive isomorphism in this city.

There was also some evidence of informally networked collectives among journalists in these cities, who had tended to move frequently among the same publications over the years. This collective behaviour was also evident online. There was friendly blogging interaction, primarily outside the workplace, but this was more active in Larger City. Blogging and other new media efforts within the news organizations were infrequent in Smaller City, and when blogs were published they were stilted and obviously mandated by management.

Thus, in Russia, there was a higher degree of isomorphism among media in Smaller City, given the greater dependence on local government and willingness to work hand-in-hand with them. This stands in contrast to US cities, where there was a greater tendency for media in Larger City to mimic one another. Larger City media in Russia had more resource options and were more thoroughly connected to online networks, which encouraged some innovation.

Evaluation

Results suggest benefits of considering both population and community factors in assessing news media behaviour. Results also demonstrate the value of comparison across media systems. Mimicry and population emergence were more common in US cities than in Russian cities: media in Russian cities were hindered by a deficiency of journalist autonomy and shortage of resources. By contrast, variation was greater within the US cities, and individual media producers regularly sought models on which to pattern their forms and practices, both locally and nationally. In Russian cities, isomorphism tended to be a result of state coercion, and collective efforts fell under the radar, loosely assembled in informal, temporary ways. These results suggest the impact of organization ecologies – both the pursuit of legitimate forms and models and the impact of a changing external environment can shape media decision-making. Results also show the importance of studying varying contexts; such contexts will differentially shape the conditions within which populations may or may not emerge.

We also see evidence of variability by community size. Mimicry of national trends may be more likely in smaller cities, but media producers are likely to adapt these trends to local conditions in smaller cities, often for immediate financial reasons. However, the pull of instrumental financial incentives seemed to wane as media owners grew comfortable with and more confident of their audiences, sources, and advertisers, and no longer 'looked at everything as a bullet that could kill us', as one alternative weekly owner in the US put it. This suggests that immediate, instrumental financial needs may undermine the dynamics of population growth, which is driven by the pursuit of public legitimacy. But then over time, growing institutionalization may diminish the impact of factors from the immediate environment, such as the state of the market.

Organization ecology and time

These findings point to the ways that the organization ecology approach can introduce the factors of time and history into our understanding of media production processes. According to the approach, entities tend toward isomorphic collectives with recognizable boundaries, pursuing legitimacy and buffering themselves from the immediate environment (though institutionalization is by no means inevitable) (Baum and Shipilov, 2006; DiMaggio and Powell, 1983). One implication is that the particular stage of development of a media outlet's population should render it more or less susceptible to external forces at the media outlet's 'gates'. External influences should have the most impact during either early periods of population formation, when processes are instrumental, strategic, and less institutionalized (Murmann, Aldrich, Levinthal and Winter, 2003). Older media organizations may attempt change during disruptive times, but in doing so, they must overcome their institutionalized constraints. In sum, the higher the level of institutional legitimacy that a media entity and its population have, the less likely that the entity will respond instrumentally to direct external forces.

Organization ecology research also helps to explain emergence and persistence of routines, and their effects, over time. Most of the literature on media routines does not address the process by which routines emerge, instead focusing on the economic, power-related and practical functions that routines serve for media operations. In an era of emerging new media forms, more study is needed on the phenomenon of organizational 'offspring' and how they adopt routines from the 'parent' organization. According to organization evolution theorists, such routines act as the 'DNA' of organizational change and stasis (Baum and Singh, 1994). We saw some evidence of this in the findings, with operators of emerging media ventures working for other companies in the community and translating previously learned routines to their new outlets. 'Imprinting' is another organization ecology concept that helps to explain dynamics of routines. New ventures, scrambling for survival, tend to adopt practices that correlate with success, and over time, these 'imprinted' practices reproduce and become change-resistant routines. As a consequence, 'the current characteristics of populations of organizations reflect historical conditions at the time of founding rather than recent adaptations' (Hannah and Freeman, 1977: xiii).

Conclusion: some thoughts on method

The study presented in this chapter used in-depth interviews, an appropriate method for exploring perceptions. Questions grounded in lived experiences were especially valuable. However, the method has limitations. Most obviously, findings are not generalizable beyond the cases. But more importantly, the interview method does not provide evidence of direct observation of practices within outlets – or interactions among outlets, which is especially important to ecology research. Also, interview responses to questions about change over time are limited to memories and perceptions about the future, offering no first-hand data across time points. Revisiting communities multiple times would aid understanding of the impact of time and history.

One other methodological challenge surfaced that is unique to studies of organizational 'ecosystems'. Because respondents know interviews are being conducted at other media outlets, including competitors and collaborators, it is necessary to promise anonymity. It is important to avoid mentioning findings from other respondents during an interview – not only for ethical reasons but because it may have a chilling effect. Respondents may not trust a researcher with their information if the researcher shares information from other interviews.

Another challenge is the gathering of data on other media within a population, as the population is a level of analysis that stretches beyond the boundaries of a single community. To explain patterns of emergence and development of new media forms and practices, observation is needed at both the geographic community level as well as the population level, which is probably national or international in scope. Without complete data on populations over time, the full dynamics of population growth cannot inform the analysis. Often, research on population dynamics tracks a single population across time, and this requires data from a (near) census of population members from 'birth' to the present (Carroll and Hannan, 2000). Such an approach allows study of the population's density and rate of growth, which are important for explaining level of legitimacy and patterns of mimicry. As population growth rises, the forms and practices of the population become better known, leading to increased legitimacy, more entrants to the population, more mimicry, and less variation. Such patterns can be tracked, and could inform analyses of media within community ecosystems. Not only could we study media behaviour as a consequence of community environment and organizational factors, we could also take into account the changing levels of media legitimacy, mimicry and institutionalization across time. All are functions of the population's development patterns.

It should be noted that there is a built-in bias in studies of populations because the sample (ideally a census) is skewed toward survivors (Aldrich and Ruef, 2007). Most entrepreneurial efforts fail (Shane, 2008), and so characteristics by unselected variations get overlooked. Studying only successful ventures falsely suggests a natural inevitability to the forms and practices that eventually dominate. There is much to be learned from processes of failure and the characteristics of unselected variations.

Finally, researchers face the challenge of prescribing community and population boundaries. What are the best typological, locational and time boundaries for the population sample? And what are the best boundaries for community sampling? A common method for population sampling is to adopt typifications of organizational forms that internal and external stakeholders perceive as appropriate (this information can be gathered by survey or interviews). Boundaries become clearer when stakeholders indicate boundary violation by 'inappropriate' organizations (Carroll and Hannan, 2000). Community boundaries may be drawn using a geographical map, but it is less arbitrary to use area stakeholders' (e.g. local media operators') perceptions as a determinant. Social network analysis may aid in determining these socially constructed boundaries.

As media ecosystems diversify and become more fluid, as legacy media shrink or change forms and new ventures sprout, and as the influence of the Internet's 'scopic' view grows, it is increasingly important for media production researchers to understand both media ecosystems across space and collective growth patterns of media across time. Comparison of these phenomena across cultures and news media systems is also important. Complex environments require complex frameworks and complementing methods to study change. As case studies in this chapter illustrate, organization ecology provides a rich theoretical framework and novel techniques to aid our understanding of how environmental conditions, relationships across news organizations within 'collectives', and change over time can all shape decision-making about media production.

Note

1. News organizations in two urban communities in the same region of the US were studied. 'Larger City' has a metro population of 1.7 million, and 'Smaller City' has a metro population of 1.1 million. Media markets differed. Smaller City lost a major daily paper and a national magazine publishing company, leaving hundreds unemployed. Larger City also suffered economically, but the media workforce environment was more stable. Seven legacy media and eleven emerging/alternative media were studied in Larger City. Twenty-two semi-structured interviews were conducted. In Smaller City, twenty-one interviews were conducted (seventeen in person, and four by phone) at eight legacy outlets and ten emerging/alternative media. Russian news organizations from two cities were studied: 'Larger City' in the Ural region with a population of 1 million, and 'Smaller City' in Central Russia at 0.6 million. Both cities are regions' capitals with diverse media markets. Larger City was wealthier, with stronger ad revenues, salaries and editorial independence. Five public issue news publications in each city were studied, including general news dailies and weeklies and business news outlets. Three local bloggers in each city were also interviewed. Fourteen in-person interviews were conducted in Larger City and eighteen in Smaller City.

References

Abbott. A. (1988) *The System of Professions: An Essay on the Division of Expert Labor* (Chicago: University of Chicago Press).
Aldrich, H. E. and Ruef, M. (2007) *Organizations Evolving* (Los Angeles: Sage).
Anderson, C. W. (2013) *Rebuilding the News: Metropolitan Journalism in the Digital Age* (Philadelphia: Temple University Press).
Baum, J. A. C. (1996) 'Organizational ecology' in S. Clegg, C. Hardy, and W. R. Nord (eds), *Handbook of Organization Studies* (pp. 77–114) (London: Sage).
Baum, J. A. C. and Shipilov, A. V. (2006) 'Ecological approaches to organizations' in S. R. Clegg, C. Hardy, T. B. Lawrence, and W. R. Nord (eds), *Sage Handbook for Organization Studies* (pp. 55–110) (London: Sage Publications).
Baum, J. A. C. and Singh, J. V. (1994) 'Organizational hierarchies and evolutionary processes: Some reflections on a theory of organizational evolution'

in J. A. C. Baum and J. V. Singh (eds), *Evolutionary Dynamics of Organizations* (pp. 3–20) (New York: Oxford University Press).

Benson, R. (2006) 'News media as a journalistic field: What Bourdieu adds to new institutionalism and vice versa.' *Political Communication, 23*(2), 187–202.

Benson, R. and Neveu, E. (2005) 'Introduction: Field theory as a work in progress' in R. Benson and E. Neveu (eds), *Bourdieu and the Journalistic Field* (pp. 1–25) (Cambridge: Polity Press).

Boczkowski, P. J. (2010) *News at Work: Imitation in an Age of Information Abundance* (Chicago: University of Chicago Press).

Bourdieu, P. (1993) *The field of cultural production*. New York, NY: Columbia University Press.

Carroll, G. R. and Hannan, M. T. (1995) *Organizations in Industry* (New York: Oxford University Press).

Carroll, G. R. and Hannan, M. T. (2000) *The Demography of Corporations and Industries* (Princeton: Princeton University Press).

Chicago Community Trust (2011) 'Linking audiences to news: A network analysis of Chicago websites.' Retrieved (1 April 2012) from http://www.marinacityonline.com/doc/2011/Linking_Audiences_0611.pdf.

Collins, R. and Makowsky, M. (2008). *The Discovery of Society, 8th edn* (Boston, MA: Mcgraw-Hill).

Cook, T. (2005) *Governing the News: The News Media as Political Institution* (Chicago: University of Chicago Press).

DiMaggio, P. J. and Powell, W. W. (1983) 'The Iron Cage revisited: Institutional isomorphism and collective rationality in organizational fields.' *American Sociological Review 48*(2), 147–160.

Epstein, J. (1967) *News from Nowhere: Television and the News* (Chicago: I. R. Dee).

Hannan, M. T., Polos, L., and Carroll, G. R. (2007) *Logics of Organization Theory: Audiences, Codes and Ecologies* (Princeton: Princeton University Press).

Hindman, D. B. and Yamamoto, M. (2011) 'Social capital in a community context: A multilevel analysis of individual-and community-level predictors of social trust.' *Mass Communication and Society 14*(6), 838–856.

Janowitz, M. (1980) *The Community Press in an Urban Setting, 2nd edn* (Chicago: The University of Chicago Press).

Jeffres, L. W. (2000) 'Ethnicity and Ethnic Media Use.' *Communication Research 27*(4), 496–535.

Kim, Y. C. and Ball-Rokeach, S. J. (2006) 'Community storytelling network, neighborhood context, and civic engagement: A multilevel approach.' *Human Communication Research 32*(4), 411–439.

Lowrey, W. (2012) 'Journalism innovation and the ecology of news production: Institutional tendencies.' *Journalism and Communication Monographs 14*(4), 214–287.

Lowrey, W. (2013) 'The emergence and development of hyperlocal news websites: An organization ecology approach.' Paper presented at the annual conference of the Association for Education in Journalism and Mass Communication. Washington, DC.

McLeod, J. M., Scheufele, D. A., and Moy, P. (1999) 'Community, communication and participation: The role of mass media and interpersonal discussion in local political participation.' *Political Communication 16*(3), 315–336.

Mohr, J. W. (2005) 'Implicit terrains: Meaning, measurement, and spatial metaphors in organizational theory' in M. Ventresca and J. Porac (eds), *Constructing Industries and Markets* (New York: Elsevier).

Park, R. (1922) *The Immigrant Press and Its Control* (New York: Harper and Brothers Publishers).

Robinson, S. (2011) 'Journalism as process: The organizational implication of participatory online news.' *Journalism & Communication Monographs* 13(3), 139–210.

Roudakava, N. (2008) 'Media-political clientelism: Lessons from anthropology.' *Media, Culture & Society* 30(1), 41–59.

Ryfe, D. M. (2006) 'Guest editors introduction: New institutionalism and the news.' *Political Communication* 23(2), 135–144.

Shane, S. A. (2008) *The Illusions of Entrepreneurship: The Costly Myths That Entrepreneurs, Investors and Policy Makers Live By* (New Haven: Yale University Press).

Stokes, S. (2007) 'Political clientelism' in C. Boix and S. C. Stokes (eds), *Handbook of Comparative Politics* (pp. 604–627) (Oxford: Oxford University Press).

Thornton, P. H., Ocasio, W., and Lounsbury, M. (2012) *The Institutional Logics Perspective: A New Approach to Culture, Structure and Process* (Oxford: Oxford University Press).

Tichenor, P., Olien, C., and Donohue, G. (1980) *Community Conflict & the Press* (Beverly Hills: Sage).

Tuchman, G. (1978) *Making the News: A Study in the Construction of Reality* (New York: The Free Press).

Tunstall, J. (1971) *Journalists at Work* (London: Constable).

Weber, M. S. (2013) 'Newspapers and the long-term implications of hyperlinking.' *Journal of Computer-Mediated Communication* 17(2), 187–201.

7
Micro vs. Macro: A Reflection on the Potentials of Field Analysis
Tore Slaatta

One rationale for the renewed focus on media production is the rapid and deep changes in the media and cultural industries. Media studies in general and production studies in particular have had problems keeping up. In many areas we simply do not know what is going on. Thus, there is a need for catching up and recruiting young researchers. But at the same time as we specialize and focus on media production, we ought to remind ourselves that our field is a sub-discipline in cultural sociology, itself an interdisciplinary subfield between humanities and the social sciences with ambitions to do critical and creative research across established disciplines and to expand methodological repertoires in the interdisciplinary borderlands. Our new emphasis on media production must therefore be understood as a strategic response to societal changes and not as an invitation to break with the fundamental understanding of media and cultural research as occupied with what John B. Thompson once coined as a 'tripartite approach' (Thompson, 1990: 307). There will always be, and should always be in media and cultural research, a sense of unity across the division of labour between researchers focusing on production, content and reception. Future media and cultural production research should continue to link these areas of research, and also investigate the *connections* between them.

In the critical tradition, the concept of production also meant some kind of reproduction. The linear thinking in early models has been repudiated, but ideas of connectivity are underlying most media research. A case in mind is the imperative *cum* that Klaus Bruhn Jensen once launched within audience and reception studies (audience-cum-content) (Bruhn Jensen, 1987, 1995). I always thought this *cum* should be extended to production-cum-content, or even production-cum-reception research. So instead of arguing, as many others is this book may do, for the need for ethnography and thick descriptions of new production practices, I will make a plea for the continued engagement with meso- and macro-levelled research questions and a particular concern for the connections between production, content and reception. Production can still be a priority. I will make my argument by way of reintroducing field theory and field analysis into the new field of production research. One might say that Pierre Bourdieu and his theories and methods for field analysis hardly need to be introduced: Bourdieu is usually hailed as the ultimate classic in cultural sociology to the degree that discussions have emerged about if there should be a 'post-Bourdieusian' cultural sociology (Born, 2010; De la Fuente, 2010). And support and criticism of Bourdieu's theory is a constant ebb and flow in international research journals and publications, reflecting on the one hand how the theoretical basis of field analysis remains a reservoir of important perspectives and fundamental ideas, and on the other how its epistemological and methodological principles are seen as problematic or unrealistic in contemporary research on cultural and media production. There is, for instance, disagreement about its methodological effectiveness and ability to grasp contemporary changes in the cultural industries. There are also disagreements about how field theory compares to institutional perspectives, not to forget the continuing challenges and critiques of field theory from ANT-camps (Action-Network-Theory, ANT) and grounded, ethnographic approaches.

However, more specific to media production research, David Hesmondhalgh argues in an article in *Media, Culture & Society* in 2006 that 'Bourdieu offers a way of thinking about the relations between the different fields (restricted and mass), which might be tested in empirical work', but generally does not offer the concepts and imperatives for empirical focus that contemporary production research needs. According to Hesmondhalgh, ethnographic approaches are more needed, and although he gives Bourdieu a fair trial, more can be said about what a field analytical approach might bring to the table. I will thus start in the first part of this chapter with a brief presentation of the line of production studies in Pierre Bourdieu's work and the way this line is kept alive today by Bourdieu's younger colleagues and former students. In the second part, I will discuss my own particular experiences with the quantitative methods of correspondence analysis in media and cultural production research, as an illustration of field theory in practice.

Field analysis in contemporary production research

A problem with the reception and critique of field theory is how little of Bourdieu's wide authorship on cultural production is usually being discussed (for an overview, see Delsaut and Rivière, 2002). This often leads to a reading of *Distinction* (Bourdieu, 1979/1984) as the most important publication concerning cultural production research, besides the obvious *Rules of Art* (Bourdieu, 1992), but a total silence around Bourdieu's other aesthetically oriented works on art and art production – for instance, his early work on photography (Bourdieu, 1965), his continued interest in the media (Champagne and Chartier, 2004), and his detailed field analytical study of French publishing from 1999 (Bourdieu, 1999). Also, most media researchers outside France seem to be unaware of the work done by Bourdieu's colleagues in more recent years – for instance, Gisèle Sapiro's work together with Johan Heilbron and others on the sociology of translation and international publishing (e.g. Sapiro, 2008, 2009a, 2009b, 2010). Also interesting for media and cultural production research are Sapiro's earlier works on French authors during and after World War II (1999), roles and positions in news journalism (2003), and most recently about the responsibilities of authors: about the historical confrontation between literature, ethics and the law. Julian Duval's work on French cinema and film production also remains unknown to the larger international research community, because he mostly publishes in French (Duval, 2006). These studies can be seen as being in a continuing line of research from Bourdieu's early work on the field of cultural production, done by the new generation of scholars at CSE (Centre de sociologie européenne, now merged with another centre at CNRS in Paris). But, although many are aware of Rodney Benson's anthology on journalism (2005) and Hallin and Mancini's adaption of the field concept in their comparative study (2005), there is generally little knowledge outside Paris of how Bourdieu's theories and intellectual legacy are still used to define contemporary research projects on media and cultural production. Few would know, for instance, that Sapiro, Heilbron and Dominique Marchetti defined a research initiative at CNRS in 2009 on 'Cultural markets of symbolic goods' (Marchetti and Sapiro, 2009). It is not only the French language that is foreign to most international scholars; some of the ideas behind it are foreign, too.

When we consider the possible contribution of field theory and field-analytical approaches to media production research, we are immediately confronted with the challenge that structural approaches are very different from process-oriented approaches. To Craig Calhoun, it was this difference that was leading him to the conclusion that Bourdieu's theory could be of little use in transnational media and communication research (Calhoun et al., 1993). But why should communication necessarily need process-oriented research designs? Exactly the opposite argument can be made: that because we tend to think of communication and cultural interactions as social processes in time and space, more structural and system-oriented approaches might yield interesting outcomes and findings that otherwise would not be seen. However, what follows on the train to Bourdieu's structural constructivism is the challenge concerning actual epistemological differences: Bourdieu's concept of the relational sticks deeper than many want to admit. The relational in a field is part of reality, or as Vanderberghe puts it, has 'more reality' than immediate experience of a subject (Vanderberghe, 1999: 42). This makes the relational dimension the very mark of Bourdieu's sociological project and what we should think of as his *epistemological specificity*. This leads us to a concern about what our preferred research objects should be, and what our methods ought to be. In my understanding of Bourdieu's project, I have come to realize the importance of stressing how different it is *as a theory* for the social sciences, and how secondary the theory is compared to actual empirical observation. As I understand it, one of Bourdieu's basic hypotheses is that his elementary and rather abstract theory, in combination with a rather rigorous method, 'will work' and 'show something' that he would call logics or structures, and that similar or related logics and structures would show up in any social universe. But to know what these structures are, we have to do the empirical work. Thus, instead of dismissing Bourdieu from production research, it can be argued that we should do it even more 'by the book' and that at least some researchers should test it, empirically, from time to time. There are four potential benefits to our field:

(1) I believe Bourdieu's theories provide researchers with a counterintuitive ability to reflect upon their research mission and the positions and perspectives (point of view) that are implicit in their scientific choices in the research process, particularly concerning the empirical focus and the use and combination of different methods. Bourdieu focused on *power relations* in society, and not all kinds of power, and thus is most suited to some kinds of studies. For instance, he stressed that his particular ambition was to analyse that kind of power that is hard to see, hard to find, and hard to understand with traditional analytical and methodological tools (Bourdieu, 1991: 163). But this does not automatically mean that other forms of power do not exist or cannot be studied. It just means that his research is more focused

on these more invisible forms of power. Similarly, his research can also be said to look for stability rather than change, or perhaps more precisely, *stability in processes of change*.

(2) I think Bourdieu's stress on cumulative knowledge is important when we consider this. Bourdieu's theory is not meant to be a general social theory that explains everything, in every detail, but rather a theory that allows for particular observations of social effects that often go unnoticed in much research. This choice or emphasis has produced a lot of resentment and critique, not the least from Latour (2005) and Boltanski (2011), who argue that Bourdieu's thinking not only fits an old-fashioned 'classical sociology' that aims at a grand description of the order of all things, but in addition puts the researcher in a potentially arrogant, authoritarian position, telling ordinary people how the world is, as a world they themselves do not know. In William Schinkel's clarifying article on Bourdieu and Latour in the *Sociological Review* (Schinkel, 2009), he argues that Latour is the best alternative. But he also argues that we should look for ways to reconcile them, although it seems difficult at the moment. I think this is the better strategy. But if future production research by definition has a general explorative rather than explanatory or field theoretical ambition, then Hesmondhalgh is absolutely right: Bourdieu is not the guy you would want to work with. Latour and Becker would go better together, in their more descriptive, bottom-up perspectives (see Becker, 2008; van Maanen, 2009; De la Fuente, 2010). But it might still be that a different perspective can be added, and observations that appear as true and obvious in one perspective look differently, if Bourdieu's theory and methodological choices are followed more closely in empirical projects on media and cultural production. In that case, we should not give it up.

(3) One of our commitments as researchers is to test and compare each other's findings and results, and thus not always strive for originality and new perspectives on new phenomena. I think ethnography sometimes risks that initial emphases on originality and the non-exemplary lead to strong claims on complexity, hybridity, and newness. More longitudinal and repetitive research designs would document both stability and change better than case studies and thick descriptions possibly can.

Rodney Benson has done a great job of translating Bourdieu and field theory into media studies (Benson and Neveu, 2005; Benson, 1999), arguing that field theory is a lot like institutional theory, and opens up space for bringing 'the media back in' (Benson, 2004). But instead of emphasizing the similarities between institutional research and field analysis, a clearer distinction could also be made. Where institutional analysis stresses values, knowledge forms, and norms, field theory stresses complexity, oppositions, and variation both in points of views and common sense, linked to a stronger stress on the relational difference between different positions in the field.

(4) I am attracted to Bourdieu's understanding of sociological research as producing a particular form of knowledge, a scientific one, which attempts to break with the knowledge in the field that is being studied. An important element in the understanding of what Bourdieu's theory is about, that also explains why quantitative objectification of the field is so important to him, is the point made by Bourdieu at one point that 'the real is relational.' It is Vanderberghe again, in his seminal article from 1999 that puts this point in its right place, and shows how important it is in Bourdieu's epistemology. Vanderberghe reminds us that already David Swartz's introduction to Bourdieu from 1997 warns the reader that in order to understand what Bourdieu is actually doing, and how deep it goes in the matter of establishing a particular and distinct scientific stand in the social sciences, we have to understand the epistemological tradition he works within (see Swartz, 1997: 31). Important influences on Bourdieu here are the line from Cassirer via Panofsky and Norbert Elias, which brings us more to Marburg than to Heidelberg, although Weber obviously is an important sociological influence on Bourdieu, as is Durkheim. The other important line is via the French philosophers of science: Canguilhem, Bachelard and Koyré.

A difficult question in the wake of this is whether Bourdieu's field theory represents a total epistemological break, or just a partial methodological break, for instance, with ethnographic approaches and grounded theory. It is strikingly different from what most of us are doing: it is not explanatory or causal research that categorizes one part of reality as explananda and another as explanandum, nor a normative one, but a *relational and realist* epistemology. The most important analytical concept here is that of homologies, which directs the researchers to look for particular patterns (logics, distributions of capital, positions) across different universes or spaces, as Bourdieu often calls them. As many ethnographers do, Bourdieu argues that theory plays an active role in constructing reality. But instead of believing in grounded theory as the least reductionist point of view, he believes in reflected positioning of the researcher himself. The researcher is the least in the way, and the research process is the least reductionist, when theory is developed from the basis of a few principles and made into a coherent abstract whole, including the researcher in a principled reflection of positions and fields. Bourdieu's understanding of what a thick description might be (and how beneficial it will be) thus also seems to be different. According to Vandeberghe, Bourdieu's idea of a cumulative social science equals the mathematical series, where the whole is never understood before the last element is fitted in, in an (in principle) infinite process of empirical research. Every valid observation, thus, should be possible to include or reconcile within the whole, as the whole itself will change, with every new observation of reality.

As a consequence, a field analytical approach will be of a different order of description than thick descriptions and on-site observations. Whether the 'epistemological break' is irreconcilable is a tricky issue. We are allowed to do ethnography also in a Bourdieusian approach, but some sort of objectification of the 'relational real' should be done *first*. A major hypothesis is that if objectification of the field *as a whole* tells a different story of the real and exposes 'the really real', then that must be used or taken into consideration when other data is collected and interpreted.

But a critical question is whether objectification of a field really brings a different and more scientifically secure basis for further analysis. Will we, with Bourdieu, get a better grip on 'the whole', on the totality, not only of the professional subfield or organization in question but of the media order and the societal context, with regards to both production and consumption patterns of cultural or symbolic goods? The challenge can be rephrased this way: If we are absolutely certain that we are most interested or exclusively interested in the micro level, and really do not want to take the larger picture into consideration, then a pure bottom-up, grounded theory approach is well suited. However, if we have a suspicion that the totality might influence the detail, then we should be careful to dismiss Bourdieu's imperatives. Should all ethnography then come with a proviso? For example:

> We acknowledge that the relational context in which our observations have been made has not fully been analysed according to the principles of field analysis, thus Bourdieu's claims thus Bourdieu's claims that positions in a field of cultural production have a defining impact on the value and meaning of our observations have not been tested.

This is obviously a provocative suggestion, and it explains why ethnographers often want to get rid of Bourdieu. In addition to the epistemological difference, there is too much work to be done first, before you can start observing and making evaluations and interpretations. And the sequencing of first doing a lot of quantitative research and then doing observations and ethnography is counterintuitive for most anthropologists. Still, this is what Bourdieu recommended.

Even if we accept the epistemology, questions remain about research efficiency, because reconstructions of fields through the use of quantitative data are immensely time consuming and labour intensive, and we do not know the outcome. The structures that might appear are often said to be invisible without the use of the correct methods of objectification. So is it really worth the actual effort? Sometimes, objectification of fields seems almost impossible to do, too, because quantitative data are unavailable or extremely hard to construct.

And the search for 'totality' – might it not taint our understanding and interpretations of details in limiting ways, so that when we see order, power, and positions almost everywhere, it is, in effect, reductionist, because other details and interesting aspects are lost? Is it too strong a claim of subsumption of details under the reign of totality in Bourdieu's approach, so that the fluid and less fixed moments and events of media production are lost out of sight, or lost in the tiresome jumping between positions and oppositions (Born, 2010)? Such issues have brought him into conflict with Latour and previously supportive colleagues such as Luc Boltanski and Nathalie Heinich (Boltanski, 2012; Latour, 2005). An alliance seems to have appeared between Latour and Heinich on the French side, and the cultural production school in the US with Howard Becker and Richard Peterson among others, all criticizing Bourdieu for his rigor and theory-driven research.

Empirical work: constructing fields

I will now present how I used field analysis in two different research projects: one on Norwegian news media from 2003 and one from an ongoing project on contemporary literature and visual arts (2012–2015). In both projects, I used the basic concepts of field theory in order to develop the research design, and then used correspondence analysis techniques in order to construct fields empirically. Otherwise, the projects are very different: the first has a historical time line, the other is a comparative and contemporary study. Although they use the same theory and similar methodologies, the latter project has had the benefit of being my second attempt to reproduce a cultural field.

The Norwegian news media order (1980–2000), and the rise of the business press

The research project on media power was part of a large-scale, national research program on 'power and democracy'. The challenge for the media part of the project was not only to estimate and discuss media power, as such, but also to understand the relative power of the media in relation to other institutions and actors in society. Surveying the literature, estimates of media power often were exaggerated and based on imprecise concepts of power.[1]

In a field perspective, a specific power of journalism and news media is linked to its construction and mediation of symbolic powers in other fields (Bourdieu, 2003, 1996). Based on considerations of general shifts in power in Norwegian society during the last twenty to thirty years, the relation between *the news media and the economic field* was selected as the main research focus. We had become particularly interested in how financial and business reporting had changed since the 1980s. Hence, we established a historical narrative of the rise of business journalism in Norway, understood as an emerging subfield within the journalistic field. As an emerging subfield, the growth of business journalism represented an emerging and expanding form of knowledge, in the Mannheimian sense, that could be studied historically. Increasing attention towards 'the economy' could be observed in traditional media, and an increasing number of people were working with 'the economy' in old and new dailies, magazines, and weeklies.

Our findings reflected how, during the period of twenty to thirty years, the economic field and the political field had changed position in the power field, much because of the changes in the value of their symbolic capital. In a field modelling exercise, we hypothesized that the economic field had generally expanded and moved upward to become the dominant field in all Western, capitalist societies. Supportive evidence was found in the educational field concerning knowledge production. Since the 1960s, university programmes and degrees in business, marketing and economic knowledge had exploded, giving way for a more mobile and dynamic financial elite and the entrance of a new generation of young, well-educated businessmen in the economic field: the representatives of the 'new economy', as Bourdieu coined them already in 1979. News stories that earlier would be seen as elite business journalism now more often figured as head news stories in omnibus media, and discourses on worth, value, profit, money, and crises emerged as news values in all genres: economics, politics, sports, culture, arts, and entertainment.

These changing symbolic relationships between the economic, the political, and the journalistic could be visualized in a field model showing the changing position of the journalistic field towards the economic field in Norway between 1980 and 2005 (see Figure 7.1).

In the second part of the project, correspondence analysis was used to construct what we defined as the Norwegian media order. We decided to use existing survey data on the media and cultural consumption patterns from two sources: Statistics Norway and TNS Gallup in Norway. We were not able to treat the two data sets in the same analysis, and thus ended up with two different plots. However, it was immediately clear from the derived plots that the news media was not 'the news media' in a simple manner: the positions that different newspapers upheld in the media order were strikingly diverse, confirming Bourdieu's observation in chapter 8 of *Distinction* that 'a newspaper is a *viewspaper (journal d'opinion)*' and in fact not only for a minority (Bourdieu, 1984: 441). The main plot showed distinct positions and oppositions, particularly within *print media consumption*. Party preferences, income levels, and somewhat random variables in the data set that could be interpreted as cultural preferences (dining out, going to rock concerts, theatre, interest in fashion, having a preference

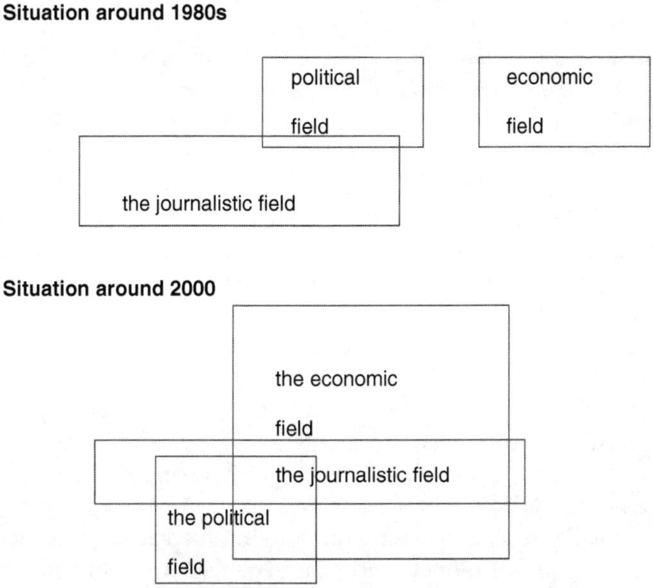

Situation around 1980s

Situation around 2000

Figure 7.1 Model of external relations to fields from 1980 and 2005

for wooden furniture, etc.) were important variables giving direction to the distributions in the news media plot. What was most striking in the positions of the newspapers was the little effect of political oppositions: the main opposition seemed to appear between the financial, specialist dailies on the one hand, and the more culturally oriented newspapers and weeklies on the other. Thus, it was interesting and remarkable in the data that the financial press in the Norwegian media order (represented by, for instance, *Dagens Næringsliv* and *Finansavisen*) clearly occupied privileged and distinct positions in both the maps.

With a different combination of questions and survey data, we produced a map showing different positions of media technologies and genres and constructed a generalized model on the basis of our interpretations along two dimensions (see Figure 7.2).

Disregarding its many shortcomings and outright methodological errors, I still think the model is interesting. But its imprecise and

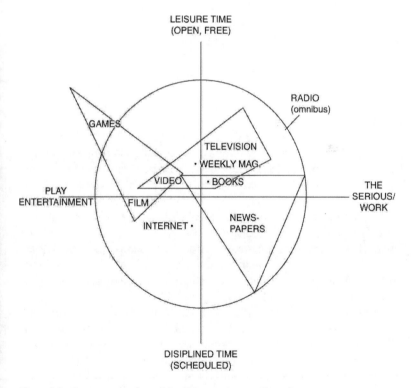

Figure 7.2 Reconstructed model of Norwegian media order

suggestive style reflects how difficult it is to use correspondence analysis on existing data sets. Some consumption patterns appeared as single macro positions (e.g. 'television' and 'Internet'), while other media appeared as positioned channels or brands (e.g. radio and newspapers). And although we could perhaps say we were on track to understand something through the labelling of the two axes, it was very hard to say what the effect of this media order was – for instance, on the distribution of power – other than that it was a certain logic in play, and capitals and powers obviously varied between technologies, between media, and between outlets. Our best finding in the project thus remained the historical documentation of the rise of the business press as an expanding form of knowledge in Norwegian society.

Art! Power! Selection and negotiation in contemporary Norwegian art

In the project Art! Power!, we are again using a field-analytical framework to study power aspects, this time comparatively in four art fields: contemporary music, literature, visual art, and stage art (theatre). The aim of the project is to produce empirically based scientific knowledge concerning how power distributions and power relations are being strengthened and weakened in the Norwegian art world today.

In the first phase, we studied relations between the art fields and external fields in the context of recent developments in cultural economics and cultural politics (digitalization and globalization). In the second phase, selected case studies were designed to analyse artists' autonomy and artistic control in art production processes in each field. One ambition in the project is to test whether it is possible – and how far it seems adequate, justifiable, and non-reductionist – to pursue field analysis towards aesthetical studies of art works. This is a huge challenge in any sociology of art, and a problem that Bourdieu has been criticized for not being able to solve (e.g. Born, 2010). But again, it is a question whether the critique emerged as a critique of the theory or from Bourdieu's own research practice and style of writing. The posthumous publication of Bourdieu's work on Manet inspired our project and a reflexive investigation of the experience, challenges and problems that appeared in the project itself.

Taking a point of departure in field-analytic theory and methodologies, the project was planned as an integrated, interdisciplinary analysis of the relations between institutional, political, and economic factors in the production of culture and their importance in structuring the space of possible actions and distributions of specific forms of capital and power in art fields on the one hand, and selected production processes of works of art in four different fields of contemporary art (literature, music, visual arts and theatre) on the other. The project, thus, thematizes the relations between an *institutional order* structured by political regulations and cultural industrial logics, and *artistic autonomy* and freedom as experienced by selected artists in actual processes of art production. The notion of 'selection' in the title of the project points to an analytical focus on the power that lies in the selection, categorization, valuation, and recognition of artists and art works. Whereas the notion of 'negotiation' points to an analytical focus on the way and to what degree artistic autonomy and the space of possibilities for artistic and aesthetic manoeuvring are challenged, when rules, structures, and borders in the art field are confronted, challenged, or transcended.

The research was organized along two axes: (1) a horizontal, integrating axis aiming at analysing the four fields of art both comparatively and individually in order to understand how the fields in various degrees and ways are structured by political and cultural industrial institutions and logics concerning selection and negotiation; and (2) a vertical axis with a series of comparable but separate case studies focusing on how the specific power structures of each field are influencing and framing actual processes and aesthetic choices in the production, performance, and reception of art and art works.[2]

It is in the field of literature (fiction novels) that we have succeeded most in constructing the field with quantitative measures. The reasons for this are the relatively high quality of data in the publishing sector and the standardized media product (the book, the fiction novel) and artist role (author) that exist in the literary field. We modelled our variables closely after Julien Duval's (2006) recent study on French cinema and Bourdieu's (1999) study on publishing from 1999, focusing on one year of publication (2011) and reducing the universe to around 250 authors through methodological and systematic considerations of who the active authors were in 2011. Among the core variables measuring authorship were productivity (number of books over a period) and genres (many authors also write children's books or non-fiction). Variables measuring forms of literary success were sales of most recent title (2011 or earlier), library loan of most recent title (2011 or earlier), literary prizes, recent media attention, and participation in festivals. Also number of translations, grants received, and sociographic factors such as age, education, gender and home region were registered. Data was confined to Norwegian authors. We experienced how difficult it generally was to construct variables on imports and foreign authors and were reminded of footnote 31 in Bourdieu's 1999 article, where he dryly

108 *Tore Slaatta*

comments, 'L'immensité des recherches nécessaires pour le mener à bien nous a conduits à abandonner ce projet' (Bourdieu, 1999). Coding of variables was done in SPSS and then imported into Coheris SPAD for further elaboration and interpretation.

The structures in the plot appeared through two main axes, confirming the main hypothesis of opposition between authors that 'count' – who win prizes, get media attention, and have high sales and library loans – and those who do not and are mostly invisible – have few publications, no prizes and little attention. The second important opposition was related to genres and sales, between authors of crime and melodrama novels on the one hand, and grant receiving, acknowledged authors with small sales on the other (see Figure 7.3).

From this macro-oriented analysis, we gain a general overview of positions and distributions of different forms of capital: economic, literary

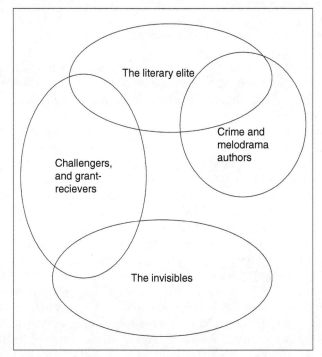

Figure 7.3 Reconstructed model of literary field 2011

and symbolic. From here, we do selected case studies of particular author careers and author styles and try to relate their positions to literary trends and readings of selected titles.

Conclusion

One of the benefits of doing this kind of work is the firm knowledge it produces of the macro trends: the structures in the field, the position and distribution of capital, and the relations between authors or groups of authors. The research process can be repeated some years later for a longitudinal check, giving a better understanding of how change plays out in the field.

As perhaps is shining through, my own ambivalence towards Bourdieu and field analysis comes not so much from a reflection over what field analysis can or cannot do, but from painful attempts of actually trying to do it. The fact is that it is terribly hard to do. But, as Bourdieu repeatedly warned, the 'real' cannot really be discovered unless we study these relations and positions `by the book' and do the hard work of quantitative objectification of a field. But then the next paradox is that – as correspondence analysis often proves – the structuring arrangements often are almost as we expect them to be. Since the efforts are so immense, should we continue doing them? The answer is, of course, yes, because we are scientists – and not all can be journalists or ethnographers in the history of cultural industries. Some have to be concerned about power and power relations in cultural fields, too. And done the right way, a proper correspondence analysis give a strong basis for further investigations and uses of qualitative and more case-based studies, expanding our understanding of positions and logics. Always interpreted, then, against the backdrop of the totality and of the field.

Notes

1. The core research team at IMK at the time included Gunnar Sæbø, Birgitta Høijer and research assistants.
2. A group of researchers from University of Oslo (Tore Slaatta, Helge Rønning, Fredrik Engelstad, Håkon Larsen, Astrid Kvalbein, Anne Lorentzen) and Telemark University College and Telemarkforskning (Per Mangset, Ole Marius Hylland, Heidi Stavrum) cooperated in the project. The research project is funded by the Norwegian Research Council. See project 212187 at www.forskningsradet.no.

References

Becker, H. S. (1982/2008) *Art Worlds* (Berkeley: University of California Press).
Bennet, T. (2005) 'The historical universal: The role of cultural value in the historical sociology of Pierre Bourdieu.' *British Journal of Sociology 56*(1), 141–164.
Benson, R. and Neveu, E. (eds) (2005) *Bourdieu and the Journalistic Field* (Cambridge: Polity Press).
Boltanski, L. (2011) *On Critique: A Sociology of Emancipation* (Cambridge: Polity Press).
Born, G. (2010) 'The social and the aesthetic: For a post-Bourdieuian theory of cultural production.' *Cultural Sociology 4*(2),171–208.
Bourdieu, P. (1984/1979) *Distinction: A Social Critique of the Judgement of Taste*, trans. Richard Nice (London: Routledge).
Bourdieu, P. (1991) *Language and Symbolic Power* (Cambridge: Polity Press).
Bourdieu, P. (1992) *Les regles de l'art*, (Paris: Éditions de Seuil).
Bourdieu, P. (1993) *The Field of Cultural Production* (Cambridge: Polity Press).
Bourdieu, P. (1996) *Sur la television* (Paris: Raisons d'agir).
Bourdieu, P. (1999) 'Une révolution conservatrice dans l'edition.' *Actes de la recherche en sciences sociales 126–127* (March), 3–28.
Bourdieu, P. (2013) *Manet: Une révolution symbolique* (Paris: Raisons d'agir/Seuil).
Calhoun, C., LiPuma, E., and Postone, M. (1993) *Bourdieu: Critical Perspectives* (Cambridge: Polity Press).
Champagne, P. and Chartier, R. (2004) *Pierre Bourdieu & les Médias* (Paris: l'Harmattan).
De la Fuente, E. (2010) 'In defence of theoretical and methodological pluralism in the sociology of art: A critique of Georgina Born's programmatic essay.' *Cultural Sociology 4*(2), 217–230.
Delsaut, Y. and Rivière, M. (2012) *Bibliographie des travaux de Pierre Bourdieu* (Paris: Le temps des cerises).
Duval, J. (2006) 'L'art du réalisme: Le champ du cinéma francais au début des années 2000.' *Actes de la recherche en sciences sociales 161–162*(January), 96–115.
Hallin, D. and Mancini, P. (2005) *Comparing Media Systems* (London: Routledge).
Hesmondhalgh, D. (2006) 'Bourdieu, the media and cultural production' *Media, Culture & Society 28*(2), 211–230.
Jensen, K. B. (1987) 'Qualitative audience research: Towards an integrative approach to reception.' *Critical Studies in Mass Communication 4*(1), 21–36.
Jensen, K. B. (1995) *The Social Semiotics of Mass Communication* (London: Sage).
Latour, B. (2005) *Constructing the Social* (Cambridge: Polity Press).
Marchetti, D. and Sapiro, G. (2009) Production et valorisation des biens symboliques. Manuscript retrieved from: http://cse,ehess.fr.document.php?id=369 (September).
Sapiro, G. (1999) *La Guerre des écrivains 1940–1953* (Paris: Fayard).
Sapiro, G. (2003) 'Forms of politicization in the French literary field.' *Theory and Society 32*(5/6), 633–652.
Sapiro, G. (ed.) (2008) *Translatio: Le marché de la traduction en France à l'heure de la mondialisation* (Paris: CNRS).
Sapiro, G. (2009a) *L'espace intellectuel en Europe* (Paris: Éditions La Découverte).

Sapiro, G. (ed.) (2009b) *Les contradiction de a globalisation éditoriale* (Paris: Nouveau Monde).

Sapiro, G. (2010) 'Globalization and cultural diversity in the book market: The case of literary translations in the US and France.' *Poetics* 38(4), 419–439.

Schinkel, W. (2009) 'Sociological discourse of the relational: The cases of Bourdieu & Latour.' *Sociological Review* 55(4), 707–728.

Slaatta, T. (2003) *Den norske medieorden* (Oslo: Gyldendal Akademisk).

Slaatta, T. (2012) *Art! Power!* The Norwegian Research Council. Available at www.forskningsradet.no (project no. 212187).

Swartz, D. (1997) *Culture & Power* (Chicago: Chicago University Press).

Thompson, J. B. (1990) *Ideology and Modern Culture* (Stanford: Stanford University Press).

Vanderberghe, F. (1999) '"The real is relational": An epistemological analysis of Pierre Bourdieu's generative structuralism.' *Sociological Theory* 17(1), 32–67.

van Maanen, H. (2009) *How to Study Art Worlds* (Amsterdam: Amsterdam University Press).

Wolff, J. (1984) *The Social Production of Art* (New York: NYU Press).

Part III
Matters of Method

8
Applying Grounded Theory in Media Production Studies
Astrid Gynnild

In order to understand the changing content, dynamics, and practices of media production, we need more theory. But time is over for *the one* theory that can explain it all for the years and decades to come. In a fast-changing digital world, we need many new theories – theories of all sizes and shapes.

Theories are important because they provide conceptual navigation tools in otherwise discernable terrains. Theories help people understand relationships and connections between otherwise fragmented bits and pieces. Theories provide interconnected terminologies and vocabularies; they may serve as conceptual bridge builders between people who would otherwise have few places to meet cognitively. An important value of a theory that is methodologically well grounded is, moreover, its ability to *explain* what is going on in a substantive area, and its ability to *make predictions* for the future – even in times of much uncertainty.

My views and perspectives on what a theory is, and what good it might do for the world, are impacted by the fact that I have been involved in the field of grounded theory for more than a decade. The aim of this chapter is thus to demonstrate and discuss the factual applicability of the classic grounded theory method in media production research, and to come up with several good arguments for using the method to its fullest potential in media production studies.

Grounded theory is a methodology and a method for inductively generating new grounded theories based on empirical data (Glaser and Strauss, 1967; Glaser, 1978, 1998, 2003). The seminal work *The Discovery of Grounded Theory* (Glaser and Strauss, 1967) is one of the most cited methods books in the social sciences. As of 24 March 2015, the book was cited more than 63,000 times on academic search engine Google Scholar alone, whereas the term *grounded theory* was referenced 344,000 times. On the general Google search engine, the concept *grounded theory* prompts nearly two million hits. There is reason to believe that many of these hits actually have little to do with grounded theory as a distinct methodology and research method, though.

As an inductive method that can make use of any kind of data, qualitative as well as quantitative, depending on context, grounded theory approaches are increasing in a growing number of disciplines – particularly in business administration, information science, medicine, nursing, sociology, psychology, and pedagogy.

Interestingly, sampling searches for the concept *grounded theory* in highly ranked media and communication journals such as *Journalism* and *Journalism Studies*, suggest that in media research, the term is often mentioned in passing. In media and communication, grounded theory citations are apparently used mostly as a quick means to undergird individual research authority; only in very few studies are the tenets of any version of grounded theory methodology actually followed.

An exception, for instance, is the audience theory of purposive attending (Martin, 2004, 2008), which explains and predicts how listeners, viewers, and readers relate to the daily news flow through relevance construction. Martin's theory of purposive attending suggests that in their daily sorting and selection of news items, people are searching for resonance; a feeling that a story rings true, confirms their views on certain topics, or informs them about issues of importance or interest. Martin explained the sub-core category relevance construction and its stages (emergent relevance/emergent attending, monitorial relevance/attending, and riveting relevance/riveting attending) as a means of cutting through the significance and credibility of news items to be able to make judgements about what to select for further attendance.

Instead of engaging in ongoing sociological debates on remodelling and jargonizing of grounded theory (Charmaz, 1995; Glaser, 2004, 2009; Stern, 1994), a phenomenon which appears to be just as widespread in media studies as in other disciplines, I will now go further into some benefits of using grounded theory when advancing media production studies. The discussion is grounded in complex data collected during more than ten years of doing interdisciplinary grounded theory research, teaching, and reviewing.

I will start the discussion with some reflections on handling research data in a world of information overload. From there, I will briefly introduce the grounded theory creative cycling of news professionals (Gynnild, 2006, 2007), which concerns the need for productive and innovative self-monitoring in journalistic work processes. The theory was generated from empirical data in complex journalism production environments during a period of two years. I will use the generation of this theory as a reference and an example of implications and applications of theory generation throughout this chapter.

I hope this provision of examples coupled with explanations might be helpful to others who are interested in testing the grounded theory method in practice. Furthermore, I will draw the lines between this particular grounded theory and the origins, tenets, and uses of grounded theory methodology in general. Finally, I will extract four particularly beneficial aspects of doing classic grounded theory studies of media production environments. The last section is supplemented with some ideas of how grounded theories might be beneficial for media researchers as well as for students, news professionals, and media managers who are seeking sustainable solutions to improve media work environments, given the many uncertainties under which the business currently operates.

What are the concerns?

What does it mean to be productive in a digital environment? More specifically, what does productivity imply for news professionals who are supposed to be online 24/7 across multiple media platforms? How do journalists resolve their professional concerns, and how do they build careers for uncertain times? These were some of the questions that came to the foreground during an extensive news production study I carried out in the first decade of the 21st century; it resulted in the theory of creative cycling (Gynnild, 2006, 2007, 2009) and a number of pedagogical and sociological follow-ups.

Nearly ten years after the theory was first published, its predictions appear to be more relevant and applicable than ever: with the outsourcing of human resources in favour of high-tech innovations, the productivity challenge of news professionals is rapidly escalating, and the news business has become an arena for survival of the fittest. How do news professionals keep pace with the constant pressures and rate of technological, managerial, and content changes in journalism? How do they find smarter ways to get work done while upholding individual integrity and personal ideals?

It often tends to be overlooked, though, that not only do the rapid changes of the media business challenge news professionals, but the changes also challenge *media researchers* in much the same ways. Thus, in the call for papers to the Advancing Media Production Research conference in Leeds in 2013, I was especially intrigued by the question, 'Can we [the researchers] keep pace with the rate of change in media production environments?' At first glance, I didn't quite understand why the question was formed as '*Can* we keep pace', instead of 'In what *ways* can we keep pace'.

But upon further reflection, the evolving dynamics of media production exemplified by co-creation, content outsourcing, social sharing, and innovative entrepreneurship imply that widespread and established research approaches may be losing relevancy. Data collected and descriptively analysed with the best of intentions might become stale before a study is published. Otherwise honourable research is at risk of becoming meaningless for the researcher and useless for students and practitioners because of its perception to be irrelevant or out of focus. And increasingly the term *newsrooms studies* is devoid of meaning in a media world where physical newsrooms are complemented by virtual meeting groups in which interdisciplinary co-creation and user-generated content rules the news environment. All in all, based on the sweeping changes in the media business, anecdotal evidence suggests that the same challenges that blew many hardworking, insightful media producers to the shore in the beginning of the 21st century might threaten established research communities in the next wave.

In the paper that I submitted to the Advancing Media Production Research conference I responded by writing,

> As posed, the question asks for a yes or a no. With grounded theory methodology (GT) as a part of the research repertoire, I would say yes. After ten years of exploring grounded theory from a variety of perspectives (Gynnild, 2006, 2007, 2012), I argue that this method appears to be close to tailor-made for reliable media production research in the digital, globalized society.

These are big words. But I still think they are true. In order to build a strong argument for doing grounded theory, I will turn to the research challenge of handling data. This issue has impacted heavily on the working conditions of media researchers as well as media producers and media audiences, but in different ways.

Getting out of the data

In the transition from a control paradigm to a chaos paradigm in the globalized news culture, information surplus is identified as a main constituent (McNair, 2006). But even if access to a growing diversity of information is increasing and database storage capacity is unlimited, knowing how to find what one is looking for is a threshold many people have yet to cross. This holds true for media researchers and news professionals in media production environments. Researchers and media CEOs as well as political decision-makers are concerned that being able to retrieve information and identify patterns by cutting across immense quantities of data is crucial for the further democratic transparency of society (Gynnild, 2014; Flew et al., 2012; King, 2011; Meyer, 2002).

The idea that analysing big data might be the best way to keep pace with the rate of change is interesting. There are many signs of information overload, and with the digital information surplus, the handling of data has become a key concern in all branches of society. In the 21st century, the biggest problem is not necessarily getting access to relevant data. Rather, the biggest problem now tends to be getting out of the data, keeping one's pace, and producing research which is generalizable enough to survive constantly ongoing changes (Glaser, 2011). The resolution to data overload, though, does not necessarily consist in computerized retrieving of even more data. A complementary way of approaching the world of computational thinking (Wing, 2010) would be to revisit human capabilities of identifying and recognizing patterns of behaviour to the extent that grounded predictions can be made with relatively simple means by changing established analytical mindsets.

In all honesty, it should be remarked that researchers have, at all times, been good at collecting more data than actually needed. Anecdotal evidence suggests that PhD candidates' analytic frustrations are often related to an experience of data overload. What made this researcher switch to classic grounded theory during her PhD study was also the search for a way to cut through immense amounts of qualitative data material.

My area of interest was the way news reporters organize their daily work in a time of rapid technological and financial change. In particular, I was interested in the emerging role of multimedia journalists. The idea was to do a phenomenological study, but with hundreds of pages of transcripts from 15 practitioner interviews stabled on my desk, I started asking myself what I actually wanted to get out of the study and whether description was the best choice in this situation.

By switching to a classic grounded theory approach, new methodological doors were opened. One, I learned that grounded theory is one of the most well-documented methods that exists. In the original literature by Glaser and Strauss (1967), and in more than twenty later books written by Glaser, the tenets of classic grounded theory are described in detail. Two, I learned that getting from the descriptive to the abstract level, getting conceptual, is a very productive way of handling large amounts of data.

Moreover, the grounded theory approach made it possible to collect a wide variety of data, conceptualized as four levels of data: baseline data, properline data, interpreted data, and vague data (Glaser, 1978). Data collection went hand in hand, in a cyclic process, with analysis and writing of memos, and theoretical reflections that derived from the data analyses. What initially appeared to be a vast amount of complex data was now systematically coded, analysed, and constantly compared according to the tenets of classic grounded theory, and comprised the empirical grounding on which the theory was gradually generated.

Short-version theory

Data included observations of, and interviews and informal conversations with, more than a hundred journalists, photographers, editors, and programmers from ten Norwegian media organizations. Data were also collected by attending editorial discussions and media conference discussions, which, in turn, were supplemented by following large international news sites and a number of American and English media bloggers to keep updated on what was going on in the substantive area internationally. The process took approximately two years and was followed by an intensive sorting and writing-up period of the theory's main concern, resolution to this concern, and the interrelationships between the dimensions of the core category guided by the large selection of memos that had been written in parallel with the coding and analysing steps.

A benefit of writing conceptually and developing grounded theories is the opportunity to scale the theory up and down according to available space. Before I provide a very short version of the theory, it should be noted that the concept of grounded theory refers to three aspects of doing research. Grounded theory is a methodology and a method as well as the outcome of a grounded theory study. This triple interconnectedness might at first sight appear quite confusing but is essential for understanding the dynamics of building a grounded theory. It implies that grounded theory is not a method that can be followed halfway. Choosing a GT approach has implications for all steps of the study.

Right now we are focusing on the outcome of a GT study of media production environments in flux: creative cycling of news professionals explains and predicts how journalists, independent of dissemination platforms, constantly explore and potentially escalate their own productive processing in both a day-to-day timespan and in the course of a career. The key word for the productive behaviour of journalists is cycling – defined as the individual ability to switch between work tasks by moving in and out and back and forth among inner (mental) and outer (organizational) framings in such a way that productive creativity is optimized.

Contrary to organizational goals of getting news reporters to be as productive as possible in as short a time as possible, the creative cycling study indicates that a main concern of journalists is *self-fulfilment through original contribution*. This proposition suggests that the assembly line, top-down organizing of work in established news organizations is counterproductive to journalistic production of meaningful news. On the other hand, it stimulates innovation and entrepreneurship outside of the newsrooms, activities that are often carried out by experienced reporters searching for new ways to manifest their potential for meaningful and original contribution to society (Gynnild, 2013).

It emerged from the data that the most important drive for journalists is to be able to work autonomously enough to make a difference in society. Journalists are journalists because they want to impact societal issues that they find essential and meaningful. Thus, creative cycling is both the dilemma and the resolution to journalists' main concern. The term *creative cycling* conceptualizes productive patterns of behaviour that go on all the time, but usually quite unnoticed. Creative cycling is an integrated part of journalists' daily work habits and consist of three interrelated stages: productive processing, breaks and shifts, and inspirational looping. The pattern is cyclic in the sense that it constantly repeats itself, but it is simultaneously highly individual and dependent on context.

Let us first have a closer look at productive processing. This dimension comprises six constantly repeated stages of journalistic work processes. The six stages of productive processing are *preparing* (e.g. the reporter starts collecting information about an event he is going to cover), *concentrating* (the reporter is fully focused on the job), *incubating/chaos* (the reporter is confused; he or she is sorting information and searching for a solution), *the aha moment* (lasts only for a few seconds; the moment when the solution is found), *elaborating* (the reporter has a clear direction and moves on), and *presenting* (the idea, story, or image is ready for sharing). In short, this dimension refers to the classic phases that creative humans undergo in the process from idea development to dissemination of a story.

The question that arose when these stages were identified was as follows: What makes individual reporters, photographers, programmers, and editors move from one stage to the next in creative processing? Why do some reporters spend most of the time preparing for a beat, whereas others might get stuck at the incubation/chaos stage, and yet others appear to produce endless amounts of aha moments but have trouble finishing projects? Further analysis of the data indicated that the productive processing of journalists is very much influenced by three types of breaks and shifts, conceptualized as *deadlines/scheduled breaks, external interruptions,* and *mental timeouts.*

Deadlines/scheduled breaks are predictable and routinized. They provide journalists with some control of the situation and make it possible to plan ahead with some certainty. External interruptions are exemplified by text messages, phone calls and the like – unexpected inquiries to which journalists have to respond on the spot. Mental timeouts, in contrast, refer to micro and macro breaks initiated by the individual reporter. Mental timeouts are the only type of breaks and shifts that are fully controlled and regulated by the individual. Problems arise when a journalist is exposed to tight deadlines and external interruptions to the extent that he or she gets out of productive balance.

The tipping point for each person varies depending on the third dimension, termed *inspirational looping.* This concept refers to the cyclic switching between six particular variables that influence the pace and direction of productive processing and breaks and shifts. In the span of a day and throughout a career, journalists switch between a variety of professional roles, temporal spans/physical locations, collaboration forms, feedback interactions, and skill levels. Moreover, during a career, news professionals typically start out at the *accessing stage,* where the main aim is to get a foot inside the newsroom. A basic dilemma during the accessing stage is that employer recognition often depends on psychological contracting – a situation where mutual expectations are not clearly formulated but based on unarticulated expectations. At the *qualitating stage,* the individual further develops and explores practical, theoretical, personal, and creative competences. Focus is now on proving one's qualities towards colleagues more than towards managers. However, at the third stage of a career, the *individuating stage,* news professionals are focused on harmonizing values and work and are more likely to take risks, such as breaking away from a position, department, or an organization to achieve their value-based goals.

Often, without explicitly being aware of their own patterns, journalists, photographers, editors, software developers, and other news professionals develop individual strategies in order to ensure self-fulfilment through original contribution. Such personal framings are interdependent with institutional framings for work. They require that he or she be simultaneously professionally flexible but firm. The complexity of journalistic work processes in the digital media world requires that each news reporter get skilled in personal and professional *self-monitoring* in order to keep up his or her productive processing without losing balance.

The industrial mindset, which still impacts work process organizing in established news organizations, stands in contrast to the whole-person paradigm introduced by Stephen Covey (2004). In the knowledge age, Covey points out, professionals need to treat each other as whole persons with feelings and thoughts. People yearn for meaning and identity, and typically search for ways in which to contribute creatively and innovatively to society by developing a distinct voice among many other voices. Covey refers to the American management philosopher, Peter Drucker, who predicts that when the history of our time is written in a long-term perspective, historians may perceive either technology or the Internet as being the most important changes in human condition. Rather, Drucker points out, the time shift is concerned with human choice. For the first time in history, vast numbers of people have an opportunity to make choices in important areas of their lives, and subsequently they have to manage themselves, they have to be their own leaders.

The full theory of creative cycling comprises 200 pages (Gynnild, 2006). The theory contributes to new insights into the need for creative freedom through individualized allocation of time and extended acceptance of more individuality of expression. With greater technological freedom and more market-oriented news management, the need for individual intervention skills increases dramatically. If a journalist does not take control of his or her professional and private time, others will do it for him or her. To improve journalistic performance and productivity then, the theory of creative cycling suggests that a crucial challenge of news professionals in a media world in constant flux is self-monitoring through extended professional and personal self-awareness. The implications of these challenges are important to news professionals themselves, and to managers, CEOs and others who facilitate complex news work environments. The grounded theory provides a new vocabulary through which the various actors in a news culture environment can interrelate, understand and potentially resolve issues of great importance to its participants. The value of the theory lies in its applicability and ability to provide sustainable predictions about consequences of future changes in the work environment.

The observant reader has probably already started questioning why grounded theory still hasn't had its breakthrough in media research, if the method is working so well. Considering the potential benefits of applying GT to media production research, it is a somewhat of a mystery that the method still is little discussed and rarely used to its fullest potential in this discipline. Especially so since the first grounded theory, which resulted in a new methodology, was generated close to fifty years ago (Glaser and Strauss, 1967) and has long been widespread across continents.

In established research schools, traditional approaches are concerned with qualitative and quantitative data analyses. When novice researchers are taught how to carry out a research study, they usually learn that theory might be applied in three ways. First, they learn that the researcher might apply existing theory to new data material or in a new field. Second, they learn that the researcher might do a purely theoretical study where he compares aspects of two or more theories, and third, the researcher might generate new theory. Even though novice analysts are informed about the option of developing new theory, anecdotal evidence suggests that colleagues and supervisors tend to be wary of the very idea of autonomous theorizing. Developing theory is by many academics still considered too risky for most researchers and definitely too risky for inexperienced researchers who are on their way to do a PhD. Maybe part of the answer to the prevalent absence of GT in Media Studies lies right there. In traditional studies, inexperienced researchers are usually taught to work deductively with data. Their starting point is theoretical knowledge from literature or earlier empirical findings, which are subsequently compared or tested in new substantive areas or on new material.

But as Fox points out,

> more often than not in social science research, there is a paucity of empirical research in the area of interest; that is, most times there are no existing substantive theories against which a methodology might set out to either support or falsify. What seems to be required in these instances is a methodology that will lead to explanations about what occurs in the area of empirical interest and from which a substantive may be developed. (Fox, 2014)

Fox refers to a number of researchers who focus on the suitability of adopting grounded theory as the inductive approach in new areas lacking conceptual frameworks (Fox, 2014). While research on human production cultures are cognitive processes that usually require much time both in the field and during analyses and write-up, the emergence of Twitter illustrates the fast innovation pace of media work environments. In a matter of months, it contributed to changing journalistic norms and habits for data collection, editorial communication, and digital news promotion. In tandem with increasing requirements of accountability and transparency in the news media, we might expect even an increasing focus on similar attributes within media research, too. We might expect from new theorizing that it fits and works, and that new theories are solid enough to be tested by professional practitioners and interested people as well as by other researchers. In other words, we might expect that new theories have explanatory power to fill theorizing knowledge gaps in rapidly changing production environments.

Glaser and Strauss' seminal work *The Discovery of Grounded Theory* (Glaser and Strauss, 1967) was published in response to the overwhelming reception of their book *Awareness of Dying* (Glaser and Strauss, 1965). In their first book, the grounded theory protocol was applied, for the first time, to the study of dying in American hospitals. This project contributed to changing conditions for dying people in the United States as well as in other Western countries. The subsequent organizational changes that resulted from the study evoked international interest in both the health industry and in academic environments. Since Glaser and Strauss split up in the early 1990s due to disagreements about procedures for collecting and analysing the data (Strauss and Corbin, 1990; Glaser, 1992), three distinct approaches that make claims to be grounded theory are identified: the Strauss and Corbin (1990) qualitative data analysis (QDA), which is often referred to as the Straussian grounded theory; constructivist grounded theory, developed by one of Glaser's early students (Charmaz, 2006); and classic grounded theory, which was first generated by Glaser and Strauss, and further developed by Glaser (1978, 1992, 1998, 2003, 2005, 2007, 2009, 2011).

A number of how-to books on grounded theory suggest a mix of approaches, and anecdotal evidence indicates that many novice researchers find it challenging to choose between the various grounded theory approaches (Glaser, 2014; Martin and Gynnild, 2012). My stance is that a mix of grounded theory approaches does not work well. Depending on the aims of the study and a researcher's favoured way of working, the researcher should select one approach or the other, and be explicit about his or her choice in order to produce reliable research results. The focus in this chapter has been on classic grounded theory, which is the most referenced and best described version of the method.

In classic grounded theory, qualitative as well as quantitative data are coded, constantly compared, and conceptualized according to distinctive cyclic steps: data collection, open coding, memoing, sampling, selective coding, theoretical coding, and write-up of the theory. The steps from two to four are repeated until data completeness. The goal of the theorizing process is the generation of a new grounded theory, which consists of a set of interrelated hypotheses that spring out of a core category. The core category is the resolution to the participants' or the study unit's main concern and will normally organize into four to six categories or dimensions which together form a grounded theory. The inductivity of the approach implies that at any point in a grounded theory study, the golden rule is to follow the data, and not be tempted to hypothesize through associative thinking. Data and the constant comparison of emerging patterns in the data decide where the researcher should go to collect data next, until data saturation is reached. Data saturation refers to the stage of a GT study where data repetition occurs and no further information is found (Glaser, 1978, 1998).

Since the outcome of a grounded theory is an interrelated set of conceptual hypotheses about patterns of human behaviour, grounded theories are abstract of time, place, and people. Thus, the accountability of a grounded theory is measured not in findings or facts, but by the theory's experienced relevance and fit for people in the field of investigation. Moreover, any grounded theory might be modified and/or further developed in order to ensure that the theory at any time is grounded in empirical data. In the ten years that have passed since the theory of creative cycling was generated, the expansion of social media, mobile technologies, and smart gadgets, coupled with escalating micro payment experiments, suggests that the theory, or rather aspects of the theory, might need to be modified.

Most probably this is the case in particular for the sub-theory of feedback switching, which might have become more dependent on new technologies. But until I have collected, analysed and constantly compared more data from the substantive field, I don't know if the theory actually needs to be modified. It should also be mentioned that the theory of creative cycling was published as a textbook in Norwegian (Gynnild, 2009), which is on the curriculum of higher education in journalism as well as media and communication in Norway. The theory has also been discussed and applied by media managers and editors and has contributed to five pages of new terms in the vocabulary of Norwegian journalism in a time when much communication tends to adopt terms and phrases from English.

The Italian grounded theorist Massimiliano Tarozzi (2012) pointed out how *translating* grounded theory is *doing* grounded theory. An important side effect of grounded theory is thus its contribution to expanding the disciplinary vocabularies in different languages. In the book *Doing Grounded Theory: Issues and Implications* (Glaser, 1998), the necessity of *doing* grounded theory is discussed at length. Misunderstandings often occur as long as the tenets of the method are only theoretically discussed; on paper, grounded theory may sound easy to grasp and test out. In practice, especially, the move from description to conceptualization is challenging for novice researchers. Thus, it is recommended that researchers who aspire to generate grounded theories should be in contact with experienced grounded theory supervisors or networks.

It appears that established descriptive research approaches may fall short in keeping pace with the rate of change in media production environments simply because they attempt to *describe* too much instead of *analysing for conceptualization*. The limitations of established approaches to media production studies also concern time, place, and ways in which data collection is carried out. With the shift to new technologies and subsequently new human patterns for news production, the classic research setting of the newsroom or studio might be too limiting for media research to explore what is actually going on. There is time for a focus shift that offers more multifaceted ways of collecting and handling data.

My main argument, then, is that grounded theory overcomes the challenges of data overload and lacking relevancy by offering not description, but conceptualization, and by providing a step-by-step approach to generating theory that is solidly grounded in empirical data. The flexibility and modifiability which is built into the method, ensures that the theorizing will always fit the data and thus be experienced as reliable by the persons or environments that are investigated.

I will finish this chapter by identifying the four benefits of doing grounded theory that I find the most important:

(1) Since grounded theory is *conceptual* and not descriptive, grounded theory is not concerned with accurate description of units or events. On the contrary, grounded theory provides a set of interrelated hypotheses about patterns of behaviour. Grounded theories provide overview through conceptually cutting through layers of empirical data. The theories are abstract of time, place, and people, and they might provide valuable predictions of future patterns based on existing data.

(2) Grounded theory is *flexible* in the sense that this approach to theory generation can make use of any kind of data, as long as they seem to be relevant for the further development of the theory. GT is also flexible in the sense that it is not unit-bound. Yet another aspect is the modifiability of grounded theories. If a generated theory no longer has "grab", is relevant, and fits and works as experienced by people in the substantive area, the theory can easily be modified by collecting and constantly comparing more data.

(3) The process of generating a grounded theory is *next-step focused*. The grounded theory stages of data collection, substantive coding, sampling, memoing, sorting, theoretical coding, and write-up of the theory are cyclically interdependent. I would say that creative cycling is actually built into the method so that the researcher keeps energy up throughout the whole study. The researcher does not wait to write till the data is collected; she starts writing from day one.

(4) The constant comparative method is a basic component of grounded theory generation and actually lays the foundation for conceptualization as well as for the flexibility and the productive next-step focus. The constant comparative method is used to instantly compare what emerges from the data, line by line, incident to incident. The constant comparative method is a premise for naming concepts for coding, sampling, and sorting. The researchers hunt for patterns, not single incidents; therein lies grounded theories' potential for explanation and prediction, since human patterns tend to be more stable than technological tools. Thus, grounded theories are impermanent in the sense that they may always be further developed through subsequent inquiries.

In this chapter, I have pointed out that in a time of information overload and constant change in the media business, the analysis, reliability, and usefulness of data is a major concern of media production researchers. The aim of this chapter was thus to demonstrate and discuss the factual applicability and benefits of grounded theory approaches in media production research. By introducing grounded theory's tenets of theorizing, exemplified by the generation of the theory of creative cycling of news professionals, I built an argument for the usefulness of grounded theories in a fluctuating but innovative business. Of particular importance is the method's capability to cut through immense amounts of empirical data through abstract conceptualization. Finally, the chapter provided some ideas on how grounded theories might be beneficial not only for media researchers, but also for students, news professionals, and media managers who want to improve media work environments and plan for the future in a time of much uncertainty.

References

Charmaz, K. (1995) 'Grounded theory' in J. Smith et al. (eds), *Rethinking Methods in Psychology* (pp. 27–65) (London: Sage).
Charmaz, K. (2006) *Constructing Grounded Theory: A Practical Guide through Qualitative Analysis* (London: Sage).
Covey, S. (1989) *The Seven Habits of Highly Effective People: Restoring the Character Ethic* (New York: Fireside).
Drucker, P. (2002) *Managing in the Next Society* (New York: Truman Talley Books/St. Martin's Press).
Evans, G. (2013) 'A novice researcher's first walk through the maze of grounded theory: rationalization of classic grounded theory.' *Grounded Theory Review* 12(1). Retrieved from http://groundedtheoryreview.com/2013/06/22/a-novice-researchers-first-walk-through-the-maze-of-grounded-theory-rationalization-for-classical-grounded-theory/.
Flew, T. et al. (2012) 'The promise of computational journalism.' *Journalism Practice* 6(2), 157–171.
Fox, S. (2014) *Thinking about Grounded Theory* [Self-published monograph]. Retrieved from http://www.amazon.com/-/e/B007H45TAS (accessed on 3 January 2014).
Glaser, B. (1978) *Theoretical Sensitivity: Advances in the Methodology of Grounded Theory* (Mill Valley, CA: Sociology Press).
Glaser, B. (1992) *Basics of Grounded Theory Analysis: Emergence versus Forcing* (Mill Valley, CA: Sociology Press).
Glaser, B. (1998) *Doing Grounded Theory: Issues and Discussions* (Mill Valley, CA: Sociology Press).
Glaser, B. (2001) *The Grounded Theory Perspective: Conceptualization Contrasted with Description* (Mill Valley, CA: Sociology Press).
Glaser, B. (2004) 'Remodeling grounded theory.' *Forum Qualitative Sozialforschung [Forum: Qualitative Social Research]* 5(2), Art. 4, 1–22. Retrieved from http://www.qualitative-research.net/fqs/.
Glaser, B. (2005) *The Grounded Theory Perspective III: Theoretical Coding* (Mill Valley, CA: Sociology Press).
Glaser, B. (2009) *Jargonizing Using the Grounded Theory Vocabulary* (Mill Valley, CA: Sociology Press).
Glaser, B. (2011) *Getting Out of the Data: Grounded Theory Conceptualization* (Mill Valley, CA: Sociology Press).
Glaser, B. (2014) *Applying Grounded Theory; A Neglected Option* (Mill Valley, CA: Sociology Press).
Glaser, B. and Strauss, A. (1967) *The Discovery of Grounded Theory: Strategies for Qualitative Research* (London: Weidenfeld and Nicolson).
Gynnild, A. (2006) *Creative Cycling in the News Profession: A Grounded Theory.* Doctoral thesis, University of Bergen, Norway.

Gynnild, A. (2007) 'Creative cycling of news professionals.' *Grounded Theory Review* 6(2). Retrieved from http://groundedtheoryreview.com/2007/03/30/1144/.

Gynnild, A. (2009) *Creativity under Pressure* (Kristiansand, Norway: Hogskoleforlaget Academic Publisher).

Gynnild, A. (2011) 'Book review: Grounded theory: A practical guide (Birks & Mills, 2011).' *Grounded Theory Review* 10(3), 63–66. Retrieved from http://groundedtheoryreview.com/2011/12/20/book-review-grounded-theory-a-practical-guide-birks-mills-20111/.

Gynnild, A. (2013) 'Journalism innovation leads to innovation journalism: The impact of computational exploration on changing mindsets.' *Journalism* 15(6), 713–730. Published online before print 22 May 2013. DOI: 10.1177/1464884913486393. Retrieved from http://jou.sagepub.com/content/15/6/713.

King, G. (2011) 'Ensuring the data-rich future of the social sciences.' *Science* 331(6018), 719–721.

Martin, V. (2004) *Getting the News from the 'News": A Grounded Theory of Purposive Attending*. Doctoral thesis, PhD. Union Institute and University.

Martin, V. (2008) 'Attending the news: A grounded theory of a daily regimen.' *Journalism* 9(1), 76–94. Retrieved from http://jou.sagepub.com/content/9/1/76.short.

Martin, V. and Gynnild, A. (2012) *Grounded Theory: The Philosophy, Method, and Work of Barney Glaser* (Boca Raton, FL: Brown Walker Press).

McNair, B. (2006) *Journalism, News and Power in a Globalised World* (New York: Routledge).

Meyer, P. (1973/2002) *Precision Journalism* (New York: Rowman and Littlefield).

Scott, H. (2009) 'Data analysis: Getting conceptual.' *Grounded Theory Review* 8(2), 89–112. Retrieved from http://groundedtheoryreview.com/2012/06/04/volume-8-issue-no-2-june-2009/.

Stern, P. N. (1994) 'Eroding grounded theory' in J. M. Morse (ed.), *Critical Issues in Qualitative Research Methods* (Thousand Oaks, CA: Sage).

Strauss, A. and Corbin, J. (1990) *Basics of Qualitative Research: Grounded Theory Procedures and Techniques* (London: Sage).

Tarozzi, M. (2012) 'On translating grounded theory: When translating is doing' in V. Martin and A. Gynnild (eds), *Grounded Theory: The Philosophy, Method, and Work of Barney Glaser* (Boca Raton, FL: Brown Walker Press).

Wing, J. (2006) 'Computational thinking.' *Communications of the ACM* 49(3), 33–35.

9
The Qualitative Interview in Media Production Studies
Hanne Bruun

In media production studies the qualitative research interview is frequently used as a tool in the generation of data, and thus in building the analytical object. However, the research contributions – including my own work – contain only to a very limited degree methodological reflections on what characterizes this kind of research interview and its application in the given analytical context. This somewhat paradoxical situation is particularly striking when compared with the situation in audience studies. Theoretical coherence and methodological transparency have been part of the quality demands for many years within this research tradition. On the basis of this difference between audience studies and production studies, the aim of the chapter is to help clarify what can be said to characterize the special configuration of the qualitative research interview genre when used in media production studies. I hope that this will help advance the validity of our research projects as well as the overall level of theoretical and methodological self-reflexivity of this growing and increasingly important research effort.

Within sociology and ethnography a helpful tradition exists of investigating what is termed 'elite interviewing', which is a tool often used to explore the practices and values of social and organizational elites. I will start off by characterizing what is understood by 'the elite', and I will suggest that the term 'exclusive informants' might be added to what 'elite' means, and why this is a more relevant conceptualization of the kind of elite informants interviewed in media production analysis. Next, Kvale and Brinkmann's (2015) seven-step model for structuring a qualitative interview research process serves as a matrix in the process of understanding what makes interviews with exclusive informants a special research interview genre. There will be an emphasis on how this genre differs from the kind of qualitative interview genre applied in audience studies. Key differences can be found in three stages in the research process: (1) in relation to the conceptualization of human agency embedded in the research question; (2) in connection with the methodological design of a study; and (3) in connection with the publication of research findings. Along the way, I make use of illustrative examples from my own research.

Elite and exclusive

In the literature on 'elite interviewing' the definition of the interview genre is characterized by two basic assumptions regarding the concept 'the elite'. Studying an elite is first and foremost the same as studying the power in society. Objects of analysis are powerful individuals or representatives of power placed in important institutions and organizations in a society. Studying this elite involves a study of more general power structures in a society that can be based on gender, class and ethnicity (Moyser and Wagstaffe, 1987). Aguiar and Schneider describe the focus on elites as 'studying up the social structure' using qualitative methodology (2012: 9). The elite is studied in order to understand the life-world and value systems of a specific elite. According to Ho, this ambition is in many ways contrary to the more or less explicitly stated value-based code of sociological and ethnographic research: '"giving voice" to marginalized others' (2012: 36). Studying the elite therefore calls for both basic meta-professional reflections and self-reflections by the researcher who him/herself belongs to an (educational) elite. The second dominant assumption that characterizes the concept of 'the elite' in the research tradition is that the elite is viewed as powerful gatekeepers of information or holders of information on the processes within and the workings of organizational structures. The elite possess a form of expert knowledge that the researcher needs to access in order to assure the quality of his or her research (Moyser and Wagstaffe, 1987: 4).

In addition to this profound connection to the concept of power, a substantial discussion of what could actually be understood by 'an elite' exists in the literature on 'elite interviewing' that is also relevant for media production analysis (see Harvey, 2011; Welch et al., 2002; Richards, 1996). Apart from the requirement to include the question of power in the definition, 'the elite' can be defined horizontally (i.e. viewed as different *types of power*), which defines these elites that are not necessarily related to or cooperating directly. In this way we can talk about a cultural, an economic, a bureaucratic and a political elite, as well as a number of sub-groups of these within specific fields. 'The elite' can also be defined vertically (i.e. viewed as *the top of a social and/or organizational hierarchy*). This often makes it difficult to determine where an elite level can be said to begin in a given structure and whether the structure is of a local, national or global nature (Moyser and Wagstaffe, 1987).

All in all, the literature on 'elite interviewing' makes it clear that the concept of 'the elite' is ambiguous, and that it is both a dynamic and relational concept. To define an elite seems also to be seen as an empirical question in relation to specific case studies on specific sectors or sociological fields (Harvey, 2011: 433; Welch et al., 2002). Depending on the context, the question arises of what types of elites a given research project will engage. Moore and Stoke (2012) suggest a typology of elite informants that seems useful in media production analysis. The typology involves the informant's access to a local, national or even an international public sphere, and it can accommodate the dynamic aspect of the concept described above. The typology is based on a definition of the various elites involved in professional football as a sector (Moore and Stoke, 2012: 450). It provides a system of three prototypes: the first is called *Macro-Elite / Celebrity* and has a high degree of power and celebrity status. Prototype two is called *Micro-Local Elite / Public 'Background' Figure*, which has a high degree of power but a lower degree of celebrity status, and the third prototype is called *Eclipsed-Faded-Fallen Elite / Celebrity* with low power but high degree of celebrity status. This system of prototypes is a dynamic and relational system, and concrete informants are often characterized by a mix of prototypical traits, and they are able to move around in the 'elite / celebrity eco-system' (Moore and Stoke, 2012: 453).

Compared to an analysis of the football industry, media production studies, however, deals with elite informants that are *professional media content producers with a direct access to the public sphere*. They are not like elites in other cultural industries (e.g. music, theatre, stand-up comedy) in varying degrees dependent on professional (mass) media institutions to reach a mass audience. This means that the informants possess a direct power over the media and the production of content taking place, which is at the same time the media researcher's analytical object. Second, many of the informants will have a high degree of celebrity status, at least in a national context. An elite / celebrity informant's current position in a particular context, will therefore have implications for the access to do research on media production, as well as for the way an interview proceeds and for the overall research results. Third, I would suggest that there are two kinds of power involved that need to be considered: first, an *objective position of power* held by the interviewee is involved, and because of this kind of power the interviewee holds a particularly attractive kind of knowledge. Second, an *interpersonal power* is of significance for the researcher and his or her opportunity to gain knowledge and/or access to construct a research object. The interpersonal kind of power can be part of the interview genre both in a specific interview situation and in the long term, when the cooperation with the researcher is completed and the research results are published. Like the informants who Moore and Stokes calls 'elite / celebrity' and some are 'eclipsed-faded-fallen' celebrities (2012: 453) and therefore no longer enjoy the same share in the objective power, media producers can easily have very high degrees of interpersonal power. This kind of power can be demonstrated by refusing to participate in an interview while their knowledge is extremely important and perhaps crucial to the research question. An example taken from my own research on the generic development of television satire from 1968 to 2010 (Bruun, 2011, 2012) is that interviews with a retired executive producer of television satire at the Danish public service broadcasting company DR for 30 years were crucial for me. *If* she had refused to participate, I would not have been able to construct my analytical object. It is the mixture between forms of objective and interpersonal power held by the professional producers of media content to a public at large that production analysis will have as a challenge when using the research interview as a data collection tool.

For two reasons *exclusive informants* might be a more accurate term for the specific kind of elite informants involved. First of all, media production analysis uses interviews with elite informants not primarily for the purpose of exploring what characterizes these elites themselves and their life-world; rather, they are interviewed as a means to gain insight into a research question related to the terms of the production of the media products in a broad sense. These media products are created within an organizational framework and under the influence of social forces such as technology, economics and cultural politics. The purpose of media production analysis is to gain insight into what is going on 'backstage', and certain individuals possess the specific knowledge that is needed in the construction of the analytical object. As in sports, exclusive rights are something that provides access to a particular kind of content that cannot be replaced by access to any other content. The same goes for exclusive informants: these individuals possess a special kind of knowledge that cannot be replaced by another person's knowledge. Second, this exclusiveness separates these informants from what journalists and sociologists call experts (Littig, 2009). Normally there are more experts in a given field of knowledge (for example, media researchers). This is not the case with exclusive informants; they are irreplaceable. This definition of the elite informants as exclusive informants has a profound impact on key stages of the actual research process, which will be discussed in the following sections of the chapter.

The role of the research question and the conceptualization of human agency

In Kvale and Brinkmann's (2015) seven-stage model of qualitative interview research, mentioned in the introduction, the first stage is to secure the accuracy of the research question since it is the starting point for all methodological issues and decisions in the following six stages. In media production analysis projects that involve interviews with exclusive informants, reflections are required on the understanding of power in the project. As mentioned, the aim of production analysis is to understand the inner workings of the media and to get access to the 'backstage' of the media organizations. Based on this type of non-publicly available knowledge, the goal is to offer explanations to media content characteristics and developments that neither media system analysis nor textual and audience analysis are able to provide. But professionals working in organizational and competitive media systemic contexts inhabit the media organizational 'backstage', and the conceptualization of agency often imbedded in the research question thus becomes important. The fundamental question for the researcher to ask is how the project understands the causal relation between the objective conditions for media production and the work done by the professional media producers. Where is the power located over how the media content/products turn out, and how is 'power' understood? Is the production of media content, for example, determined by political, economic, or organizational forces, or determined by genre conventions? Or is the production of media content on the contrary, determined by the creative talents employed and the innovative work performed individually and in cooperation by the media producers? Frandsen (2007) identifies two prototypical approaches to the location of 'power' in her analysis of this structure-agency-theme within the media production analysis research tradition linked to the object of analysis. If the researchers are interested in film production and audio-visual fiction, they tend to focus on human agency and creativity. Structural power is considered either an opponent or a teammate in the realization of the expressive and artistic ambitions of the professionals. If the researchers are interested in news production, there is a tendency to focus on functionalist or critical-theoretical approaches to the structural forces and to highlight the collective dimensions of media production rather than the creative abilities and expressive needs of the individuals involved.

Whether one subscribes to one or the other approach to the dichotomy, it has implications for the research interview genre. Are the interviewees considered to be powerful human agents in their own world and perhaps with the ability to change and determine how the external world looks? Another option is to consider the interviewees to be powerless victims of structural forces within and outside of the organization. In such a framing the interviewees are considered to be more or less aware of their own powerlessness. The interviewee may even be regarded as someone who is the victim of a delusion or uses a psychological defence mechanism against the ethical dilemmas that acknowledged powerlessness might produce. A third option is to consider the relationship between human agency and structure as the basic empirical questions to be highlighted. The dichotomy is therefore replaced by an interest in the *interaction* between powerful human agents and powerful structures.

The goal of this chapter is *not* to decide what is the 'correct' approach to the question of power, but simply to point out the need for us to proactively consider this basic question in the research projects. The approach taken will have profound implications for not only the project's theoretical coherence but also the possibilities of creating an object of analysis. How will the approach to human agency in the project, for example, influence the informants' motivation to participate in the interview itself, and how will it influence the ability to create trust between the researcher and the informant? Moreover, it should be considered how the approach to human agency will affect the image of the interviewees that the researcher ends up drawing in his/her disseminations. If the result is that the exclusive informants are depicted as 'puppets on a string', it might provoke many professionals' self-image and probably also that of the researcher's. If informants, by contrast, are depicted as powerful individuals, it can be seen as a glorification or an indictment.

Besides the importance of the approach to human agency in the projects, another basic challenge to media production studies is to make the exclusive informants see the immediate value of participating. The researcher's job is to (re)pose the research question in such a way that it contains a motivation to help the researcher. Welch et al. recommend that the researcher makes the project stand out as independent research (and not consultant work), with herself in the role of 'an informed outsider who is willing to listen' (2002: 624) in order to try to bridge the gap between a professional researcher and the professional informant, but without trying to deny it. How the research question is 'pitched' to the exclusive informants of various kinds is therefore crucial to think through carefully. My own experience is that it is a good idea to include appeals to the informants' creative work, professional experiences and personal impact. It is also important to include an understanding of the professions of the different kinds of exclusive informants. Furthermore, it is often relatively easy to get interviews with informants from top management of media organizations, probably because they are the most objectively powerful, and because they are often very accustomed to talking about the media organization's work and social significance with more or less informed 'outsiders'.

Getting in and the fear of 'cold calling'

The considerations described above will influence the next stage of the research process. Kvale and Brinkmann call this stage 'design' (2015: 129), and it deals with the planning of the study's specific approach. This stage is obviously not unproblematic in audience research, but in comparison with production analysis somewhat easier, as it is possible to *replace* informants in the recruitment process. In production analysis there are certain people who you need to talk to. Lack of access to these individuals can be devastating for the research project's validity, and at worst, it could mean that a research project must be shelved. Because the objective of the analysis is to gain insight into what is going on 'backstage', and to publish this insight, it can be perceived as dangerous, uncomfortable or just annoying and time-consuming for media organizations' employees. Gatekeepers often surround them (Mikecz, 2012), and in addition, they are able to prevent access to other kinds of information. At the same time, they are busy people who must have good reasons to answer the researcher's (many) requests and be able to see that helping will not be hugely time consuming or difficult. The nightmare of any media production researcher is that contact to these exclusive informants is not obtained – a phenomenon called 'cold calling' in the literature on 'elite interviewing' (Thomas, 1995: 8).

The topic 'getting in' is for these reasons of profound importance in many contributions to production analysis. As mentioned, a lot of professional media production takes place in organizations and private companies on a competitive media market. Therefore informants are not so keen and often not even allowed to tell outsiders, even with very noble intentions, anything about what is going on in the production processes, or inform about future plans and strategies, etc. Doing this could provide competitors in the media market with business insights and/or lower the informant's professional market value. The paradox is that because it is difficult to get access and thus produce knowledge about the 'backstage' of media production, the need for documentation is correspondingly large. To offer the exclusive informants anonymity is typically not an option because this will compromise the validity. To avoid potential personal and organizational consequences, it is far easier not to give the researcher access to the 'backstage'.

To sum up, to gain access is a difficult and time-consuming work. Furthermore, if it is achieved, the way it is achieved can have consequences. Frandsen distinguishes between two basic ways. Access obtained may take the form of a *trade* or a *gift* (2007: 48). If access is obtained as part of a trade-relationship, clear expectations of the services and roles of the parties are involved. In this relationship the researcher's role is close to the role of the action researcher or the consultant's. Often, trade relations mean that research results are confidential or imposed some restrictions concerning publication of the results. The trade-relationship is often of limited interest to researchers who are employed to contribute to public knowledge and gain professional merit doing so. Access can also be given as a gift, and if this is the case, the expectations placed on the researcher's services are of a more obscure nature, because the relationship involves a moral and symbolic dimension. It can give the researcher some troubles in finding a role in the relationship to the donor without offending or even harming the donor in, for example, a critical analysis of what has been given access to (Frandsen, 2007: 49). All in all, achieved access must be analysed for what motivates one's trading partner or donor, and its consequences for the analytical platform of the project. By far, the majority of production analytical research done is characterized by access given as a gift, and a gift economy will therefore typically play a role in the research interviews.

The gift-relationship also framed my project on the generic development and production cultural history of television satire (Bruun, 2011, 2012) and my project on the political television talk show (Bruun, 2014). However, the construction of *a specific object* for analysis seems to influence the relationship and the possibilities for getting access as a gift. In the project on political talk shows, getting access to conduct interviews was difficult. The exclusive informants were far more cautious, even wary, of my intentions and motives compared to the satire project. Some of the reasons for this striking difference might be that what happens to the journalistic genres in television is under much closer political scrutiny especially within a public service organization and from the outside world than entertainment. Another reason for the differences between the two projects is connected to the fact that two very different groups of media professionals were involved: satire producers, writers, actors, stand-up comedians and entertainment editors versus journalists and current affairs editors. In this way the set of values framing specific genres and media might play a role in the specific economy of the gift-relationship and thus for the researcher's opportunities to create an object for analysis and to publish findings.

Exclusive informants and the interview as an asymmetric social relation

The literature on qualitative research interviews highlights the asymmetric power relations between researcher and informant as a key challenge for the researcher. The interviewees, however, are automatically and relatively unexamined and seen as the underdog (Kvale and Brinkmann, 201: 37–38). This assumption must be questioned in interviews with exclusive informants. Welch et al. (2002) point out that in an 'elite interview' the asymmetry is basically turned upside down. Reactions to the asymmetry can be a patronizing and impatient attitude towards the researcher. Furthermore, the researcher is entering into an organizational hierarchy and must expect the informants to use the participation in the research interview in a professional context. For example, the researcher can be used as a kind of 'useful idiot' inside the organization and/or in relation to the external world (Welch et al., 2002: 621).

Evidence of this 'upside-down' asymmetry can undoubtedly also be found in interviews with exclusive informants, and it can lead to the described characteristics due to the particular types of powers held by the exclusive informants. Perhaps less paranoid, reactions to the asymmetry can also be regarded as a reflection of the interview as *a meeting between professionals from different fields*. In this meeting, status is at stake and negotiated, and therefore it is also a dynamic relationship. Negotiations on what is regarded as high status, and not least who has elite status, will influence the interview situation and the research process in its entirety. They are, among other things, interlinked with the motives to participate at all, from the exclusive informant's point of view. In understanding the kind of power relationship at work it is worth remembering that the researcher has access to the public sphere either as an expert in the media's coverage of the media or as a writer of books and articles in more or less exclusive public forums. From this point of view, the relationship can be considered a bit more symmetrical, which may play a role in both the lack of desire to participate in an interview and the willingness to participate in order to influence the researcher's accounts. A researcher's status as a professional contributor of content to the media and to the public cultural debate might entail that s/he gets media producers to participate, which otherwise would have ignored the researcher. But the same status could also cause problems if the preliminary or published results of the research are not considered to exercise an appropriate gratitude in relation to the donor of access as a gift. Because media production studies deals with more or less publicly known informants, personal market value and reputation play a central role. This should not be denigrated as untimely star whims by the researcher, but be accepted partly as a major ethical challenge in the discipline and as part of the research results. In my project about changes in the production culture of television satire, career management and legacy of course played a role in the interviews I conducted. Another common interest was naturally, and luckily, to explain to me who came from another professional context, how the conditions in the media industry were, in order to influence the results of the analysis. A common story was that the media industry, and comedy industry in particular, was influenced by random, lucky and unlucky coincidences and especially by important individuals and not by deliberate strategy, planning and systemic coercion. At the same time, the same informants complemented this with a story about the influence of media market competition, the audience ratings, and economics that often had devastating impact on the working conditions and the programmes.

Building trust

All in all, motives for participating in research interviews are not to be considered sources of error that must or can be avoided. Instead, they should be analysed in an interactional perspective, which means that status negotiations also inform about the research object, thus contributing to the research results (Ortner, 2009; Alasuutari, 1995: 85–115). For that reason, the need to build trust in the researcher's project, and not least ethos, is crucial. Trust can probably be built or undermined based on the informant's knowledge of the researcher's previous research, media performances, and personal merits and communication skills, as Frandsen highlights (2007: 47).

The literature based on management research in organizations and companies is very preoccupied by the trust-building dimensions of the way the researcher contacts potential informants, and focuses mostly on letters and emails as the tools. In my experience, oral and person-to-person-powered forms of approaches are much more fruitful in media production studies probably due to two things. First, they mirror the way these professionals work themselves. Second, the researcher makes use of the core features of the value system in the media industries, where personalized professional networks and the appreciation of individual creativity and professional skills are seen as extremely important. This means that to call people on all levels of power and scales of celebrity status seems to be a much more fruitful form of approach in the media industry. Another fruitful form of approach is going through 'spokespersons' for your project, followed up by calls and subsequent emails or social network media interaction to give more detailed descriptions and ensure appointments and agreements. 'Snowballing' strategies can also be strongly recommended. This form of approach is not only designed to gain access to more of the exclusive informants, but can also be used in relation to informants with a very high degree of celebrity status bypassing the gatekeepers.

An equally important way to build trust is that the researcher appears to have background knowledge of the subject in question and a professional understanding of the problems in the informant's world (Mikecz, 2012; Harvey, 2011; Ryan and Lewer, 2012). This should, in my experience, be supported by the researcher's particular insights into the *media products* produced. As an example, in my study on the changing production culture of political debate talk shows, I managed to get an interview with the commissioning editor of the channel *TV 2 News*. His acceptance was undoubtedly based on the fact that in my initial phone call to him I was able provide him with a short outline of the generic development of the political talk show in Danish and international television since the late 1980s.

The actual questions asked during the interview must also be able to build trust, and they must be of such a nature that they can actually obtain new knowledge. As pointed out in the literature on 'elite interviewing', *critical questions* asked on the basis of knowledge and insight into the informant's professional world and its problems builds trust and creates new knowledge (Kvale and Brinkmann, 2015: 186; Welch, 2002: 616; Thuesen, 2011: 620). According to Welch et al. (2002), the aim is therefore to strike a balance between being an insider and outsider, critical and fair at the same time. If the researcher is trained in qualitative audience studies, asking critical questions might pose a challenge. The argument is that critical questions will make the informant defend her/himself, and very easily this becomes counterproductive to the aim of building trust in an asymmetrical relationship. In media production studies, however, the interview is, as suggested in this chapter, to be regarded as a meeting between professionals. The exclusive informants are professionals and even celebrities familiar with being interviewed and/or performing in the media often as interviewers themselves. A key challenge for striking the balance between trust and obtaining new knowledge in interviews with exclusive informants is actually to avoid repetition of the already published anecdotes and the official, packaged information available in different forms of additional materials on a media product's genesis (Caldwell, 2008; Gamson, 1995). A strategy to avoid this kind of 'frontstage–backstage' information with no or very limited new information is to point out that your aim is to ask another kind of question than journalists, and very importantly, to publish in other types of genres and publications (Borer, 2012). However, the researcher might also come across informants who inform the researcher about a backstage behaviour that turns out to be unusable because it is deep backstage and/or perhaps legally problematic.

Interviews, where 'frontstage–backstage' or 'deep backstage' discourses take up large parts of the interview, are not necessarily useless but can actually inform us about the object of analysis. Caldwell (2008) regards the 'frontstage–backstage' information to reflect the many types of self-reflexivity that characterizes the production culture of television drama production in the United States. Legally problematic information may also characterize a production culture's understanding of itself even if the knowledge obtained cannot be published. In order not to risk offending or to demotivate the exclusive informant by completely rejecting these kinds of information, the literature on 'elite interviewing' recommends the researcher 'to go with the flow' and let the informant 'run with the story' (Ryan and Lewer, 2012: 82). The fact that exclusive informants have agendas for the interview must therefore be regarded as part of the research findings.

Publication, power and ethics

As indicated in the section about getting access and the gift economic ethics of the relationship between the researcher and the exclusive informants in most production analytical research, both have an impact on the reporting of research findings. Kvale and Brinkmann (2015) regard 'publication' as stage seven in the research process, and in the book, this stage is mostly treated as a matter of writing readable reports. For media production studies, on the other hand, this last stage involves risks far beyond boring or confusing one's readers.

The requirement to document what is going on 'backstage' in order to validate the conclusions means that it is necessary to quote interview statements as part of the presentation of comprehensive data material. And because we have to do it with exclusive informants, each informant's statement is of great value and is irreplaceable. Although it is tempting to offer confidentiality and anonymity in order to get access to information from these exclusive informants, it will harm the validity of the research. Furthermore, because media production studies focus on specific cases and informants in a relatively small professional media industry, the informants are easy to identify anyway (as an example of this problem see Grindstaff, 2002). As mentioned above, this means that in this kind of research a conceptualization of the relationship between human agency and structural forces must be given a proactive consideration. A way to demonstrate an ethical research process is to offer the informants the opportunity to read manuscripts before publication. This can be used to straighten out misunderstandings and small factual errors. But the researcher might run into informants that do not like the analysis. This might happen even though the researcher has briefed the informant, has built a trustful relationship with the informant, and does not her/himself regard the analysis as controversial. Although a researcher might choose to publish anyway, unless you are contractually prevented from doing so, the decision might have consequences for your future research opportunities, depending on informants' mixture of objective power and interpersonal power. Whether it is a risk that a researcher should run can only be determined concretely. There is little doubt that the research questions in media production studies as a research tradition are characterized by what *can* be investigated without running into problems with the publication of the research results.

Two conditions must be noted, however, that can help to allay the fear of not being able to publish your research and the risk of being unable to do media production research in the future. First, a very high heart rate, new products, and changes mark the media industry where competition, strategically sensitive issues, or actions have a relatively short lifespan. Often, what is perceived as sensitive while the researcher is doing the interviews, therefore, might well be much less sensitive, or passed, when research results are published. The much slower heart rate, workflow, and publication rates of academic research are in this sense a big advantage. Second, the media and academic research are two relatively independent fields, each with its target audience. Academic research publishing increasingly takes place in quite closed, professional forums, as neither the general public nor the media industries frequent.

Despite this somewhat dismal reassurance, there is a point where the exclusive informants' power and not least the research's ethical considerations continue to be important. When it comes to sensitive personal issues or matters that may be relevant to the professional market value or legacy of the informant, the distance between the world of the media industries and of academic research vanishes. Despite high job mobility and change in the production cultures of the media industries, such an obsolescence of sensitive personal issues and matters cannot be assumed. First, their celebrity status as well as their creative and professional skills are to be regarded as a commodity – and its market value and reputation must be protected. Second, if the researcher wants to continue to do media production research, s/he will need the cooperation of a relatively limited number of established media organizations of various kinds, where the informants circulate at a high frequency. Rumours about the researcher's ethos in terms of treatment of informants in previous research and/or contributions to the public debate can therefore easily be known beforehand, for better or worse.

Concluding remarks

The aim of this chapter has not been to provide a complete analysis of what can be said to characterize the research interview genre used in media production studies, nor to deliver a kind of recipe for how to then actually interview exclusive informants and process the data collected. The aim has been to focus on key points, which separate this research interview genre from the kind used in audience studies. Against this background, the aim has been to help strengthen the ability among media researchers to switch between and reflect on the use of different qualitative research interview genres in media studies in general. This could be said to be a core methodological competence for researchers and students working on research questions that switch between or increasingly cut across the traditional divisions between audience/user and production studies approaches in media studies in general. Furthermore, I have argued that the research interview genre in media production studies deals with a specific kind of elite: 'exclusive informants'. This makes it a special genre of the qualitative research interview. Discussing its consequences and even ramifications for the questions we ask would contribute to strengthen basic qualities like theoretical coherence and methodological transparency, and to secure the validity of the research contributions.

References

Aguira, L. L. M. and Schneider, C. J. (eds) (2012) *Researching amongst Elites* (Farnham: Ashgate).
Alasuutari, P. (1995) *Researching Culture: Qualitative Method and Cultural Studies* (London: Sage).
Borer, M. I. (2012) 'Interviewing celebrities: Strategies for getting beyond the sound bite' in L. L. M. Aguira and C. J. Schneider (eds), *Researching amongst Elites* (pp. 89–102) (Farnham: Ashgate).
Bruun, H. (2011) *Dansk tv-satire. Underholdning med kant* (København: Books on Demand).
Bruun, H. (2012) 'Changing production cultures in television satire.' *Northern Lights* 10(1), 41–57.
Bruun, H. (2014) 'Conceptualizing the audience in political talk show production.' *European Journal of Communication* 29(1), 3–16.
Caldwell, J. T. (2008) *Production Culture* (Durham: Duke University Press).
Frandsen, K. (2007) 'Produktionsanalyse: Teoretiske og metodiske problemstillinger' in H. Bruun and K. Frandsen (eds), *TV-produktion – nye vilkår* (pp. 23–54) (Frederiksberg: Forlaget Samfundslitteratur).
Gamson, J. (1995) 'Stopping the spin and becoming a prop: Fieldwork on Hollywood elites' in R. Hertz and J. Imber (eds), *Studying Elites Using Qualitative Methods* (pp. 83–93) (London: Sage).
Grindstaff, L. (2002) *The Money Shot: Trash, Class, and the Making of TV Talk Shows* (Chicago: University of Chicago Press).
Harvey, W. S. (2011) 'Strategies for conducting elite interviews.' *Qualitative Research* 11(4), 431–441.
Ho, K. (2012) '"Studying up" Wall Street: Reflections on theory and methodology' in L. L. M. Aguira, and C. J. Schneider (eds), *Researching Amongst Elites* (pp. 29–48) (Farnham: Ashgate).
Kvale, S. and Brinkmann, S. (2015) *InterView: Learning the Craft of Qualitative Research Interviewing*, 3rd edn (London: Sage).
Littig, B. (2009) 'Interviewing the elite – Interviewing experts: Is there a difference?' in A. Borger, B. Littig, and W. Menz (eds), *Interviewing Experts* (pp. 98–116) (Chippenham: Palgrave Macmillan).
Mikecz, R. (2012) 'Interviewing elites: Addressing methodological issues.' *Qualitative Inquiry* 18(6), 482–493.
Moore, N. and Stokes, P. (2012) 'Elite interviewing and the role of sector context: An organisational case from the football industry.' *Qualitative Market Research: An International Journal* 15(4), 438–464.
Moyser, G. and Wagstaffe, M. (eds) (1987) *Research Methods for Elite Studies* (London: Allen & Unwin).
Ortner, S. B. (2009) 'Studying sideways: Ethnographic access in Hollywood' in J. T. Caldwell, M. Banks, and V. Mayer (eds), *Production Studies: Cultural Studies of Media Industries* (pp. 175–189) (New York: Routledge).
Richards, D. (1996) 'Doing politics. Elite interviewing: Approaches and pitfalls.' *Politics* 16(3), 199–204.
Ryan, S. and Lewer, J. (2012) 'Getting in and finding out: Accessing and interviewing elites in business and work contexts' in L. L. M. Aguira and C. J. Schneider (eds), *Researching amongst Elites* (pp. 71–88) (Farnham: Ashgate).

Thomas, R. J. (1995) 'Interviewing important people in big companies' in R. Hertz and J. Imber (eds), *Studying Elites Using Qualitative Methods* (pp. 3–17) (London: Sage).

Thuesen, F. (2011) 'Navigating between dialogue and confrontation: Phronesis and emotions in interviewing elites on ethnic discrimination.' *Qualitative Inquiry 17*(7), 613–622.

Welch, C., Marschan-Piekkari, R., Penttinen, H., and Tahvanainen, M. (2002) 'Corporate elites as informants in qualitative international business research.' *International Business Review 11*(1), 611–628.

10
When You Can't Rely on Public or Private: Using the Ethnographic Self as Resource
Michael B. Munnik

The problem of access is enduring and significant for fieldwork-based research on media production, but some periods are more challenging than others. When scholars gathered in Leeds in 2013 to discuss advancing the field, the United Kingdom news media were in a turbulent time. The phone-hacking practices of certain newspapers and the subsequent scrutiny of the Leveson Inquiry had scholars wondering whether the notoriously uncooperative private press, attempting to show goodwill and best behaviour, might open its doors to independent research in the context of an imminent change in the regulatory regime (Brock, 2012; Grayson and Freedman, 2013). Meanwhile, the public broadcaster, the British Broadcasting Corporation (BBC), was under intense scrutiny for its failure to broadcast an investigation into the criminal behaviour of one of its star presenters, Jimmy Savile. What had been a *slightly more open* door for production research was closing, and my own research on relations between journalists and Muslim sources in Glasgow, Scotland, suffered because of this process. Whatever goodwill gestures may or may not have occurred among private broadcasters and the press, they did not manifest in an invitation to pick up the BBC's slack.

Fortunately, I had strategies in place that allowed me to complete the project and my doctoral thesis, including a field-based approach, a source-journalist approach, and an approach cumbersomely called 'the ethnographic self as resource'. In this chapter, I emphasize the latter in detail as a tool for advancing media production analysis. In this case, my prior professional experience as a broadcast journalist in Canada enriched my Scottish study. It is wise for scholars to develop alternative, defensive strategies, for as Chris Paterson and Anna Zoellner note, no media organization supports 'accountability and transparency' to the extent that participation in academic research is 'automatic' (2010: 106).

Acute problems of access

My doctoral research investigated the relationship journalists from mainstream news organizations in Glasgow build with source contacts from Muslim communities and groups in the city (Munnik, 2015). Overtures to several private news organizations were simply ignored, though I had been prepared for this (Schlesinger, 1980: 341). Due to a prior professional acquaintance, I gained access to the Herald & Times Group, which produces the *Herald* and *Sunday Herald*, both Scottish national newspapers, and the *Evening Times*, a Glasgow daily; even so, my request for one week was answered with an offer of two days, which was whittled down to one before I arrived – clearly insufficient for any kind of scholarly inquiry. The site, therefore, which I imagined would host the bulk of the fieldwork was BBC Scotland. I had previously worked for the Canadian Broadcasting Corporation (CBC), so I was already familiar with the environment and the language of a public broadcaster, and I felt I could hit the ground running and convince the corporation's gatekeepers that my presence would not be burdensome (cf. Paterson and Zoellner, 2010). As well, I had the public testimony of Georgina Born's ethnography: she notes a 'closure' that belied the BBC's 'rhetoric of accountability' during John Birt's tenure has director-general in the mid-1990s; but she adds the caveat that BBC Scotland offered 'an extraordinary amount of cooperation from people at all levels', making her feel 'completely welcome' and offering 'astonishingly open access' (2004: 17). I had an encouraging conversation with a manager at the headquarters on Glasgow's Pacific Quay in June 2012, and at the end of August, I spent three days there on a pilot study.

This went as well as can be expected, given the circumstances. The day before I arrived, staff had been informed of job cuts: 35 positions gone, across the service. One cannot help putting the wrong foot forward when entering such an environment (in a necktie, no less) and asking questions about how people do their job. But I endeared myself and got through my visit with copious notes and the promise of more to come. As my chief interlocutor said on my last day, when I told her there were people I had yet to talk with and encounters I wanted to see, 'There's lots of time. We'll see you back.' I returned to Edinburgh to write up the pilot.

As my writing progressed, I sent her an email asking to build a schedule for the autumn. I suggested three days a week from October to Christmas – not as much as makes a proper anthropological ethnography, but more than BBC Scotland would probably want to give me. When I heard nothing back, I sent another email, then called, worried that I had asked too much in my opening gambit. Finally, I received a reply on 24 October, which included the line, 'At the moment there is a lot going on in the newsroom and it may not be the best time for an observer to be around' (personal correspondence, 2012). I pulled my head out of the sand of my doctorate and looked about.

I had dismissed the coverage of Jimmy Savile as so much prurient British journalism – posthumous revelations that the popular television presenter had used his influence to engineer sexual encounters with underage girls. I caught the headlines at the corner shop when I bought my milk, but I did not look any further than that. After receiving the email from my interlocutor, I watched the *Panorama* documentary (BBC, 2012b) on BBC's iPlayer and fathomed just how bad it was. And how widespread. And how managers were implicated in attempts to hide the news at an embarrassing moment for the broadcaster. And how, in an effort to show its journalistic strength or in an error facilitated by uncertainty about oversight, the BBC fell deeper into the muck by wrongfully identifying Lord McAlpine as a paedophile (BBC, 2012a). Although BBC Scotland was not directly implicated, its director, Ken MacQuarrie, led one of the internal inquiries into this series of unfortunate events (2012). In addition, the corporation is linked through its web network, so even in Scotland it would wish to keep unknown eyes away from sensitive documents.

Internal events specific to BBC Scotland were at the same time adding pressure to my intended field site. In response to the job cuts that had been announced as I began my pilot study, a Scottish parliamentary committee requested a meeting with union leadership and with local management. They wanted to understand how these cuts would be carried out and what impact they might have on Scotland, not least with a national referendum on independence due in two years' time. The committee's minutes show a souring of management's relationships with employees and with politicians (Scottish Parliament, 2012, 2013). The union voted in favour of a strike in the spring of 2013, and though it was ultimately averted, the acrimony endured. My periodic entreaties to my chief interlocutor were rebuffed, as I was continually encouraged to try again later, when things had settled down. I managed to interview some of the journalists at greater length, but my observation and widespread access to employees and management began and ended with my pilot study.

External scandals and internal conflict conspired to make the likeliest candidate for production research an inhospitable place right at the moment I needed access. I do not wish to single out BBC Scotland – the private sphere were no more welcoming and often far less. I was unable to rely on the private or the public news sector for much help with my research.

The strategy

This deficit in data from one field site did not spell disaster for the project because of the research strategy I mentioned in my introduction: conducting fieldwork in multiple news sites, engaging with sources as well as journalists, and making rigorous use of my prior professional experience in journalism. Taking a multi-site approach mitigates the cost when access to a specific site is reduced or denied. This is not always appropriate for production research – there are particularities to certain media outputs, ownership structures, and ideological frames which might compel a researcher to restrict the sites included in the study. My research question concerned the relation of journalists to sources, however, which is a basic and widespread practice. Moreover, to engage with multiple sites gives a more accurate account of the environment in which journalists and sources work. Whether we view it as a field (Bourdieu, 2005; Benson and Neveu, 2005; Willig, 2013), a social world (Becker, 1982; Dickinson, 2008), or an ecosystem (Anderson, 2013), we have sociological models that relate newsworkers to activity beyond the bounds of their newsrooms. Jeremy Tunstall pioneered this approach with his sophisticated concept of the 'competitor-colleague' (1971). In my case, I secured twelve interviews with journalists working for three different news organizations, and I mustered a small amount of observation with the Herald & Times Group to supplement my BBC pilot.

Tunstall also notes that journalists are oriented to their sources, which brings me to the second strategy: considering sources as well as journalists. This views newswork from a different angle, including the voices of those who contribute to the news by offering comment, helping clarify details, or acting as a conduit to other informed sources. Such work illuminates the strategies of sources (cf. Ericson et al., 1989), but it also gives us indirect access at the actions and justifications of journalists. This strategy enriches the content of the study and counters what Philip Schlesinger calls 'media-centrism' (1990). My study included interviews with eighteen sources as well as observation of a community group actively working on its media strategy and trying to present itself as a helpful, knowledgeable, and reliable source for journalists.

What I wish to discuss in more detail here, however, is the third strategy I employed: the ethnographic self as resource. Anthropologists Peter Collins and Anselma Gallinat (2010) argue that researchers should include their own experiences as data in their project. Indeed, they suggest that researchers do this already but invisibly: 'the anthropologist as a competent member of society will always and already draw on their stock of experiences in making sense of the world' (p. 12). Collins and Gallinat are not recommending autobiography, whereby the researcher's story becomes the dominant or even the only narrative of the project; rather, experiences of the researcher join those of participants in constituting the research data, and the researcher is 'aware of the responsibility she has...to hold up her own as well as others' accounts for critical inspection' (p. 10). The authors outline some of the hazards, including using the self as 'a ploy,' incautious implication of family and friends, and a retreat into narcissism (pp. 15–16). But, these dangers aside, Collins and Gallinat make this approach imperative: 'anthropologists *should* include personal experiences as data in their analysis. Not to do so seems to us at best an opportunity lost and at worst a moral transgression' (p. 17, emphasis mine).

In the volume they edited, both authors contribute chapters which illustrate how their ethnographic selves became resources for their research. Collins' contribution (2010) speaks primarily of signalling empathy: he notes that employing memory and experience during the field encounter help to draw out data from participants. However, the visible inclusion of his own stories also *introduces* data, and in this regard, Gallinat (2010) reveals more fully the potential of their approach. Gallinat researches a phenomenon called *Ostalgie*, or a nostalgia among former East Germans for their socialist past. Gallinat grew up in the German Democratic Republic (GDR), and as she was conducting fieldwork in 2001, she inquired after a trend she had read of called *Ostalgie* parties, in which people would dress in and celebrate the retro kitsch of socialism. Although her 2001 informants did not describe such events, she recalled encounters from her own youth with *Ostalgie* parties. She then wrote a narrative of those encounters, including details of her ambivalence, her relationship with her peers, and her family's critical relation to the GDR state.

In analysing this material, Gallinat forestalls criticisms of selective memory, arguing that, '[j]ust as for me, it can be argued for each one of them [my participants] that they presented their memories in a way that suited their personal agenda in relation to this interview with me'; further, '[m]y own power of recollection seems no more fraught here than that of my informants' (2010: 39–40). Gallinat gives her method an ethical edge that recalls the conviction of authors who contributed to *Writing Culture* (Clifford and Marcus, 1986) – an important text in what is sometimes called the reflexive turn in anthropology. Although Gallinat as researcher has 'the final say' on the inclusion and interpretation of stories, '[t]he detailed representation of my own experiences...renders these subjective aspects more explicit and allows the reader to critically engage with them' (2010: 40). This task is essential: knowing about her family's stance against the socialist state gives me tools to interrogate her interpretations. Collins reminds us that we implicate our memories and experiences throughout the fieldwork encounter; Gallinat exposes those memories and experiences by including them as data to be analysed.

Models in media research

Responsibility, as Gallinat's example suggests, is key to making this approach work. Lying is a risk, and it is easy to be insufficiently critical of one's own stories. Moreover, if I contradict or diminish insights from my participants by saying, 'Well, that's not how we did it when *I* was back at the CBC...', I am not engaging openly with the stories of others. But sometimes, the 'that's how I did it' motif is precisely in order. Allan Bell is a journalist and a linguist, practising both disciplines at the same time; and though he does not identify as an anthropologist, he implicated his journalistic self as a resource twenty years before Collins and Gallinat's volume. In *The Language of News Media* (1991), Bell includes as data his experiences as an editor and the texts he and his colleagues had written. He is careful to note the uneven application of this approach: 'the constant demands of working in a daily news service left me so far removed from my research interests that I did not even retain examples of news copy which I recognized at the time as having research importance' (p. 31). What he did retain, though, he uses to powerful effect, notably in his empirical analysis of the editing process. His insights gain force because of his dual role as an analyst of language and the one doing the copy editing, and he includes in his monograph copies of news texts with his editing marks on them to compare with the published version. He is, in effect, saying, 'Here is the material the journalist gave me; here are the changes I made; here, to the best of my recollection, are the reasons why I made these changes; and here is the effect I believe these changes have.'

Bell can be reflexive about this process, as with a story he edited on wool markets. The lead he shaped 'is five words shorter [than in the original copy]. It also carries more punch because most of the words are contentful adjectives and nouns, including the strong *demand*' (p. 81). However, Bell notes 'a semantic price for these syntactic and discourse changes': he has widened the attribution from one individual to an entire delegation, not all of whom may agree with the substance of the lead statement (p. 82). Though he was comfortable with this change as a journalist, as an analyst he is right to note the potential for the edit to cause a drift in accuracy. Bell's reflections on this process and his role within it are as ethnographically valuable as the edited news texts he produces. Such concrete evidence of the editing process is hard to access, and Bell observed back in 1991 that the increase of editing by computer would make this evidence scarce to verging on invisible (p. 81).[1]

Colleen Cotter's more recent contribution, *News Talk* (2010), covers similar terrain but from a more austere analytical position. Cotter inhabited the same roles as Bell but sequentially, moving *from* practical journalism *to* scholarly analysis of journalistic language. Cotter, too, draws on her own experiences, though only '[t]o a limited extent' (p. 5), briefly summarizing her background and sprinkling references throughout the text to what she did or observed during her journalistic career. She declares that her objective is to study news talk 'from the vantage point of the practitioner' (p. 1), in which she can easily include herself, especially as her fieldwork took place in newsrooms of American daily newspapers – the very profile of her previous employers. Yet Cotter's experience is present only by suggestion. She frames herself as a practitioner in order to authorize her analysis of the practices she witnesses and the accounts of other journalists. Her ethnographic insights are sound and credible, but I would categorize Cotter's book as one of Collins and Gallinat's lost opportunities.

Making it personal

My experience with CBC Radio in the first decade of the 21st century has had a significant influence on the scholarly work I have subsequently undertaken. It is understandable for a scholar to study a subject he or she knows well: Charlotte Aull Davies notes that 'we cannot research something with which we have no contact, from which we are completely isolated' (1999: 3). Scholars have produced thorough research that is sited in their self, acknowledging and incorporating their vocation, as with the media examples above, their interests (e.g. Faulkner and Becker, 2009), or their biological identification (e.g. Davis, 2015). My years of employment in news production gave me a lexicon that I could transfer to qualitative fieldwork and a set of analogous experiences that informed questions to participants. The basic one-of-usness with which I presented myself when negotiating access may have reassured the gatekeepers that I would be at least unobtrusive and at best sympathetic.

Paterson and Zoellner identify these as some of the advantages for scholars of media production, but they also raise concerns about keeping scholarly distance (2010: 103). In preparing for fieldwork, I had to consider whether my identification as a former journalist would encourage me to take too light a touch in the critical scrutiny of journalistic practices – *tout comprendre c'est tout pardonner* and all that? And would my familiarity make me blind to practices and assumptions which I should interrogate? Asking naive questions requires participants to form answers for them, and these may generate valuable data for the ensuing analysis; glossing over them because both the researcher and the participant already know what these terms mean or how these processes work results in a deficit of foundational data. This is not a new concern for ethnographic research[2]: as much as Davies valorizes the scholar's connection to the topic of research, 'depending on the extent and nature of these connections, questions arise as to whether the results of research are artefacts of the researcher's presence and inevitable influence on the research process' (1999: 3).

Collins and Gallinat address these concerns, noting that Marilyn Strathern (1987) and Kirin Narayan (1993) have troubled easy assumptions about 'native anthropology' both, as it were, 'at home' and 'over there'. Their approach is not mere reflexivity, though Collins calls reflexivity 'the first precondition' to adopting this approach (2010: 234). Rather, they defend the inclusion of the self through rigorous visibility. As a researcher, how I introduce my memory and experience matters in terms of the conversational quality of the semi-structured interview. The stories I choose to share inspire participants to share certain responses, just as Collins shared about gardening, sports, and moving home to build rapport and elicit responses during his fieldwork among Quakers in Britain (2010: 230–234). These stories should not escape later analysis. I must pay attention to my questions as well as their answers when reviewing transcripts.

Therefore, in speaking with a BBC Scotland editor about what I mean by 'relations with Muslim communities in the city', I described work I had been assigned by CBC editors in Ottawa: they had commissioned demographic research to identify prevalent minority populations, comparing results with programme logs to get a sense of which communities they were 'missing' in local coverage. High on the list were

Lebanese and Somali populations, which they bundled as 'Muslims'; this was, perhaps, unfortunate, as many Lebanese people in the city identified as Christians. Nevertheless, I felt there were sound journalistic reasons in a post-9/11 context to forge deeper connections with Muslims in Ottawa, and some of my work for this project brought me in contact with Indian community groups, even though this ethnic category did not feature as prominently in the demographic research. My editors defined the target communities religiously, and they knew of my own religious interests. As a casual and freelance journalist, I had cultivated a niche in the newsroom by pitching stories concerning religion. By doing so, I became recognized by colleagues and editors as 'the one who knows about religion', though I did not have a formalized beat in the subject. Since they had labelled this group by religion, they assigned the task of building relationships to me.

I describe more of this work below, but my purpose here is to show that, in narrating this work to my participant in Glasgow, I was entering into dialogue – not merely asking questions but sharing stories. He asked me a few questions about the project and then declared that BBC Scotland had begun some work like this several years ago but that it was not completed: management priorities from London shifted to a focus on 'bi-medial' reporting, and journalists could no longer commit the time to relationship-building exercises that did not produce the immediate goods of story ideas for broadcast. The project I had done must have stayed with him, because later in our conversation, he returned to it, wondering if it might be possible to initiate such a scheme now. Privately, I wondered how this would work at a time when his station was cutting jobs, and I intended to follow this question up with him on a subsequent visit but never got the chance.

The story that I shared, which was more detailed than a typical anecdote for prompting information during an interview, elicited several responses: curiosity, a description of a former practice and how it was abandoned, and a proposal that such a practice might have merit for the current newsroom context. It also gave me insight into the Scottish and particularly Glaswegian setting for my research. Whereas I mentioned reaching out to Lebanese and Somali populations, the target demographic he considered was South Asian. This advanced my study and suggested more questions to ask him and the journalists who report to him.

As with Collins, my conversational exchange contributed to the research. I narrated the targeted outreach to which I was assigned at the CBC many times during my fieldwork, both to explain the purpose of my research and to clarify what I meant with certain questions. As with Gallinat, the information I contributed in those conversations is relevant to my research questions. I introduced the story in the field, and now I need to make it transparent. I do not have the space here for more than a brief sketch of what I did; a fuller account and analysis is available elsewhere (Munnik, 2015: 188–196).

To expand CBC Ottawa's breadth of Muslim sources, I began by searching through programme logs for names and contact details of Muslims we had already spoken with, and I consulted colleagues for 'good' sources in their contact files. I also searched through databases such as Google for community groups that defined themselves religiously or, where relevant, ethnically. I contacted these people and organizations, explained who I was and what my project was, and asked two things of them. I asked them to provide suggestions of other Muslims in their networks who might be useful for me to get to know and to keep my contact details on file, so that if they had a story idea which they thought might interest the CBC, they could contact me in the first instance. These requests required me to spend time with these sources, explaining what a 'story' was and what elements were desirable in a well-crafted pitch.

Further, I was encouraged by editors to attend meetings and events within these communities – not necessarily to bring back a story for immediate broadcast, though that is always helpful, but to be a visible presence for the broadcaster. I was to talk with people, hand out business cards, and build relationships. In practice, I was released from my typical duties to do this work less often than would be necessary to develop a strong, effective network. The demands of daily radio programming and a diminishing workforce were high. However, it did happen from time to time, and these moments were initiated both by me and by my editors, suggesting some degree of commitment to the idea from higher up the hierarchy.

The results of this initiative were uneven. I was received warmly by the people I contacted, and I was directed to sources we had not hitherto engaged with. If I turned up at an event and met a source I had previously met or spoken with, he or she remembered me and made some reference to my project. The public broadcaster already had the reputation of being favourably disposed to stories from minority communities, and so my task was enabled by a sense of goodwill and cooperation. However, I do not recall a single instance of one of these sources contacting me unsolicited with a story idea. I continued with the work for over a year, but in the spring of 2009, the CBC announced hundreds of job cuts across the service as a response to financial pressures. One of those jobs was mine, and by the summer's end, I no longer worked for the organization. I do not know if other journalists in the Ottawa station were able to maintain the network I had developed, but with such a reduced workforce, I doubt they were able to make it even as much of a priority as it was when I worked there.

The objectives of the project, as explained to me, were threefold: to improve the diversity of sources represented in our coverage; to increase our audience within these targeted demographics; and to bring fresh, original stories into our coverage. Insofar as a network of Muslim sources was aggregated and expanded, the first objective was successful. I cannot venture a guess concerning the second – it would take time for market research to establish the motivations for such an increase, and there is no guarantee of respondents in such research drawing a straight line between being contacted by a CBC reporter or having one cover a community event and choosing therefore to listen to CBC Radio or watch CBC Television over alternative news outlets. I consider the third objective a failure, in that there was no reciprocal relationship with these sources. They were happy to speak with me when I contacted them, but they did not contact me themselves. The CBC did not benefit by getting an edge over competing news media for stories from Muslim communities, and with our reputation, we would have been a likely port of call for story ideas anyway, whether we reached out deliberately or not.

In recounting this narrative, I must be cautious. More so than Bell, I did not save materials from this work while I was doing it, such as contacts files, notes from conversations, or programme logs. I also did not have the bifurcated role Bell inhabited: when I conducted this work, I was thinking exclusively of my role as a journalist; I was not considering whether this might be useful information for an academic study in the future. Conjuring it after the fact, for research purposes, I am relying on memory and experience, just as my participants relied on these when answering my questions.

Finally, this experience helped my analysis of the data my fieldwork generated. I could relate general descriptions of journalistic practice to my training and work, and I had a specific frame through which to interpret statements from non-Muslim journalists about Islam in its global and local expressions and sources and subjects that were identified as Muslim. My creation of categories for coding and understanding was informed by my past.

From design to fieldwork, to the inclusion of data and the analysis thereof, my journalistic self was implicated in my research. Writing it into the study has helped me and my readers. It allows me to put analogous descriptions from my data in a wider context – for example, the 'community patch' system adopted by Glasgow daily the *Evening Times*, in which reporters are assigned geographic districts and expected to build a network of sources and community leaders, providing new stories for the newspaper. When I scrutinize relationships between journalists and Muslim sources in Glasgow, I do not merely allude to my prior professional experience as a device to authorize my interpretations: I have recounted some of that experience, and the reader can assess these interpretations with more information at hand. Writing my memory and experience into the study thus makes visible that which would otherwise be hidden.

Conclusion

Media production analysis is resource intensive. In times of austerity, it is easier to pore over news content and make judgements from it. Indeed, electronic media and a widening of what counts as journalism have contributed to an abundance of material. Scholars of media production believe, however, that there is value in assessing the processes, not merely the product. As hard as it is to make the case for a budget for such research, it is harder still when the researcher has little confidence that requests for access will be granted. As my experience shows, even when the scholar presents a research question in which the organization is curious, other factors can trump it. Even when the scholar speaks the specialized language and knows the practices, his presence can still be burdensome.

But that language and experience – that inside scoop – can still be put to use in producing meaningful research. My training in journalism and my years of work with a public broadcaster became tools in my analysis, and my specific work building relationships with Muslims in Ottawa became an asset in assessing how those relationships work in Glasgow. When doors were closed to both private and public media institutions, I had another door to open: the door of my memory, which led to another newsroom thousands of miles away and several years ago. With the visible inclusion and cautious application of my experience, I used my journalistic self as a resource for my research, examining the question without derailing the study into an autobiography. In this way, I can enrich and even advance my examination of journalistic practice. This is not the solution for every scholar nor is it applicable for every research question. But when the self is so integrated with the scholarship, it is not only an advantage – it is an imperative.

Notes

1. Though see Daniel Perrin, Chapter 11 of this volume, for a description of 'progression analysis', which employs an exhaustive, intensive technological method that allows researchers to catch up with the minute edits that take place on newsroom computers.
2. Neither are researchers who do not share common experiences with their participants immune from this risk. Philip Schlesinger, who had not worked as a journalist when he embarked on his ethnography of the BBC in the 1970s, describes a process of 'captivation' (1980: 353–355), in which he began to adopt the logic of the journalists he studied during his long engagement.

References

Anderson, C. W. (2013) *Rebuilding the News: Metropolitan Journalism in the Digital Age* (Philadelphia: Temple University Press).

BBC. (2012a) 'BBC settles with Lord McAlpine', http://www.bbc.co.uk/news/uk-20348978 (webpage), date accessed 31 May 2013.

BBC. (2012b) 'Jimmy Savile – What the BBC Knew', *Panorama*, http://www.bbc.co.uk/iplayer/episode/b01nspvr/sign/Panorama_Jimmy_Savile_What_the_BBC_Knew/ (online video player), date accessed 24 October 2012.

Becker, H. S. (1982) *Art Worlds* (Berkeley: University of California Press).

Bell, A. (1991) *The Language of News Media* (Oxford: Blackwell).

Benson, R. and Neveu, E. (2005) 'Introduction: Field theory as a work in progress' in R. Benson and E. Neveu (eds), *Bourdieu and the Journalistic Field* (pp. 1–25) (Cambridge: Polity).

Born, G. (2004) *Uncertain Vision: Birt, Dyke and the Reinvention of the BBC* (London: Secker & Warburg).

Bourdieu, P. (2005) 'The political field, the social science field, and the journalistic field' in R. Benson and E. Neveu (eds), *Bourdieu and the Journalistic Field* (pp. 29–47) (Cambridge: Polity).

Brock, G. (2012) 'The Leveson inquiry: There's a bargain to be struck over media freedom and regulation.' *Journalism* 13(4), 519–528.

Clifford, J. and Marcus, G. E. (eds) (1986) *Writing Culture: The Poetics and Politics of Ethnography* (Berkeley: University of California Press).

Collins, P. (2010) 'The ethnographic self as resource?' in P. Collins and A. Gallinat (eds), *The Ethnographic Self as Resource: Writing Memory and Experience into Ethnography* (pp. 228–245) (New York: Berghahn Books).

Collins, P. and Gallinat, A. (2010) 'The Ethnographic Self as Resource: An Introduction' in P. Collins and A. Gallinat (eds), *The Ethnographic Self as Resource: Writing Memory and Experience into Ethnography* (pp. 1–22) (New York: Berghahn Books).

Cotter, C. (2010) *News Talk: Investigating the Language of Journalism* (Cambridge: Cambridge University Press).

Davies, C. A. (1999) *Reflexive Ethnography: A Guide to Researching Selves and Others* (London: Routledge).

Davis, D. L. (2015) *Twins Talk: What Twins Tell Us about Person, Self, and Society* (Athens, OH: Ohio University Press).

Dickinson, R. (2008) 'Studying the sociology of journalists: The journalistic field and the news world.' *Sociology Compass* 2(5), 1383–1399.

Ericson, R. V., P. M. Baranek and Chan, J. B. L. (1989) *Negotiating Control: A Study of News Sources* (Milton Keynes, UK: Open University Press).

Faulkner, R. R. and Becker, H. S. (2009) *'Do You Know...?' The Jazz Repertoire in Action* (Chicago: University of Chicago Press).

Gallinat, A. (2010) 'Playing the native card: The anthropologist as informant in Eastern Germany' in P. Collins and A. Gallinat (eds), *The Ethnographic Self as Resource: Writing Memory and Experience into Ethnography* (pp. 25–44) (New York: Berghahn Books).

Grayson, D. and Freedman, D. (2013) 'Leveson and the prospects for media reform.' *Soundings: A Journal of Politics and Culture* 53(1), 69–81.

MacQuarrie, K. (2012) 'Findings of the Editorial Standards Committee of the BBC Trust: Newsnight, BBC Two', BBC Trust http://downloads.bbc.co.uk/bbctrust/assets/files/pdf/appeals/esc_bulletins/2012/newsnight_2nov.pdf, 2 November 2012.

Munnik, M. (2015) *Points of Contact: A Qualitative Fieldwork Analysis of Relationships between Journalists and Muslim Sources in Glasgow*. PhD, University of Edinburgh.

Narayan, K. (1993) 'How native is a "native" anthropologist?' *American Anthropologist* 95(3), 671–686.

Paterson, C. and Zoellner, A. (2010) 'The Efficacy of Professional Experience in the Ethnographic Investigation of Production.' *Journal of Media Practice* 11(2), 97–109.

Schlesinger, P. (1980) 'Between Sociology and Journalism' in H. Christian (ed.), *The Sociology of Journalism and the Press* (pp. 341–369) (Keele, UK: University of Keele).

Schlesinger, P. (1990) 'Rethinking the sociology of journalism: Source strategies and the limits of media-centrism' in M. Ferguson (ed.), *Public Communication: The New Imperatives: Future Directions for Media Research* (pp. 61–83) (London: Sage).

Scottish Parliament (2012) 'Education and Culture Committee – Official Report 30 October 2012', http://www.scottish.parliament.uk/parliamentarybusiness/28862.aspx?r=7922&mode=pdf.

Scottish Parliament (2013) 'Education and Culture Committee – Official Report 22 January 2013', http://www.scottish.parliament.uk/parliamentarybusiness/28862.aspx?r=7991&mode=pdf.

Strathern, M. (1987) 'The limits of auto-anthropology' in A. Jackson (ed.), *Anthropology at Home* (pp. 16–38) (London: Tavistock).

Tunstall, J. (1971) *Journalists at Work: Specialist Correspondents: Their News Organizations, News Sources, and Competitor-Colleagues* (London: Constable).

Willig, I. (2013) 'Newsroom ethnography in a field perspective.' *Journalism* 14(3), 372–387.

11
Investigating the Backstage of Newswriting with Process Analysis
Daniel Perrin

Stance and the practice of stancing

What product-oriented approaches conceptualize as journalistic *stance* in news items is, from a process perspective, the result of newswriting: a complex and emergent interplay of situated production, reproduction and recontextualization activities (Catenaccio et al., 2011; Van Hout, Pander Maat and De Preter, 2011; Perrin, 2013) with individuals' psychobiographies, social settings such as newsrooms, and contextual resources such as 'glocalization' (Khondker, 2004). In this first section of the chapter, I address stance from such a process perspective, as *stanc-ing*. The rest of the chapter then draws on the case of stance vs. stancing to explain and contextualize Progression Analysis, a multi-method approach to newswriting that is informed by Applied Linguistics (AL).

By *stancing*, I understand the practice of taking and encoding a particular position. *Position* refers to implicit or explicit commitments that are based on judgements and assessments, and thus are related to subjective properties such as opinions, attitudes and emotions. In journalism, positions are encoded through collaborative practices of text production (Perrin, 2011b) within individual, organizational, institutional and societal frames of reference. The process of encoding stance is guided by professional values and principles such as 'newsworthiness' (e.g. Schultz, 2007) or 'news values' (e.g. Schultz, 2007; Bednarek and Caple, 2014; Huan, 2015) and audience design (e.g. Bell, 2001). On an operative level, stancing results in using or omitting specific semiotic and, in particular, linguistic means, such as camera angles, evaluation markers and reported speech.

These semiotic and linguistic means in the final products have been analysed in detail for various domains, even diachronically and using large corpora (Biber, 2004). Various media genres have attracted researchers' interest, in particular the apparently impartial genre of hard news reports (e.g. White, 2012). In media products, stance has been identified on two levels. First, stance appears in journalists' own voices, as authorial stance or 'speaker subjectivity'. Second, stance is the consequence of 'reporting reporting' (Caldas-Coulthard, 1994); it is attributed to and encoded in the reported speech of quoted sources, such as experts, eye-witnesses, spokespersons from interested parties, decision-makers and people concerned by their decisions.

Investigating the omitted

Stance, however, extends beyond manifest semiotic and, in particular, linguistic means. On the one hand, it is also expressed through the inclusion or exclusion of entire semiotic systems such as visual signs (Economou, 2008); for example, in video genres such as television news (Pounds, 2012). On the other hand, it results in consequences far beyond formulations. Stance determines the selection of certain topics, topical aspects, sources and quotes – and the omission of others. Whereas the selected variants appear in the media product, the omissions do not. Process analyses, as explained in this article, help researchers overcome the 'limitations of discourse analysis' (Philo, 2007; also Van Hout and Macgilchrist, 2010) when analysing the 'backstage' part (Goffman, 1959: 2) of newswriting.

From an applied linguistics and transdisciplinary perspective, a process-oriented approach to stancing enables researchers to identify real-world problems of language use related to stance – and to contribute to sustainable solutions to these problems (Perrin, 2012). Discussing problems of language use and their solution requires a definition of *language awareness*, by which I understand 'the ability to reflect upon and manipulate language(s); a sensitivity to what is implied rather than stated; and an analytical attitude towards language' (Ehrensberger-Dow and Perrin, 2009: 277, based on Jessner, 2009).

Journalistic stancing practices and the related awareness are situated in a complex and dynamic environment, which I separate into four levels. On a macro level, stancing reflects an institutional role and position in the intertextual chains of newsflows and public discourse. On a meso level, stancing is performed within the collaborative process of text (re-)production in the newsroom. On a micro level, stancing represents individual journalists' decisions within writing processes. On a meta level, finally, stancing consists of critically reflecting on one's own or other agents' stancing practices. These four levels are illustrated by practical example in the next section.

The Fami case from the Idée Suisse project

Discussing in detail the real-life stancing practices observed in newsrooms challenges principles of data protection. Media items are accessible in digital archives and authors can easily be identified. Therefore, this article draws on a case study that, according to the research policy all stakeholders have ratified, is old enough to be published. Recent data allow for similar analyses but are not yet ready to be published as detailed case studies. The data for the case study this article draws on, the Fami case, were recorded within the Idée Suisse project, 2005–2010.

In this transdisciplinary project (e.g. Perrin, 2012), applied linguists, media and communication scholars and media practitioners analysed how policy-makers, media management and journalists understood and enacted the mandate according to which the Swiss public broadcasting company SRG SSR has to foster public understanding between societal groups in Switzerland, such as the young and old, the well educated and less educated and those living in rural and urban areas. Within this research framework, the Fami case shows how, in the conflict between storytelling and facticity, the journalist O.K. decides for the story and against factual details that would undermine his elegant dramaturgy. By doing so, he combines practices of stancing on all levels. The next sections focus on meso and micro stancing.

Meso stancing

The day before he shot the pictures and produced the item, O.K. had the idea of portraying a family in a refugee centre telling their story of how they had experienced Iraq, why they had fled the war, how they came to Switzerland and when they hoped to return to their country. Instead of exposing himself to dangers in Iraq just to report on 'very repetitive scenes of violence', he wanted to exemplify 'through an individual' the problems of this war and the flood of refugees to Europe in general and to Switzerland in particular.

O.K. gradually decided to reduce and concentrate the complexity of his topic towards a straight and lean five-step plot: step one opens a contrast between the war in Baghdad and the refugee centre in Couvet and notes the protagonist's fear of reprisals; step two supports step one with testimonies referring to the past; step three is an infographic piece explaining the trip from Iraq to Switzerland; step four quotes the protagonist's prospects; and step five contextualizes these prospects in a future-oriented conclusion. These five steps determine both the media product and the writing process.

During preparations with the cameraman, O.K. had mentioned that the refugee they were going to interview and stage as the item's protagonist belonged to a privileged class. Later, in the cutting room, he said: 'spending eight thousand dollars to pay a human smuggler..., not all Baghdadis can do this.' Cutter: 'Let's not be so naïve to think this is only a poor refugee, perhaps he has seen other people being made miserable too.' Journalist: 'No doubt, but...he also could have hidden [it], saying: me, I was a trader, you know, constructing another identity, at least, he was honest enough to say OK, I was in the military.'

Micro stancing

In O.K.'s initial draft then, the first opening sequence ended with suspension points: 'former career officer ..'. As a recording of O.K.'s writing process shows, the suspension points were then replaced by 'threatened [with] death...' (Example 1, revisions 159–160). After numerous follow-up revisions, the refugee status of the protagonist was clearly referred to, whereas the status of the father as a former career officer was blurred.

> De confession sunnite, cette famille ne souhaite pas s'exprimer à visage découvert, la peur de représailles, pour cet ancien militaire de carrière^{159}..$^{159}|_{160}^{160}\{^{162}[$, menacé mort... $]^{162}|_{163}^{163}\{^{167}$ ... $^{167}|_{168}^{168}\{$, $^{170}[$les menace de$|_{170}]^{170,\ 256}[$la guerre civile. $]^{256}\}^{168}|_{172}^{257}\{$le traumatisme aussi de la guerre civile.$\}^{257}\}^{160}$

Ex. 1 Workplace session in S-notation, indicating the sequence (small numbers) of insertions (in curly braces) and deletions (in square brackets) in the evolving text.

Source: tsr_tj_070222_1930_kohler_familleirakienne_snt_1

In the cutting room session, however, the insertion 'his wife and his two children' (Example 2, revision 4), immediately followed by a 'for' (revision 5), directs the focus towards the man's family. When speaking the offtext, O.K. added an 'also' (revision 6). Thus, in the broadcasted version, the emphasis had shifted from military to family matters (Fig. 5, lines 22–25).

```
De confession sunnite, cette famille ne souhaite pas
s'exprimer à visage découvert, la peur de représailles,
pour cet ancien militaire de carrière,
⁴{ ⁵{pour }⁵|₆sa femme et ses deux enfants, |₅}⁴ le trau-
matisme ⁶[aussi]⁶ de la guerre civile.
```

Ex. 2 Cutting room session.

Source: tsr_tj_070222_1930_kohler_familleirakienne_snt_2

When speaking the offtext in the booth, O.K. spontaneously changed some formulations (Example 3, changes between /slashes/). One of these changes completes the chain of revisions related to the protagonist's status as a former career officer in Saddam Hussein's army.

```
014  Off:   /Du jour au lendemain/ laisser une vie
             derrière soi
             /From one day to the next/, leaving a life
             behind you,
015          quitter l'enfer de Bagdad
             leaving the inferno of Baghdad
      ...        ...
051  Off:   Dans l'immédiat la confédération n'envisage
             pas
             For the time being the government does not
             envisage
052          de renvoyer ces familles /en Irak/.
             sending these families back /to Iraq/.
```

Ex. 3 Changes in the booth, indicated between /slashes/.

Source: tsr_tj_070223_1930_kohler_familleirakienne_item

In the end of the production process, O.K. had done everything necessary to incorporate his initial stance and incrementally refine his plans: He had contrasted the distant war with the local peace in a concise five-step story. By exemplifying what it means to be Iraqi refugees in Switzerland, he had contextualized instead of reproduced the 'very repetitive scenes of violence' from Iraq. In contrast, everything superfluous to the telling of the concise five-step story had been omitted or deleted during the workplace session or the collaboration in the cutting room. For example, as shown above, O.K. had renounced discussing or emphasizing that the father of the refugee family had been a career officer under the Saddam Hussein regime and that his family must have belonged to the privileged classes in Iraq before and even still during the war. Such findings require methodological access to the backstage processes of newswriting.

Progression Analysis in its methodological context

In this section, I outline a typology of four methodological perspectives of AL-informed research in newswriting. They provide empirical evidence of material, cognitive, social, or socio-cognitive aspects of text production in the newsroom. Respective state-of-the-art methods focus, for example, on material differences between text versions, individuals' writing strategies, variation of practices within and across organizations' newswriting and communities' metadiscourse reflecting their communicational offers.

The material focus: tracking intertextual chains with version analysis

From a material perspective, AL-informed research into newswriting emphasizes the intertextual nature of its object: new texts and text versions are created and differ from earlier ones. Material changes to the semiotic products are captured with version analyses. By *version analysis* I understand the method of collecting and analysing data in order to reconstruct the changes that linguistic features undergo in intertextual chains. The methods and procedures applied originate in comparative text analysis.

Prototype version analyses trace linguistic products (e.g. Sanders and Van Wijk, 1996) and elaborate on the changes in text features from version to version, be it at one single production site or across a series of sites. In the Fami case, the version sent to the booth for speaking and the actually spoken version of the news differ in crucial details (see above, Example 3). Another case study, from a project similar to Idée Suisse, traced the changes made to a quote from a politician's original utterance when it passed through the intertextual chain of correspondents, local and global news agencies, broadcasters and the follow-up discourse in social media (Perrin, 2011a). Other medialinguistic studies, also, draw on version analyses to reveal how texts change throughout the intertextual chains (e.g. Van Dijk, 1988; Bell, 1991: 56ff.; Luginbühl, Baumberger, Schwab and Burger, 2002; Robinson, 2009; Lams, 2011).

Comparing various versions of texts from various sites and stages of production is sufficient to gain empirical evidence of material text changes. However, in itself, it provides hardly any data on the meaning of material activity. In order to develop such knowledge, additional methodological approaches are required. They focus, for example, on whether the writers were conscious of their actions; whether the practices are typical of certain text production institutions; or how the practices and related norms are negotiated in communities and organizations.

The mental focus: identifying writing strategies with Progression Analysis

From a cognitive perspective, AL-informed writing research emphasizes individuals' language-related decisions in writing processes. What exactly do authors do when they produce their texts? What are they trying to do, and why do they do it the way they do? Such mental reflections of material changes are captured with progression analyses. By *Progression Analysis* I understand the multi-method approach of collecting and analysing data in natural contexts in order to reconstruct text production processes as a cognitively reflected activity in context.

Progression analysis combines ethnographic observation, interviews, computer logging and cue-based retrospective verbalizations to gather linguistic and contextual data. The approach was developed to investigate newswriting (e.g. Perrin, 2003; Sleurs, Jacobs and Van Waes, 2003; Van Hout and Jacobs, 2008) and later transferred to other application fields of writing research, such as children's writing processes (e.g. Gnach, Wiesner, Bertschi-Kaufmann and Perrin, 2007) and translation (e.g. Ehrensberger-Dow and Perrin, 2013). With Progression Analysis, data are obtained and related on three levels.

- Before writing begins, Progression Analysis determines through interviews and observations what the writing situation is (e.g. Quandt, 2008). Important factors include the writing task, the writers' professional socialization and experience, and economic, institutional, and technological influences on the workplaces and workflows. In the Idée Suisse project, data on the self-perception of the journalists investigated, such as O.K. in the Fami case, were obtained in semi-standardized interviews about their psycho-biography, primarily in terms of their writing and professional experience, and their work situation. In addition, participatory and video observations were made about the various kinds of collaboration at the workplace.

- During writing, Progression Analysis records every keystroke and writing movement in the emerging text (see above, Examples 1 and 2) with keylogging (e.g. Flinn, 1987; Lindgren and Sullivan, 2006; Spelman Miller, 2006) and screenshot recording programmes (e.g. Degenhardt, 2006; Silva, 2012) that run in the background behind the text editors that the writers usually use; for instance, behind the user interfaces of news editing systems. The recording can follow the writing process over several workstations and does not influence the performance of the editing system. From a technical point of view, it does not influence the writers' performance either, since it operates automatically and without changing the user interfaces of the editing software. Nevertheless, knowing about the recording alters writers' behaviour, with decreasing effect over time. This is why, in projects such as Idée Suisse, the first four weeks of data are excluded from analyses.
- After the writing is over, Progression Analysis records what the writers say about their activities. Preferably immediately after completing the writing process, writers view on the screen how their texts came into being. While doing so, they continuously comment on what they did when writing and why they did it. An audio recording is made of these cue-based retrospective verbal protocols (RVP). This level of Progression Analysis opens a window onto the mind of the writer. The question is what can be recognized through this window: certainly not the sum of all (and only) the considerations that the author actually made, but rather the considerations that an author could have made in principle (e.g. Camps, 2003; Ericsson and Simon, 1993; Hansen, 2006; Levy, Marek and Lea, 1996; Smagorinsky, 2001). The RVP is transcribed and then encoded as the author's verbalization of aspects of his or her language awareness, writing strategies and conscious writing practices. As doing an RVP strongly influences writers' awareness, this level of Progression Analysis is normally limited to one RVP per writer, at the end of the investigation.

In sum, Progression Analysis allows researchers to consider all the revisions to the text and all of the electronic resources accessed as well as the information omitted during the production process; to trace the development of the emerging text; and, finally, to reconstruct collaboration at workplaces from different perspectives. The main focus of Progression Analysis, however, is the individual's cognitive and manifest processes of writing. Social structures such as organizational routines and editorial policies are reconstructed through the perspectives of the individual agents involved, the writers under investigation. If entire organizations are to be investigated with respect to how they produce their texts as a social activity, then Progression Analysis has to be extended by another two methods: variation analysis and metadiscourse analysis.

The social focus: revealing audience design with variation analysis

From a social perspective, AL-informed writing research focuses on how social groups collaborate when they write. Examples include investigations on how editorial teams customize their linguistic products for their target audiences, and analyses of the linguistic means, such as gradients of normativity and formality, an organization chooses for specific addressees. Such social language use is captured with variation analyses. By *variation analysis* I understand the method of collecting and analysing text data to reconstruct the special features of the language of a certain community of discourse and/or practice (Pogner, 2012). The basis for comparing versions is discourse analysis.

Variation analyses investigate the type and frequency of typical features of certain language users' productions in certain communication situations such as writing for a specific audience. What variation analysis discerns is the differences between the language used and the related practices in one situation type from that of the same users in another (e.g. Koller, 2004) or from the language and practices of other users in similar situations (e.g. Fang, 1991; Werlen, 2000). In the Idée Suisse project, for example, variation analyses revealed whether language properties of the newscast *Tagesschau* and the newsmagazine *vor* [10], competing in the same German television programme of the Swiss public broadcaster, differ in explicit stancing practices, according to their programme profiles (Perrin, 2013: 10–12) – and if they are different from those of *Téléjournal* from the French-speaking division of the media organization.

Such broadly based variation analysis is able to show the special features of the language used by specific groups of writers. However, what the method gains in width it loses in depth. Why a community prefers to formulate its texts in a certain way and not another cannot be captured by variation analysis, which, similar to version analysis, neglects access to mental aspects of writing. It is possible to regain some of that depth using a procedure that examines not only the text products, but also the institutionalized discourses connected with them – the comments of the community about its joint efforts.

The socio-cognitive focus: investigating policy-making with metadiscourse analysis

From a socio-cognitive perspective, AL-informed writing research focuses on text producers' collaboration and metadiscourse (e.g. Clayman and Reisner, 1998; Mey, 2005; Moschonas and Spitzmüller, 2007; Lundell, 2010), such as correspondence between authors, quality control discourse at editorial conferences, and negotiations between journalists, photographers and text designers. What do the various stakeholders think about their communicational offers? How do they evaluate their activity in relation to policies – and how do they reconstruct and alter those policies? Such socio-cognitive aspects of language use are captured by metadiscourse analyses. By *metadiscourse analysis* I understand the method of collecting and analysing data in order to reconstruct the socially and individually anchored (language) awareness in a discourse community. The basis for analysing the metadiscourse of text production is conversation and discourse analysis.

Metadiscourse analyses investigate spoken and written communication about language and language use. This includes metaphors used when talking about writing (e.g. Gravengaard, 2012; Levin and Wagner, 2006), explicit planning or criticism of communication measures (e.g. Peterson, 2001), the clarification of misunderstandings and conversational repair (e.g. Häusermann, 2007) and follow-up communication by audiences (e.g. Klemm, 2000). In all these cases, the participants' utterances show how their own or others' communicational efforts and offers have been perceived, received, understood and evaluated. The analysis demonstrates how rules of language use are explicitly negotiated and applied in a community.

In some case stories from the Idée Suisse project, cutters challenge the journalists' ethics and aesthetics or appear as representatives of a critical audience, such as in the dialogue between journalist and video editor in the Fami case (see above). On a macro level of the project, interviews and document analyses reveal policy-makers' and media managers' contradictory evaluation of and expectations towards the broadcasters' – and the journalists' – ability to fulfil the public mandate of promoting public understanding. Whereas media policy-makers expect the Swiss national broadcasting company to foster public discourse through stimulating contributions, media managers tend to consider this public mandate to be unrealistic (Perrin, 2011a: 8).

Thus, the focus of metadiscourse analysis scales up from negotiations about emerging texts at writers' workplaces, to organizational quality control discourse and related discussions in audiences and society at large. Integrating metadiscourse analyses extends the reach of newswriting research from a single author's micro activity to societal macro structures. However, for empirical evidence of writers' actual behaviour, metadiscourse analysis must be combined with progression analyses.

In sum, by applying and combining methods of the four types, researchers investigate real-life writing from product and process perspectives, as cognitive and social backstage activity, and on micro and macro levels. In contrast, analysing only the frontstage products of newsmaking, as often practiced in empirical approaches to media and public discourse, risks falling short of explaining newswriting in general and crucial practices such as stancing in particular, in their variegated dynamics and purposes, as a playful, epistemic and communicative activity in complex contexts. However, applying, let alone combining, innovative methods in multi-perspective real-life writing research causes methodological problems which can be carefully addressed – albeit not completely solved yet.

Key challenge: combining perspectives and methods

In this last section of the chapter, I explain challenges of combining perspectives and methods in projects of writing research. Researchers investigating real-life writing and text production (e.g. Brizee, Sousa and Driscoll, 2012; Olson, 1987; Pogner, 1999; Spilka, 1993; Sullivan and Lindgren, 2006; Thompson, 2009) tend to combine a multitude of approaches and perspectives in order to develop a vivid, life-like representation of their object under investigation (for an overview see, e.g., Grésillon and Perrin, 2014).

The methodological question arises as to how methods can be combined when rooted in different theories or even incompatible scientific paradigms (Kuhn, 1996; Kuhn, 1962). Working with multi-method approaches that involve various theoretical traditions requires methodologically pragmatic approaches (Feilzer, 2010; Johnson and Onwuegbuzie, 2004) and a distinctive meta-theoretical position towards ontology and epistemology as developed, for example, in social constructivism and, in particular, in Realist Social Theory (e.g. Archer, 2000; Sealey and Carter, 2004; Perrin, 2015).

From a methodologically pragmatic position, triangulating different methods results in sometimes contradictory, but always multidimensional, complex, life-like reconstructions of the object under research. Triangulation helps shift the reconstructions (e.g. of the multi-level practice of stancing) toward a state in which they are perceived by ideally all relevant knowers as adequate. Objectivity, in this understanding, emerges from triangulating theories, methods, results and interpretations (Denzin, 1978; Flick, 2004). It consists of as close as possible an approximation to a real world – a formal object which is, after all, neither the material object itself (as in radical positivism) nor an arbitrary construction (as in radical constructivism).

Such multi-perspective views shed light on the following facets of situated newswriting and text production:

- source materials, such as handwritten notes, pictures, sound bites, footage and previously published texts in intertextual chains;
- the sequences of material revisions in the writing process, such as insertions and deletions on a micro level and their complex combinations;
- the text products, such as drafts and final versions as well as interim versions from various stages in collaborative text production;
- the macro products, such as entire newspapers, news programmes and all the language versions of a multilingual production;
- the non-textual work context, such as writers' biographies, social environments and workplace equipment;
- writers' thoughts and thought patterns, such as mental representations of ideas, decisions, strategies, practices, procedures and routines;
- the normative framework, such as cultural norms, editorial mission statements, style sheets and language policies; and
- the discursive evaluation of products and processes in follow-up discourses involving individual and collective authors, audiences and further stakeholders, such as editors' comments, readers' blog posts, or political discussions (e.g. about legitimizing censorship).

The four types of methods distinguished above complement each other in providing access to the various facets of one and the same object: the newswriting process in context (Figure 11.1).

Language as →	Product	Activity		
		Cognitive	Social	Socio-cognitive
Method type →	Version analysis	Progression analysis	Variation analysis	Metadiscourse analysis
Object facets ↓				
Source materials	text chain			
Work context		workplace, ...		
Thought patterns		writing strategy		
Revisions		writing activity		
End products		newspaper article, broadcast news piece, blog post, ...		
Macro products			volume, news program, website, ...	
Normative frame			esthetics, mission, policy, ...	
Evaluation				norm discourse

Figure 11.1 Methods of AL-informed writing research as complementary approaches

As shown above, each perspective requires suitable methods. Questions about cognitive practices of stancing, for instance, can only be addressed by reaching beyond material activity; the same is true for social practices and their interactions, such as a broadcaster's strategy of telling the news to an audience ranging from the yet uninformed to experts in the topic of the news. Investigating stretches of language in a 'one-size fits all approach' (Richardson, 2007: 76) is not enough to allow newswriting research to explain what is special about text production in the newsroom (e.g. Philo, 2007) and to reveal the backstage activities and structures, such as omitting facts in favour of dramaturgy, that 'cannot be directly observed' (Ó Riain, 2009: 294).

This explains the need for novel multi-method approaches, such as Progression Analysis. Combining ethnography with computer-based workplace tracking, Progression Analysis helps reveal the backstage activities, which, actually, can 'be directly observed' in detail. Moreover, the obvious need to overcome the 'one-size fits all approach' calls for even more complex multi-method approaches, such as extending Progression Analysis with metadiscourse analyses – despite their tendency towards theoretical vagueness at the interfaces between methods, methodologies, theories and research paradigms involved. For many applied researchers, it might be more important to understand real-life problems than to eliminate the theoretical problems related to combining methods from potentially conflicting paradigms. But this is a question of stance.

Note

This chapter draws on existing publications by the author. Paragraphs and formulations have been reproduced from Grésillon and Perrin (2014) and Perrin (2013) without explicit cross-references.

References

Archer, M. S. (2000) *Being Human: The Problem of Agency* (Cambridge: Cambridge University Press).

Bednarek, M. and Caple, H. (2014) 'Why do news values matter? Towards a new methodological framework for analysing news discourse in Critical Discourse Analysis and beyond.' *Discourse & Society* 25(2), 135–158.

Bell, A. (1991) *The Language of News Media* (Oxford: Blackwell).

Bell, A. (2001) 'Back in style: Reworking audience design' in P. Eckert and J. R. Rickford (eds), *Style and Sociolinguistic Variation* (pp. 139–169) (Cambridge: Cambridge University Press).

Biber, D. (2004) 'Historical patterns for the grammatical marking of stance: A cross-register comparison.' *Journal of Historical Pragmatics* 5(1), 107–136.

Caldas-Coulthard, C. R. (1994) 'On reporting reporting: The representation of speech in factual and factional narratives' in M. Coulthard (ed.), *Advances in Written Text Analysis* (pp. 295–309) (London: Routledge).

Camps, J. (2003) 'Concurrent and retrospective verbal reports as tools to better understand the role of attention in second language tasks.' *International Journal of Applied Linguistics* 13(2), 201–221.

Catenaccio, P., Cotter, C., Desmedt, M., Garzone, G., Jacobs, G., Lams, L. and Van Praet, E. (2011) 'Position paper: Towards a linguistics of news production.' *Journal of Pragmatics* 43(7), 1843–1852.

Clayman, S. E. and Reisner, A. (1998) 'Gatekeeping in action: Editorial conferences and assessments of newsworthiness.' *American Sociological Review* 2(63), 178–199.

Degenhardt, M. (2006) 'CAMTASIA and CATMOVIE: Two digital tools for observing, documenting and analysing writing processes of university students' in L. Van Waes, M. Leijten and C. M. Neuwirth (eds), *Writing and Digital Media* (pp. 180–186) (Amsterdam: Elsevier).

Denzin, N. K. (1978) *The Research Act*, 2nd edn (New York: Mc Graw-Hill).

Economou, D. (2008) 'Evaluation in news images: Comparative studies of the detention of refugees' in P. R. R. White and E. A. Thomson (eds), *Communicating Conflict: Multilingual Case Studies of the News Media* (pp. 253–280) (London: Continuum).

Ehrensberger-Dow, M. and Perrin, D. (2009) 'Capturing translation processes to access metalinguistic awareness.' *Across Languages and Cultures* 10(2), 275–288.

Ehrensberger-Dow, M. and Perrin, D. (2013) 'Applying a newswriting research approach to translation.' *Target* 25(1), 77–92.

Ericsson, K. A. and Simon, H. A. (1993) *Protocol Analysis: Verbal Reports as Data*, rev. edn (Cambridge: MIT Press).

Fang, I. (1991) *Writing Style Differences in Newspaper, Radio and Television News* (Minnesota: Center for Interdisciplinary Studies of Writing, University of Minnesota).
Feilzer, M. Y. (2010) 'Doing mixed methods research pragmatically: Implications for the rediscovery of pragmatism as a research paradigm.' *Journal of Mixed Methods Research* 4(1), 6–16.
Flick, U. (2004) *Triangulation* (Wiesbaden: Verlag für Sozialwissenschaften).
Flinn, J. Z. (1987) 'Case studies of revision aided by keystroke recording and replaying software.' *Computers and Composition* 5(1), 31–44.
Gnach, A., Wiesner, E., Bertschi-Kaufmann, A. and Perrin, D. (2007) 'Children's writing processes when using computers: Insights based on combining analyses of product and process.' *Research in Comparative and International Education*, 2(1): 13–28.
Goffman, E. (1959) *The Presentation of Self in Everyday Life* (New York: Anchor).
Gravengaard, G. (2012) 'The metaphors journalists live by: Journalists' conceptualisation of newswork.' *Journalism 2012*(13), 1064–1082.
Grésillon, A. and Perrin, D. (2014) 'Methodology: From speaking about writing to tracking text production' in D. Perrin and E.-M. Jakobs (eds), *Handbook of Writing and Text Production*, Vol. 10 (pp. 79–111) (New York: De Gruyter).
Hansen, G. (2006) 'Retrospection methods in translator training and translation research.' *Journal of Specialised Translation* (5): 2–40.
Häusermann, J. (2007) 'Zugespieltes Material: Der O-Ton und seine Interpretation' in H. Maye, C. Reiber and N. Wegmann (eds), *Original / Ton. Zur Mediengeschichte des O-Tons* (pp. 25–50) (Konstanz: UVK).
Huan, C. (2015) *Journalistic Stance in Chinese and Australian Hard News*. PhD Thesis (Macquarie University, Sydney).
Jessner, U. (2009) 'A DST-model of multilingualism and the role of metalinguistic awareness.' *Modern Language Journal* 92(2): 270–283.
Johnson, R. B. and Onwuegbuzie, A. J. (2004) 'Mixed methods research: A research paradigm whose time has come.' *Educational Researcher* 33(7), 14–26.
Khondker, H. H. (2004) 'Glocalization as globalization: Evolution of a sociological concept.' *Bangladesh e-Journal of Sociology* 1(2), 12–20.
Klemm, M. (2000) *Zuschauerkommunikation. Formen und Funktionen der alltäglichen kommunikativen Fernsehaneignung* (Frankfurt am Main et al.: Lang).
Koller, V. (2004) 'Businesswomen and war metaphors: "Possessive, jealous and pugnacious"?' *Journal of Sociolinguistics* 4(1), 3–22.
Kuhn, T. S. (1962) *The Structure of Scientific Revolutions* (Chicago: University of Chicago Press).
Kuhn, T. S. (1996) *The Structure of Scientific Revolutions*, 3rd edn (Chicago: University of Chicago Press).
Lams, L. (2011) 'Newspapers' narratives based on wire stories: Facsimiles of input?' *Journal of Pragmatics* 43(7), 1853–1864.
Levin, T. and Wagner, T. (2006) 'In their own words: Understanding student conceptions of writing through their spontaneous metaphors in the science classroom.' *Instructional Science* 34(3), 227–278.
Levy, C. M., Marek, J. P. and Lea, J. (1996) 'Concurrent and retrospective protocols in writing research' in G. Rijlaarsdam, H. Van den Bergh and M. Couzijn (eds), *Theories, Models and Methodology in Writing Research* (pp. 542–556) (Amsterdam: Amsterdam University Press).

Lindgren, E. and Sullivan, K. (2006) 'Analysing online revision' in K. Sullivan and E. Lindgren (eds), *Computer Keystroke Logging and Writing: Methods and Applications* (pp. 157–188) (Amsterdam: Elsevier).

Luginbühl, M., Baumberger, T., Schwab, K. and Burger, H. (2002) *Medientexte zwischen Autor und Publikum. Intertextualität in Presse, Radio und Fernsehen* (Zürich: Seismo).

Lundell, Å. K. (2010) 'The before and after of a political interview on TV. Observations of off-camera interactions between journalists and politicians.' *Journalism* 11(2), 167–184.

Mey, J. L. (2005) 'Discourse and metadiscourse.' *Journal of Pragmatics* 37(9), 1323–1324.

Moschonas, S. and Spitzmüller, J. (2007) *Metalinguistic discourse in and about the media. On some recent trends of Greek and German prescriptivism*. Paper presented at the 2nd Language in the Media Conference: Language ideologies and media discourse. Texts, practices, policies, Leeds.

Ó Riain, S. (2009) 'Extending the ethnographic case study' in D. Byrne and C. C. Ragin (eds), *The SAGE Handbook of Case-based Methods* (pp. 289–306) (London: Sage).

Perrin, D. (2003) 'Progression analysis (PA): Investigating writing strategies at the workplace.' *Journal of Pragmatics* 35(6), 907–921.

Perrin, D. (2011a) *Medienlinguistik*, 2nd edn (Konstanz: UVK).

Perrin, D. (2011b) '"There are two different stories to tell": Collaborative text-picture production strategies of TV journalists.' *Journal of Pragmatics* 43(7), 1865–1875.

Perrin, D. (2012) 'Transdisciplinary action research: Bringing together communication and media researchers and practitioners.' *Journal of Applied Journalism and Media Studies* 1(1), 3–23.

Perrin, D. (2013) *The Linguistics of Newswriting* (Amsterdam, New York et al.: John Benjamins).

Perrin, D. (2015) 'Realism, social cohesion, and media policy making: The case of Swiss public broadcasting.' *European Journal of Applied Linguistics* 2(1), 111–133.

Peterson, M. A. (2001) 'Getting to the story: Unwriteable discourse and interpretive practice in American journalism.' *Anthropological Quarterly* 74(4), 201–211.

Philo, G. (2007) 'Can discourse analysis successfully explain the content of media and journalistic practice?' *Journalism Studies* 8(2), 175–196.

Pogner, K.-H. (1999) 'Discourse community, culture and interaction: On writing by consulting engineers' in F. Bargiela-Chiappini and C. Nickerson (eds), *Writing Business: Genres, media and discourses* (pp. 101–127) (Harlow: Longman).

Pogner, K.-H. (2012) 'A social perspective on writing in the workplace: Communities of Discourse (DC) and Communities of Practice (CoP)' in A. Rothkegel and S. Ruda (eds), *Communication on and via Technology* (pp. 83–107) (Berlin et al.: De Gruyter Mouton).

Pounds, G. (2012) 'Multimodal expression of authorial affect in a British television news programme.' *Discourse, Context & Media* 1(2–3), 68–81.

Quandt, T. (2008) 'News tuning and content management: An observation study of old and new routines in German online newsrooms' in C. Paterson and

D. Domingo (eds), *Making Online News: The Ethnography of New Media Production* (pp. 77–97) (New York: Peter Lang).

Richardson, J. E. (2007) *Analysing Newspapers: An Approach from Critical Discourse Analysis* (Houndmills: Palgrave Macmillan).

Robinson, S. (2009) 'A chronicle of chaos: Tracking the news story of hurricane Katrina from *The Times-Picayune* to its website.' *Journalism* 10(4), 431–450.

Sanders, T. and Van Wijk, C. (1996) 'Text analysis as a research tool: How hierarchical text structure contributes to the understanding of conceptual processes in writing' in C. M. Levy and S. Ransdell (eds), *The Science of Writing: Theories, Methods, Individual Differences and Applications* (pp. 251–270) (Mahwah: Erlbaum).

Schultz, I. (2007) 'The journalistic gut feeling.' *Journalism Practice* 1(2), 190–207.

Sealey, A. and Carter, B. (2004) *Applied Linguistics as Social Science* (London et al.: Continuum).

Silva, M. L. (2012) 'Camtasia in the classroom: Student attitudes and preferences for video commentary or Microsoft Word comments during the revision process.' *Computers and Composition* 29(1), 1–22.

Sleurs, K., Jacobs, G. and Van Waes, L. (2003) 'Constructing press releases, constructing quotations: A case study.' *Journal of Sociolinguistics* 7(2), 135–275.

Smagorinsky, P. (2001) 'Rethinking protocol analysis from a cultural perspective.' *Annual Review of Applied Linguistics* 21, 233–245.

Spelman Miller, K. (2006) 'Keystroke logging: An introduction' in K. Sullivan and E. Lindgren (eds), *Computer Keystroke Logging and Writing: Methods and Applications* (pp. 1–9) (Amsterdam: Elsevier).

Spilka, R. (ed.) (1993) *Writing in the Workplace: New Research Perspectives* (Carbondale: Southern Illinois University Press).

Van Dijk, T. A. (1988) *News Analysis: Case Studies of International and National News in the Press* (Hillsdale/London: Erlbaum).

Van Hout, T. and Jacobs, G. (2008) 'News production theory and practice: Fieldwork notes on power, interaction and agency.' *Pragmatics* 18(1), 59–86.

Van Hout, T. and Macgilchrist, F. (2010) 'Framing the news: An ethnographic view of business newswriting.' *Text & Talk* 30(2), 169–191.

Van Hout, T., Pander Maat, H. and De Preter, W. (2011) 'Writing from news sources: The case of Apple TV.' *Journal of Pragmatics* 43(7), 1876–1889.

Werlen, I. (2000) '"Zum Schluss das Wetter": Struktur und Variation von Wetterberichten im Rundfunk' in J. Niederhauser and S. Szlek (eds), *Sprachsplitter und Sprachspiele* (pp. 155–170) (Bern: Lang).

White, P. R. R. (2012) 'Exploring the axiological workings of "reporter voice" news stories: Attribution and attitudinal positioning.' *Discourse, Context & Media* 1(2–3), 57–67.

Part IV
Beyond the Newsroom

12
From 'Poetics' to 'Production': Genres as Active Ingredients in Media Production

Ana Alacovska

All media production happens within 'genre-specific worlds' (Tunstall, 1993: 201). Most of the discourses that float in and around production worlds – whether aesthetic and ethical or economic and managerial – in fact belong to genres (Bruun, 2011, 2010; Dornfeld, 1998: 91). Genres are thus an emic conceptual force with which production studies must reckon. Most current sociological studies, however, either completely disregard genres or treat them conveniently as outcomes of production and utilitarian labels by which managers, directors and marketers label and promote classes of cultural products as 'genres' (Bielby and Bielby, 1994). Yet by treating genres merely as imposed classification systems that link producers and audiences on the market, we preclude the possibility of enriching the analytical repertoire of production studies with a category that possesses structural, formal and ontological autonomy. In this way we forfeit a potentially nuanced and comprehensive understanding of how producers work in practice in genre-based production worlds, cope daily with workplace anxieties, and forge professional identities as genre-specialists.

In this chapter I present the rough contours and the rationale of my (post-doc) proposal for a genre-based production study that honours the effectiveness of genres in media production (Alacovska, 2015) by treating them as active ingredients in the production process, wherein genres inform the formation of professional identities and impinge on production norms and values by way of their ontological and structural autonomy.

In doing so, I displace the analytical lens from genres as 'a backward-looking category', distilled taxonomically and descriptively from 'finished' past textual instances, to genres as 'forward-looking categories' orienting and guiding the work of future authors by way of furnishing modes of 'fitting in' or 'matching' an object-to-become with appropriate modes of authorial conduct and compositional skills (Guillén, 2000: 35–36). Genres *enable* and *facilitate* the 'process of formation, making, poièsis' (p. 36).

This is thus essentially an argument in favour of the convergence between poetics, on the one hand – that is, the textual study of 'a finished work as a result of a process of construction' whereby a producer's agency is inferred backwards from genre clues, textual functions and formal devices (Bordwell, 2008: 12) – and on the other hand, media production – that is, the empirical study of actual flesh-and-blood producers and their work-in-progress as embedded in specific workplaces or production worlds oriented towards specific genres (see Paterson and Domingo, 2008, on the production of 'online news').

Such convergence entails examining producers' genre understating and practices in reference to a genre's deep structural manifestation; its fixed, objective definition as opposed to fluctuating semantic 'surface manifestations' or discursive formations (see Mittell, 2004). This means analytically uncoupling genre from social structure, diachronic change and socially agreed-upon value-judgements, so as to investigate the powerful role genres play in concrete, spatio-temporal instances of media production by way of examining what producers actually do with and in genres, their structural/formal/functional properties. Rather than using producers' perceptions and interpretations to build genre definition, evaluation or classification, I start from an 'objective' genre definition, based on invariable structural/functional properties, and then proceed to examine how these properties are mobilized and deployed in the act of production and professional self-definition. In this way, genres are accorded power to furnish modes of acting and self-perception. Such an approach then subscribes to the 'strong program' in cultural sociology, also called 'structural hermeneutics' which recognizes the power of culture (understood as the structural patterning of myths and genres) to influence social life (see Alexander and Smith, 2001).

I do not wish to deny, though, that genres do not change over time. They do, and therefore biological metaphors of the birth, the blooming, and the death of genres permeate genre theory. In sociology, Born (2010), for example, rightly calls for a diachronic study of 'genres-in-process' as a precondition for determining the value and quality of industrially produced cultural objects. However, although genres by necessity require a flux, they also presuppose an obdurate presence of 'family resemblances' or synchronic set of features and functions that remain invariable for extended periods of time that are intertextually shared and historically reproduced. The convergence between poetics and production focuses on the reproduction of stasis (maintenance of proximal, communal and 'familial' relationships with other producers and their texts) rather than on the production of novelty (seeking disconnection, rapture or distal relationships). This is based on the premise that the historically specific, stable internal genre structure is constitutive of producers' nominally differentiated production choices and their ties to the professional community (Swales, 1990; Bazerman, 1988). As such, the structural and functional dynamics of genres deserves to be taken seriously in the studies of professional media producers, as it was in the studies of workplace writers in legal, medical or academic professions (Schryer, 1993).

Extending the insights gleaned from a four-year qualitative study, interviews, and ethnography of the production of travel guidebooks (a factual and performative genre), I here sketch the research design of my ongoing genre-based study of Scandinavian crime fiction, or Nordic Noir (a full-fledged fiction genre that is a mixture of thriller, whodunit, and mystery), within Danish book publishing.

The story of a 'rogue writer': becoming aware of the power of genres

In mid-April 2008, a memoir by 'TK' about the ethics, work and 'professional hedonism' of a travel guidebook writer was published by a 'serious publisher' (as TK informed me in a message just before the memoir's publication). Once out, the memoir caused a scandal of quite disproportionate dimensions.

As part of the global online media promotion of his 'tell-all', TK admitted to unethical production practices that led to his 'scandalous' *inventing* and *fabricating* large portions of a guidebook on Colombia he had authored for Lonely Planet. Strained by a 'thrifty' budget, 'draconian' deadlines, and 'numb editors that never respond to your emails', he was not able to visit Colombia in person and so gathered all the details from 'a chick at the Colombian embassy', culled information from the Web, and summarized tips he had received from random travellers. He further confessed to black-market vending in Brazil to complement his 'paltry wage' while he was commissioned by Lonely Planet. To prevent incurring a 'giant' personal debt, TK subsidized his guidebook work by accepting 'freebies' from hotels and restaurants about which he thus wrote 'necessarily' positive reviews that otherwise should have been 'objective, true and reliably accurate'.

Emblazoned prominently on every guidebook is a statement by Lonely Planet of its official 'responsible' production policy:

> our writers don't research using just the internet or phone, and they don't take freebies in exchange for positive coverage. They personally visit thousands of hotels, restaurants, cafes, bars, galleries, palaces, museums and more. They tell it how it is.

However, TK did not only act in contravention to Lonely Planet policies or his contract. More crucially, TK had breached – if only inadvertently – the industry-wide unwritten genre-specific code of conduct and thus hit a raw nerve. All of a sudden, travel guidebook writers became self-righteous and eager to defend their conscientious craft and the dignity of 'the genre'. Some writers whom I had interviewed just days before now immediately wrote back in defence:

> We don't fake reviews. We check everything we write about. ... This is a serious genre. This is our job. We are in the service of our readers. And the guy who did this, *he* is a real bastard.

Aghast at the moral impropriety of guidebook-making thus exposed, the global press was filled with sensational headlines making the trade sound cheap and shoddy and the genre contrived and sleazy. These headlines included: 'The truth about writing Lonely Planet guidebooks' (*The Guardian*); 'Author for the Lonely Planet admits he never set foot in the place' (*The Sunday Times*); 'The travel industry's dirty little secret' (*The New York Times*); 'The "Hell" of travel writing' (*Los Angeles Times*); 'Guidebooks: don't believe everything you read' (*Time Online*); 'Can you trust your travel guidebook?' (*Washington Post*); and 'The death of the guidebook: lost in a cutthroat world' (*The Age*).

BBC Worldwide, the then owner of Lonely Planet, reacted swiftly to TK's allegations by setting in motion a quasi-juridical investigative process to assess the 'accuracy' and 'impartiality' of many guidebooks and by defending publicly the ethical stature of their writers.

The writers were convinced, however, that the revelations were not only an affront to their hard work and steadfast ethics but also an indictment of the way the company treated its contractual workers. Many understood the tell-all as blowing the whistle on the travel publishing industry's 'dirty little secret' – that is, that publishers allow (and even encourage) their poorly paid writers to accept freebies from airlines, hotels and tour operators in return for write-ups in order to underwrite production costs. The hiring of an incessant stream of unvetted and underpaid writers, together with accelerated publishing schedules, unclear commissioning procedures and ambivalent 'don't ask don't tell' policies on freebies, were all blamed for compromising the 'accuracy' and 'impartiality' of travel guidebooks.

The scandal had an even more forceful impact on audiences, whose genre-related horizon of expectation and trust has been brutally deceived. Apart from righteous indignation, audiences demonstrated operative genre-specific knowledge of the ways authors (should have) worked to attain 'accuracy' and 'impartiality'. Pondering over the boundaries between factual and fictional genres, one guidebook-user wrote in Thorn Three, the online traveller community harboured by Lonely Planet:

> I am shocked! I've always thought all those writers traveled incognito, and they have been there. Show up unexpectedly, inspect, see how 'ordinary' people are treated and not receive red carpet treatment. You can't do an honest, reliable job if you are not there, and if they try to bribe you.... Send out 'Comedy! Fiction!' stickers to current vendors for the old Colombia edition! A spontaneous outpour of marihuana-fuelled imagination!

The scandal of a factual and performative genre

It is only when research fields become distressed by unanticipated events that the researcher can sneak a glance at the underlying rules, commonplaces and habitualities of behaviour and discourse that remain unspoken during periods of 'normalcy' (Latour and Woolgar, 1986). Indeed, TK's 'fakery scandal' evinced the power that genres hold over the travel guidebook production world. The power of genres could otherwise remain unnoticed, if only because a production researcher would not otherwise be immediately concerned with the role of genres in production worlds, nor would the producers themselves ponder unprompted upon ingrained and often unarticulated genre knowledge and competence.

The scandal was not only about the moral accountability and corruptibility of travel writers, chastised for questionable production techniques such as accepting freebies or regurgitating word-of-mouth as fact. Nor was it solely about 'evil' managers and editors who induced unethical behaviour and rendered their authors docile through murky commissioning policies, paltry terms of recompense and unrealistic deadlines. The scandal was, above all and despite all, about a genre: about what *mattered* to writers and readers, but also managers; about its genre-poetics; that is, the legitimate and conscientious production techniques and procedures pertinent to the genre.

A producer's actions, production routines and professional attitudes can be judged as ethical, good or conscientious only in relation to the genre's immanent and autonomous properties. TK's actions were perceived, sensationalized and hyperbolized as unscrupulous and unethical – as absolute mendacity and outright fabrication – because he transgressed the norms, values and procedures intrinsic to the guidebook genre. TK has admitted to callous disrespect of the genre-specific values and norms pertaining to: 1) 'factuality', meaning every guidebook is 'accurate' and 'impartial' description predicated on 'an actual' journey and based on fact-gathering and eye-witnessing; and 2) performativity, meaning every guidebook is meant to guide, to be enacted in travelling practice by audiences who expect truthful and reliable guidance. Indeed, other 'fakery scandals' in media production have made manifest a 'factual' genre's effectiveness in inflecting producers' moral (ethical) and immoral (aesthetic freedom/economic coercion) choices and behaviour (see Winston, 2000, on the British documentary scandal in the late 1990s, and Mittell, 2004, on the American quiz show scandal in the 1950s).

In light of the empirical evidence that genres exert power over the ways in which producers, both individual and institutional, act as appropriate 'genre participants', I here explore the possibility of developing a research design for a genre-based production study whereby genres will be accorded analytical, structural and formal autonomy.

Genres in media/cultural production

In studies of cultural production the notion of genre is invariably seen as a conduit between the humanities' interest in cultural objects (textual content) and the emphasis of social sciences on context (the political economy of production, industrial and organizational fiats) (Jensen, 1984; Born, 2010; Bruun, 2010).

At present, however, sociological studies of cultural production treat genres as outcomes of production or yardsticks for measuring novelty and putative novelty rather than as active ingredients with an agentic import for social (economic, managerial or labour) processes. Through this prism, cultural producers label, categorize or promote cultural products as genres because genres conveniently link audience tastes (purchasing preferences) with classes of cultural products (a company's offering). Hence the pivot of sociological analysis is either on nominal destabilization or radical disruption of established genre conventions. The calibration between genre-specific sameness and difference is a precondition for achieving aesthetic novelty in products, involving either marginal differentiation or disruptive innovation, which in turn is a requirement for market positioning, sustainability and success. To this end, Born (2010: 192) influentially calls for a sociological study of the history of 'genres-in-process' against which it is possible to 'access the degree of inventiveness or redundancy of the cultural object in question'.

The sociological interest in genres in the studies of cultural production is thus closely connected to the effort at understanding the creation and management of novelty or originality. In this regard, the sociological focus on genres is situated on three planes: (1) on genres as risk-minimizing tools by means of which 'mass media' managers such as network executives (Bielby and Bielby, 1994) or marketing directors (Ryan, 1991) reproduce genre-based *sameness or formats* to capitalize on known audience tastes and expectations; (2) on the ingenuity and originality of particular charismatic artists who 'invent' 'new genres' by waging wars on old traditions to accumulate symbolic capital later transferable into monetary gain (see Born, 1995, on Boulez; DeNora, 1995, on Beethoven); or (3) on the evaluative potential of genres as legitimation devices by which a long series of cultural intermediaries, critics, journalists, or academics assess the quality/novelty – and by implication build the legitimacy – of certain classes of textual/product offering (see Lena and Peterson, 2008, for an overview).

However, recently sociologists of culture started to notice (without probing further) that all cultural producers (not only 'charismatic artists') are in fact *genre participants*, since every cultural worker is inevitably involved in 'genre environments' – genre-bound 'circles', 'scenes', 'firms' (Lena and Peterson, 2008) – and hence all producers are emotionally as well as economically embedded in 'genre-specific worlds' rather than general 'art worlds' (Hesmondhalgh and Baker, 2011). Bearing in mind the centrality of genres in the life-and-work worlds of cultural producers, it would be potentially insensitive to empirical realities and analytically impoverishing to deny the structuring and enabling function of genres in studies of cultural/media production.

As decades of audience reception studies have taught us, genres are not merely outcomes of the materialist and hegemonic structures of the culture industries but are constantly acted with and acted upon by audiences in a variety of interpretations (Radway, 1984; Livingstone, 1990).

Genres enable and govern textual reception and, a fortiori, textual production. Because creative workers are by default 'creative producers' we should not be blinded to the fact that every producer is in fact also a genre recipient. Genres precede and follow the work of producers. No author works outside specific genres, because genres are first and foremost categories of labour and production, if only acquired through sustained 'professional reception'; hence we must expect that genres exert an influence over producers as much as they have been documented to exert influence over audiences, as I show below (Radway, 1984; Livingstone, 1990).

According to Livingston (1990) the 'text-reader metaphor' has been far more influential than the 'author-text metaphor' and, not surprisingly, as a result, we have seen a migration of literary, phenomenological and formalist concepts towards reception studies, which in turn has enormously enriched its analytical repertoire, to the detriment of production studies.

What can we learn then from the sophisticated use of the category of genre in audience/reception studies?

Lessons from audience/reception studies (and hermeneutics)

The notion of genre holds a prominent if not central location in the analytical repertoire of audience/reception studies, alongside notions such as codes, themes, or semiosis. Drawing inspiration directly from the venerable tradition of reader-response criticism, whose proponents (Holland, 1975) have argued staunchly for a theory of reception inferred from *actual readers'* responses instead of from abstract and assumed interpretive activities of *imagined readers* (Iser, 1981), audience/reception studies have empirically documented the role of genres in the ways readers engage with texts. By concentrating their analyses on specific genres, audience/reception studies reveal that readers' interpretative strategies are constituted by a genre's structural properties, formal conventions and expectations (Livingstone, 1990, and Ang, 1982, on soap operas; Hill, 2007, on reality TV; Radway, 1984, on romances). For example, Livingstone (1990) argues that viewers of soap operas 'decode texts' in accordance with genre systems because it is actually the genre structure that stimulates viewers' engagement: viewers foresee cliffhangers, tease out convoluted plot lines, guess at the resolution of subplots, or assess the morality of central characters.

In addition, audience/reception studies have ethnographically researched historically situated, genre-based case studies of viewing/reading/listening (a counterattack to the positivistic and behaviouralist generalizations of use-and-gratification studies) showing how certain genres actually 'get in action' in recipients' daily practices and hence exercise tangible and identifiable effects on recipients, sometimes detrimental and sometimes beneficial. For example, Radway (1984) has shown how romances can both emancipate women from and sometimes subjugate them to patriarchal norms and normative femininity. Tufte (2000) described in detail how telenovelas prop up fantasies about social mobility and cultural citizenship in Brazil.

These studies have thus empirically corroborated the entrenched hermeneutical tenet which holds that all textual understanding and a fortiori interpretation is unavoidably genre-bound (Hirsch, 1967). In other words, reception studies have empirically investigated the text-reader link by charting the ambiguous and multifarious ways in which genres are enacted or get into action in reception practice and how they exercise power over the ways recipients think, feel, perceive of and imagine themselves. Indeed, both hermeneutics in a phenomenological guise (Iser, 1981) and structuralist/formalist/semiotic literary theories (Todorov, 1990; Culler, 1975/2002) – the theoretical foundations most heavily exploited in reception studies – have long axiomatically maintained that readers necessarily read in reference to a genre because genres provide the set of references, the orienting frameworks and evaluative procedures that enable and facilitate meaningful reader-text interaction. For example, Todorov argues (1990: 19) that 'readers read in function of the generic system, with which they are familiar thanks to criticism, schools, the book distribution system, or simply by hearsay'. Similarly, Iser (1981: 190) contends that by virtue of common formal and structural properties, genres 'map out' a reader's attitude and participation by steering them into the right reading 'position'. More starkly, Ricoeur argued that readers' lives become more intelligible and meaningful when they apply narrative models, plots or characterizations derived from genres – that is, genres constitute narrative identities (1991: 188).

However, these theories have also been observant of the 'author-text' metaphor. They have maintained, albeit tangentially, that authors themselves work (write, compose, craft) their texts always in reference to a genre's formal, structural and cultural properties. According to Todorov (1990: 18), genres offer 'the models of writing for authors' as 'authors write in function of (which does not mean in agreement with) the existing genre system'. Genres *govern* the production of texts by way of authors having mastered a specific 'genre system' and having accumulated 'genre competence'; that is, having internalized a genre's specific codes, topics or characterizations. Genres establish what is pertinent and sensible but also strategic *to do* in production practice (Culler, 1975/2002). Consider, for example, the way Culler describes how it is genres that 'make possible' an author's agency:

> To write a poem or a novel is immediately to engage with a literary tradition or at the very least with a certain idea of the poem or the novel. The activity is made possible by the existence of the genre, which the author can write against, certainly whose conventions he may attempt to subvert, but which is none the less the context within which his activity takes place, as surely as the failure to keep a promise is made possible by the institution of promising. (Culler, 1975/2002: 135)

The genre-mediated relationship between authors and texts in literary studies and hermeneutics is mainly considered a question of poetics, namely 'structuralist poetics', which involves a study 'of the devices, conventions and strategies of literature, of the means by which literary works create their effects on readers (Culler, 1975/2002: xiii). From this definition it becomes immediately clear that structuralist poetics privileges the working or effectiveness of 'the literary works' instead of the actual activities of flesh-and-blood authors who actually create the 'effect' by mobilizing and acting with specific genre codes, structures and cultural norms in their production practice. This is not surprising given the dismissal by hermeneutics and poetics of any empirical engagement with authors and their work practices as demeaning forms of 'psychologism' or 'sociologism'. Under direct pressure from 'death-of-the-author' obituaries, cultural producers have been even further stripped of meaningful or purposeful agency and intention. In poetics 'the authors' are in fact only 'imagined authors' or 'implied authors' (Booth, 1988), whereas the intentions, interventions and work of locally and socially situated producers are the product of sustained guesswork, inferred backwards and reconstructed from finished and finalized genre-specific textual instantiations.

If audience/reception studies could productively hijack the notion of genre from hermeneutics to investigate empirically the act of reading/watching and even Internet use (see Das, 2010; Lomborg, 2011) as audience engagement with a genre's formal and structural functions and values, why can production studies not empirically probe a genre's role in enabling production by investigating the ways in which producers engage with genre-specific structures, formal properties and conventions in the act of production?

A theory of production induced from producers' subjective accounts about their genre-specific work experiences, as well as ethnographic observation of their genre-related work, as opposed to inferences from texts, can appropriate some of the methodological innovations of audience/reception studies. Reception studies have overcome the methodological obstacles to empirical studies of the essentially private, mental, and cognitive processes of reception by diverting attention to socialized modes of reading/watching taking place in book clubs (Radway, 1984) or on the streets of neighbourhoods (Tufte, 2000). In this regard, production studies could not only investigate collaborative modes of authorship (such as screenwriting, Conor, 2014) but also the modes of engagement in professional genre-based associations, movements, fairs and award systems – such as, for example, horror writer societies, crime fiction fairs, science fiction academies, jazz musician unions, and so forth.

However, it still remains unclear how to bridge the yawning gap between 'poetics', which builds on philosophical, interpretive and structural evidence for genre-driven authorial agency, and 'production studies', which build on valid, systematic and rigorous gathering of empirical evidence such as life stories, biographies and observations of practice. Does this convergence hold the passkey to empirically grounded, genre-based studies of production practices whereby the notion of genre would be accorded full analytical valency so as to capture the power of genres to influence social life?

Towards a poetics-production convergence

The path towards a poetics-production convergence has already been trodden by media scholars such as Mortensen and Svendsen (1980), Jensen (1984) and Dornfeld (1998), and lately and most consistently Bruun (2010, 2011). What is extremely productive in these studies is their treatment of professional producers as professional readers of sorts. 'Professional producers' have learnt the ropes of their trade (i.e., how to make texts) by intense, sustained and focused reading, often as a compulsory part of educational curricula. According to this logic, professional producers are in fact interpreters and cultural production is tantamount to interpretation. Every producer produces texts through an explicit interpretation of preceding, proximal yet rival textual instances grouped in genres. Given that interpretation is inevitably genre-bound, genres could be seen as conduits of producers' tacit, layered and conventionalized professional knowledge. By implication, genres underpin production values and producers' belief systems, as well as the ethics within production cultures.

Mortensen and Svendsen (1980) offered an early and revealing insight that genres are profoundly built into journalists' daily work within Swedish newsrooms: 'The "good journalist" has learned to command the journalistic genres. These enable him to produce adequate material, finish to deadline, treat usual subjects with authoritative sources and to present them in an uncontroversial and reader-friendly manner' (p. 175). Bruun (2010) shows in her study of the production of television satire at DR, the Danish PBS, that genres are ingrained in 'the ways media professionals are thinking, organizing practices and verbalizing the many professional competences involved in specific productions' (p. 734). Bruun (2011) therefore openly calls for 'an explicit genre approach' (p. 51) to media production. Similarly, Joli Jensen (1984) makes an argument for 'an interpretive approach to culture production' wherein genres are treated as 'an arena of negotiation' as 'it is in and through it that ideas, values and beliefs are worked' (p. 114). Moreover, Dornfeld (1998) demonstrates convincingly in ethnographic detail how the producers of *Childhood*, a documentary film, constantly self-evaluate their performance, judge the quality of the outcome and even self-censor in reference to the genre of documentary. Furthermore, Zoellner (2009) shows how in the UK documentary development, genres function as 'interpersonal "objective" criteria' (p. 519) by which commissioning and funding decisions are justified and professionalism defended.

Alas, although insightful and empirically well grounded, such accounts of the 'active role' of genres in production process are sporadic, mutually independent, geographically detached, and have remained unappreciated in subsequent production studies. For all their empirical insightfulness, these studies do not develop a consolidated theoretical framework that will connect issues of a genre's formal, structural and aesthetic properties with production values, working procedures and workplace norms. This perhaps plays into their failure to gain robust traction in spite of having empirically evinced the salient role that genres play in professional production and professional self-definition.

It is important to take seriously these studies' call for a genre-based study of cultural production while aiming at developing an overarching methodological and theoretical agenda. How we are to treat genres in such studies empirically and theoretically is still open to debate. Given the space constraints here, I will only be able to chart but by no means comprehensively elaborate on one possible way that will enable us to accord genres analytical valency as active ingredients in production practice. This is essentially a proposal for putting structuralist poetics in dialogue with sociological poetics and ethnopoetics.

From sociological poetics to ethnopoetics: towards genres as resources for action and 'equipment for living'

In openly attacking the sterility of text-based formalist/structuralist studies of genres, 'sociological poetics' involves the analysis of devices, plots and aesthetic values as organizing principles of speaking, communicative intentionality and performance (Bakhtin and Medvedev, 1985). The main tenet of sociological poetics is that 'speech genres' exercise an ideological influence over the material circumstances of production. Indeed, sociological poetics has been extremely influential in subsequent studies of communicative genres because of its recognition that the intrinsic textual dynamics directly shape, rather than being merely shaped by, the surrounding extra-linguistic environment. Through this prism, genres are neither infinitely malleable to socio-economic impositions nor products of classifications. Genres *do* things, enable action/activities, because they provide the social, affective and behavioural resources to be mobilized by producers in text-producing activities. Producers in turn deploy genre resources to accomplish certain communicative actions and fulfil communicative exigencies: to amuse or insult (jokes), to invite (invitation), to admonish (proverb) (see Miller, 1984).

If genres guide and organize interpersonal communication, how do they organize writing? What do genres afford textual producers to do?

Extending the empirical scope of 'sociological poetics' into pragmatism, socio-linguistic and rhetorical studies of language use investigate how genres 'get into action' in professional writing contexts and workplaces. By concentrating on professional workplace writers such as academics (Bazerman, 1988), tax accountants (Devitt, 2004), and veterinary physicians (Schryer, 1993) these studies probe how a specific genre's formal and conventional properties are reactivated and enacted in work processes, as well as in professional identity formation. Genre-based studies of professions provide an especially useful framework and innovative methodology for the treatment of genres not so much as entities to be defined but as active ingredients that permit professionals to accomplish their daily tasks as well as to uphold their professional self-identification.

Genre-based studies of professions have meticulously documented that the work of professional writers is enabled through intuitive and embodied genre awareness acquired through protracted genre use/reading. Through reading, professional writers internalize and, a fortiori, reproduce a genre's formal codes, structures and norms. At the same time, their knowledge of genres and intuitive genre competence together facilitate a sense of professional affiliation and belonging to genre-based professional communities. In order to investigate genre awareness and intuition, these scholars have pursued the 'think aloud' method. The 'think aloud' method proved extremely useful for eliciting expert knowledge while the subjects actually undertake/perform text-production. The 'think aloud' method would elucidate writers' relationships to implicit audiences and make manifest producers' engrained genre knowledge and competences only if the researcher is fully conversant with the genre's structural prerogatives. It is only against a specific genre system that the researcher can interpret/evaluate a producer's skills, attitudes, behaviour and ethical/aesthetic choices (Bazerman, 1988) and also follow how a genre's resources facilitate the formation of professional identities (Schryer, 1993).

Bearing in mind that media producers take pride in the work they produce, which is always by default a genre-bound work, as well as the fact that producers concentrate their work in a specific genre and claim professionalism through 'genre specialization' (Tunstall, 1993), it is especially important to understand the *active* role of genres in the forging of occupational solidarity and professional reflexivity of media producers. In this regard we can learn a great deal from 'ethnopoetics' and the (emic) treatment of genres by linguistic anthropology as 'equipment for living', wherein genres are '*strategies* for dealing with *situations*' and hence are 'active categories' with which genre users-producers make sense of their place in the world (Burke, 1998: 597). From here, ethnopoetics or 'the ethnography of speaking' studies 'the regimens of calibration, that is expectations and values, bearing on the degree to which individual performances should conform with or depart from what is taken to be normative for the genre' (Bauman, 2008: 10). In each individual performance, the genre serves as a nexus for communicative relationships as well as an enabler of communicative practice. From here the discrepancy or overlap between 'the intrinsic qualities' of the genre (formal features in morphological and structuralist guises) and 'the performer's virtuosity' will reveal the 'regimes of calibration' operative in a specific communicative event. Indeed, Bauman (2001) demonstrates that open-market vendors who are skilful genre users-producers enhance the value of pantyhose by deploying in their selling practices the structural codes and expressive means of the genre of 'spiel'. Recognizing the power of genres, social actors try to align their actions and performance with genres, which also leads to alignment of their conduct with other community members (other vendors on the market, for example). In short, genres provide the resources and benchmarks for measuring virtuosity, expertise and specialization in text-production.

Given the theoretical developments and methodological inventions in socio-linguistic studies of genres in professions and workplaces, as well as linguistic anthropology's treatment of genres as resources for living, it is very puzzling that cultural/media production studies do not tap into their potential. We can learn from sociological poetics and ethnopoetics how to analytically treat and empirically investigate genres as active ingredients in production practice. If genres are approached as active ingredients carrying social import, then the investigative lens will be on what producers do with, through and in genres, which is much better attuned to the ways professional media producers go about their work. In addition, the concept of genre would help us understand the layered and complex authorial/producer orientations to their actual and implicit audiences, as well as their projections of imagined professional selves. Moreover, media production studies can make constructive use of the 'think aloud' method so as to grasp the often hidden and easily dismissed as unfathomable processes of artistic/creative creation. In sum, the notion of genre is well poised to dissolve the disciplinary walls that now divide medium-based production studies of television/radio/film/book/digital media and hence to contribute to the theoretical and methodological solidification of a general media production study.

In lieu of a conclusion: towards a genre-based study of the production of Scandinavian crime fiction

Here I outline the usefulness of the notion of genre for the practical and epistemological design of a genre-based study of media production. In a practical sense, genres can be used as scoping devices and as a passkey for research access. Given the variety of media industries, we can scale down the research design by national regions of production: a focus on the Danish book publishing field instead of the more expansive Scandinavian publishing. Yet such national industry-sector analysis still comes across as too extensive. Instead, the notion of genre delimits the scope of a national study to manageable field coordinates (Bourdieu, 1996): the study of Scandinavian crime fiction in the Danish publishing industry.

Genres are a field's centripetal forces. The genre-bound field of production consists of genre-defined positions of actors, both institutional and individual, including: crime fiction publishing houses (Aarhus-based Klim or Modtryk); departments within larger publishers (*krimi* subdivisions at larger publishers); literary agencies that specialize in crime fiction (Nordin, Salamonsson); crime fiction rights sales auctions; crime fiction writers (crime fiction writers' unions); fairs (Krimimesse in Horsens); or crime writing academies and literary awards (Det danske krimi akademi). The collaborative or combative relations among these positions will always pertain to and be driven by a genre's specificity.

The feasibility of such genre-based production analysis is facilitated by genres themselves, which act as passkeys to research sites. Bruun (2011) lauds a researcher's genre knowledge as the strongest methodological weapon to be used in securing access to the notoriously difficult-to-access sites of media production. Once access has been granted, the empirical study will follow through think aloud, interviews and ethnography, all the genre-based field positions. Both the data-gathering and analysis will be conducted in reference to genre-specific structural/formal properties.

In order to investigate the effectiveness of the genre of Scandinavian crime fiction in the Danish publishing field, I propose: (1) establishing the 'analytical autonomy' of genres, and (2) following a genre's 'concretization' or its enactment in historically situated production contexts (see Kane, 1990; Alexander and Smith, 2001).

Firstly, the establishment of a Scandinavian crime fiction genre's 'analytical autonomy' involves a definition of its structural and formal properties. Various textual and literary analyses have already established the genre's dominant structural and functional characteristics which tend to become conventionalized over time (Nestingen and Arvas, 2011). The structuralist approach to genres identifies the genre-specific intertextual relationship of characterization, plot lines, moral judgements, or appropriate themes that constitute a set of formal techniques or models for production. In this way, the structurally and symbolically patterned codes that provide the guidelines for the way people work, feel, aspire and act become manifest. Such 'objectively' inferred sets of techniques serve as an analytical backdrop against which producers accounts are evaluated.

Secondly, we can follow how a genre's structural patterning becomes a resource for action and equipment for living by investigating the 'concretization' of the formal and functional properties in specific events of production. This involves following (through 'think aloud', interviews and ethnography) how actors (crime fiction publishers, writers, foreign rights sellers, authors' agents) act with and upon the genre properties in specific production spaces such as book fairs, promotional campaigns, editing rooms, boardrooms and rights sales meetings. Producers' lived experiences of production and their biographical accounts, as well as the observations of their practices, are always cross-referenced with the functional and formal models inferred 'objectively' from past textual instances belonging to the genre of Scandinavian crime fiction. The aim is therefore not to understand how producers classify or define the genres, but to grasp how genres do their work – frame producers' accounts as phenomenal genre instantiations and shape producer practice as genre-practice. The investigative emphasis then is on how producers go about achieving 'good' Scandinavian crime fiction in between revisions; how they justify changes in draft revisions; how they balance formal (aesthetic) choices with market or career choices (ethical); how they relate to the characters they create or to implicit readers; how they use the genre to forge professional images, frame virtuosity, and sell expertise; how they cope with genre anxiety.

Note

The work on this chapter has been generously supported by the Danish Council for Independent Research – the Humanities (individual post-doc grant number: DFF – 4001–00112B).

References

Alacovska, A. (2015) 'Genre anxiety: Women travel writers' experience of work.' *The Sociological Review* 63:S1, 128–143.

Alexander, J. and Smith P. (2001) 'The strong program in cultural sociology: Elements of structural hermeneutics' in H. J. Turner (ed.), *Handbook of Sociological Theory* (pp. 135–150) (London: Springer).

Ang, I. (1982) *Watching Dallas: Soap Opera and the Melodramatic Imagination* (London: Methuen).

Bakhtin, M. and Medvedev, P. N. (1985) *The Formal Method in Literary Scholarship: A Critical Introduction to Sociological Poetics* (Cambridge: Harvard University Press).

Bauman, R. (2001) 'The ethnography of genre in a Mexican market: Form, function and variation' in R. J. Rickford and P. Eckert (eds), *Style and Sociolinguistic Variation* (pp. 57–77) (Cambridge: Cambridge University Press).

Bauman, R. (2008) *A World of Other's Worlds: Cross Cultural Perspectives on Intertextuality* (New York: John Willey).

Bazerman, C. (1988) *Shaping Written Knowledge: The Genre and Activity of the Experimental Article in Science* (Madison: University of Wisconsin Press).

Bielby, T. W. and Bielby, D. D. (1994) 'All hits are flukes: Institutionalized decision making and the rhetoric of network prime-time program development.' *American Journal of Sociology* 99(5), 1287–1313.

Booth, W. (1988) *The Company We Keep: An Ethics of Fiction* (Berkeley: University of California Press).
Bordwell, D. (2008) *Poetics of Cinema* (London: Routledge).
Born, G (1995) *Rationalizing Culture: IRCAM, Boulez, and the Institutionalization of the Musical Avant-garde* (Berkeley: University of California Press).
Born G. (2010) 'The social and the aesthetic: For a post-Bourdieuian theory of cultural production.' *Cultural Sociology* 4(2), 171–208.
Bourdieu P. (1996) *The Rules of Art* (Palo Alto, CA: Stanford University Press).
Bruun, H. (2010) 'Genre and interpretation in production: A theoretical approach.' *Media, Culture & Society* 32(5), 723–737.
Bruun, H. (2011) 'Genre in media production.' *MedieKultur* 27(51), 22–39.
Burke, K. (1998) 'Literature as equipment for living' in D. Richter (ed.), *The Critical Tradition* (pp. 593–598) (Boston: Bedford Books).
Conor, B. (2014) *Screenwriting: Creative Labour and Professional Practice* (London: Routledge).
Culler, J. (1975/2002) *Structuralist Poetics: Structuralism, Linguistics and the Study of Literature* (London: Routledge).
Das, R. (2010) 'Meaning at the interface: News genres, new modes of interpretive engagement.' *Communication Review* 13(2), 140–159.
DeNora, T. (1995) *Beethoven and the Construction of Genius: Musical Politics in Vienna, 1792–1803* (Berkley: University of California Press).
Devitt, A. (2004) *Writing Genres* (Carbondale: Southern Illinois University Press).
Dornfeld, B. (1998) *Producing Public Television, Producing Public Culture* (New Jersey: Princeton University Press).
Guillen, C. (2000) 'From Literature as System: Essays toward the theory of literary history' in M. McKeon (ed.), *Theory of the Novel: A Historical Approach* (pp. 34–50) (Baltimore: John Hopkins University Press).
Hesmondhalgh, D. and Baker, S. (2011) *Creative Labour: Media Work in Three Cultural Industries* (London: Routledge).
Hill, A. (2007) *Restyling Factual TV: Audiences and News, Documentary and Reality Genres* (London: Routledge).
Hirsch, D. (1967) *Validity in Interpretation* (New Haven: Yale University Press).
Holland N. (1975) *The Nature of Literary Response: Five Readers Reading* (New Hampshire: Yale University Press).
Iser, W. (1981) *The Act of Reading: A Theory of Aesthetic Response* (Baltimore: John Hopkins University Press).
Jensen, J. (1984) 'An interpretive approach to culture production' in R. Willard and B. Watkins (eds), *Interpreting Television: Current Research Perspectives* (pp. 98–118) (Beverly Hills: Sage).
Kane, A. (1991) 'Cultural analysis in historical sociology: The analytical and concrete forms of the autonomy of culture.' *Sociological Theory* 9(3), 53–69.
Latour, B. and Woolgar, S. (1986) *Laboratory Life: The Construction of Scientific Facts* (Princeton: Princeton University Press).
Lena, J. and Peterson, R. (2008) 'Classification as culture: Types and trajectories of music genres.' *American Sociological Review* 73(5), 697–718.
Livingstone, S. (1990) *Making Sense of Television: The Psychology of Audience Interpretation* (Oxford: Pergamon Press).
Lomborg, S. (2011) 'Social media as communicative genres.' *MedieKultur* 27(51), 55–71.

Miller, C. (1984) 'Genre as social action.' *Quarterly Journal of Speech* 70(2), 151–167.
Mittell, J. (2004) *Genre and Television: From Cop Shows to Cartoons in American Culture* (New York: Routledge).
Mortensen, F. and Svendsen, N. E. (1980) 'Creativity and control: The journalist betwixt the readers and editors.' *Media, Culture & Society* 2(2), 169–177.
Nestingen, A. and Arvas, P. (2011) *Scandinavian Crime Fiction* (Cardiff: University of Wales Press).
Paterson, C. and Domingo, D. (2008) *Making Online News: The Ethnography of New Media Production* (New York: Petar Lang).
Radway, J. (1984) *Reading the Romance: Women, Patriarchy and Popular Literature* (Chapel Hill: The University of North Carolina Press).
Ricoeur, P. (1991) 'Narrative Identity' in D. Wood (ed.), *Paul Ricoeur: Narrative and Interpretation* (pp. 188–199) (London: Routledge).
Ryan, B. (1991) *Making Capital from Culture: The Corporate form of Capitalist Cultural Production* (Berlin: Walter de Gruyter).
Schryer, F. (1993) 'Records as genre.' *Written Communication* 10(2), 200–234.
Swales, J. M. (1990) *Genre Analysis: English in Academic and Research Settings* (Cambridge: Cambridge University Press).
Todorov, T. (1990) *Genres in Discourse* (Cambridge: Cambridge University Press).
Tufte, T. (2000) *Living with the Rubbish Queen: Telenovelas, Culture and Modernity in Brazil* (Bloomington: Indiana University Press).
Tunstall, J. (1993) *Television Producers* (London: Routledge).
Winston, B. (2000) *Lies, Damn Lies and Documentaries* (London: BFI).
Zoellner, A. (2009) 'Professional ideology and program conventions: documentary development in independent British television production.' *Mass Communication and Society* 12(4), 503–536.

13
Production Studies and Documentary Participants: A Method
Willemien Sanders

It was only after I finished my PhD thesis that I learned that my research related to *production studies*. Departing from the question of ethics in documentary filmmaking, I investigated both the perspective of filmmakers and participants on ethical issues in the documentary filmmaking practice, using quantitative and qualitative research methods respectively (Sanders, 2012). For the latter, I extensively interviewed four participants who had participated in documentary film projects. The analysis of the participants' interview accounts resulted not just in an understanding of their take on ethical issues in documentary filmmaking, but also in an understanding of the complexity of their involvement in documentary film projects, which included contributing unsolicited content and the taking on of production responsibilities, such as arranging for locations and recruiting additional participants. Hence, I theorized them as co-creators, who contribute to their own representation in the resulting film. My research was firmly situated within documentary film studies and I refrained from including perspectives from media ethics and journalism ethics explicitly, arguing that the former is too general and the latter too specific. I also excluded discussion of other – more or less documentary – formats such as docusoaps and reality TV. Instead, I approached documentary filmmaking as an artistic practice of its own.

Although I have tried to use additional methods to research participation in my case studies, this did not work out for several reasons, which I will address below. This prompted me to think of yet other ways to include participants in my research. In this chapter I propose a method to do so. Below, I will first argue the role participants play in production processes and briefly discuss the context of participant research in terms of technologies of representation and self-presentation. I will then talk about the challenge of access to documentary production more extensively, discuss visual research methods, and propose a three-level method, including using both the film text and raw and test footage. With raw and test footage I mean the material not included in the final film (raw footage) as well as any footage not intended to be included, such as set-ups for interviews and location shoots, sound checks, and rehearsals (test footage). For reasons of convenience, I will refer to all this material as raw footage.

In this chapter, I will focus on documentary filmmaking, because it seems to be the least institutionalized practice (less so than docu-soaps and current affairs reports), and because single documentary projects are generally smaller than documentary and non-fiction series, which makes them more accessible at a practical level. Arguably however, the method should be applicable for other non-fiction and reality genres as well, provided material with the participant is pre-recorded (that is, raw material exists).

Participants and production studies

The proliferation of non-fiction formats includes documentary films, docu-soaps, reality TV, scripted reality, unscripted entertainment, and interactive Web documentaries, all of which often rely on the participation of 'ordinary people' in processes of representation. This proliferation has inspired attention for those contributing in front of the camera in quite different ways, most notably with respect to reality TV. Apart from an interest in the experiences of reality TV participants (Patterson, 2013; Shufeldt and Gale, 2007), there are questions about the use of ordinary people as labourforce (Hearn, 2006) and about the production of celebrity (Boyle and Kelly, 2010; Curnutt, 2009; Grindstaff, 2014).

The basis for these investigations is often the media text. Participation – be it of ordinary people, 'ordinary celebrities' (Grindstaff, 2014: 324), or celebrities – is seldom investigated as a contribution to production processes as such.[1] Hearn (2006) bases her argument about the way participants construct and mould their image within an enforced tight production framework on an analysis of the media text and a few very general and partly anonymously published quotes from participants. This can, in my view, impossibly result in a profound understanding of the meaning of participation. Production studies researchers have mainly focused on professional creators in institutional contexts (see, for instance, Caldwell, 2008; Dornfeld, 1998; Hemmingway, 2008; Mayer et al., 2009; Silverstone, 1985). Documentary participants have so far been theorized in terms of ethics, exploitation and vulnerability (see Sanders, 2012, for an extensive discussion), and in terms of performance within the documentary text (see, for instance, Lacey and McElroy, 2010; Marquis, 2013). However, (amateur) participants contribute to documentary production as do filmmakers and other professionals in the creative and media industries (Sanders, 2012). But non-fiction participants usually are not regarded as part of the institutional context in which non-fiction projects are produced, and are thus easily excluded from production studies research. Scholars who do investigate the participation of ordinary people in reality TV rely predominantly on interviews to do so (Boyle and Kelly, 2010; Grindstaff, 2009; Patterson, 2013). Although labour-intensive, interviews seem to be an obvious method if you want to find out how people think about their experiences (Galletta, 2012).

The lack of participant research in documentary studies mentioned above might be related to documentary's problematic but nonetheless long-standing claims to truth and the myth of transparency. Truth claims continue to fuel romantic ideas about participants displaying spontaneous and authentic actions and behaviour. Turner illustrates this when he discusses 'the putative ordinariness of the participants' (2010: 43) as a key issue in the critical discussion of reality TV. About this ordinariness he says: 'Not such a problem with the more documentary "fly-on-the-wall" (or what in the UK tends to classify as "docu-soap") end of the format' (2010: 43; see also Bonner, 2003), confirming the perpetual myth of participants just being themselves, going about their business, in observational documentary texts. However, to properly understand the meaning of participation in the production of culture through documentary film, the way participation is unavoidably constructed, it is necessary to include participants in empirical approaches such as production studies. My first argument, therefore, is to consider participants in documentary and in non-fiction in general as integral to the production process and hence include them in empirical studies of such production processes, rather than view them as objects for the camera's attention. A short exploration of the technologies of representation will elucidate this point.

Technologies of representation

The technology to represent – or reproduce – reality was traditionally ascribed to photography, and, Winston (1995) argues, realist painting before that. With the development of film, this claim to capturing reality transferred to the now moving images, and non-fiction started its development into the variety of forms and formats mentioned above. Specifically in documentary film, the relationship between the person behind and the person in front of the camera has, traditionally, been considered one of inequality (see, for instance, Gross et al., 1988; Rosenthal, 1988; Winston, 1988), raising a variety of questions about ethics and documentary film and filmmaking.

The technology for representing others, in the meantime, developed, to include not only video, cine film, and streaming media, but also lightweight cameras and sync sound, ever smaller video recorders, surveillance cameras, and mobile telephones and screens. In line with 'home' photography, people started to make home videos, capturing themselves and others, and sharing the material with family members and friends. Such technologies thus facilitated early forms of representation and self-presentation. The development of these technologies also facilitated groups and individuals who felt underrepresented in the mainstream media to produce and distribute their own stories. More recently, technological developments have opened up opportunities for a much wider distribution of such materials. The Internet and social media platforms as well as mobile devices make it possible to share material instantly, with people known personally but also with an unknown worldwide crowd (see for research on the latter, for instance, Hew, 2011; Lange, 2007; Leurs, 2012). The coexistence of technologies for representation and technologies for self-presentation prompts questions about how these might be related. In other words, in a society in which individuals increasingly use technologies to present themselves to the outside world – through video and through sites and technologies such as Facebook, LinkedIn, and Twitter – and in societies in which this is also demanded from them – for instance, through company websites with personal profiles – how do individuals respond to being *re*presented? And what is their role in processes of representation?

With respect to reality TV, Andrejevic (2004), relying on media reports, interviews with participants, fans, and producers, and audience surveys, places participation in relation to the creation of personality as commodity and participation as self-commodification. Curnutt (2009) used in-depth interviews, correspondence, pictures and articles to research the participation of Susie Meister in *The Real World* (1992–). He concludes, among others, that his case study suggests 'a broader compulsion to participate with the media at the level of its manufacture' (Curnutt, 2009: 15). Grindstaff (2009), based on participant-observation while functioning as production assistant and on interviews with makers and participants, concludes that there is a wide variety of motivations to participate, including a desire for celebrity or for a prize, publicity for a cause, sharing a life-changing experience, sharing information, getting acknowledged, countering stereotypes, increasing minority visibility, and experiencing something out of the ordinary. In relation to such motivations, participants consider their role and its possible interpretation by viewers (Grindstaff, 2009).

In the research discussed above, there appears a tension between understanding participation as commodification and understanding participation as an embodied experience in a complex production process. More research is needed to better understand this tension and the involvement and perspective of participants in technologies of representation. The question I am addressing here is how to research such experiences of, on the one hand, participation, which echoes an active involvement (Sanders, 2012), and on the other hand, being represented, which reflects a passive submission to the maker's whims. Previous interview-based research has indicated that documentary participants and filmmakers have complex relationships (Nash, 2009). Also, power-relationships shift: both filmmaker and participant depend on each other, though the former in fear of loss of the participant, and the latter in fear of being damaged through the representation (Nash, 2009). In addition, documentary participants contribute to projects in various ways, at various levels, and to various extents by, for instance, continuous negotiation of their disclosure and consent, by contributing unsolicited content, and by taking on production responsibilities (Sanders, 2012). As discussed above, conducting interviews has been the preferred method of data collection to capture the dynamics and complexities of documentary and reality TV participation, necessarily relying on reconstruction, memory, and reflection. Therefore, my second argument, to which the majority of this chapter is devoted, is to use visual methods rather than 'just' interviews to research participation. However, the perpetual myth of authenticity and spontaneity mentioned above underlies some of the specific challenges that surround research on participants' contributions, the main one being getting access to the production process, which I will discuss next.

The challenge of access

In order to tap into the experience of what it is like to participate in a documentary film production, it seems to make sense to collect data about this as the experience is unfolding; that is, during the period in which the participant is involved in a project. In an effort to defend film studies as a distinct discipline, Roberts calls for rigorous methodologies for production studies and for theorizing 'from within' (2011: 3). This 'from within' would ideally include production sites and shoots. In the case of documentary film, a number of challenges exist for the researcher not involved in the production process; several barriers hinder such access. These barriers include the filmmaker's pursuit of spontaneity and authenticity and the researcher's extra demands on the participant. Below, I will discuss these based on my own experiences working in the documentary field and preparing participant research for my PhD thesis.[2]

Spontaneity and authenticity

Certainly in the case of documentaries, but I would say at the core of all non-fiction programmes, is the idea that such programmes capture and include authentic and spontaneous behaviours and actions of their participants (see Turner, 2010, quoted above). Although this is very much open to question, in terms of ontological as well as epistemological issues, this idea legitimizes its production as non-fiction and invites that understanding by the audience. A reflection on the behaviour and actions involved is considered a threat to this perceived authenticity: if a participant is invited to describe, evaluate, and reflect on the experience of participating while that participation is ongoing, she might reconsider that experience and the behaviour and actions displayed in it. As a consequence, such reconsidered behaviour loses its authenticity and spontaneity and is thus perceived as less 'true' or 'real'. Allowing a researcher to enter the production ground and ask the participant to reflect on, reconsider, or even think or talk about her behaviour in any way, is thus considered a threat to the spontaneous and authentic behaviour and actions needed for a proper documentary work. Patterson observed that reality TV participants in her research had become 'learned in the art of media interviews' through their experience as participants, using 'mediaspeak or talking points' (2013: 60). This might be less the case in individual one-off documentaries, but it is plausible that respondents will increasingly consider their self-presentation and what makes proper or valid speak. The question of authenticity thus becomes increasingly complex.

Extra demands on participants

Another impediment to access to participants during production is the nature of the relationship between filmmaker and participant. Certainly in traditional documentary projects, the relationship between filmmaker and participant is considered complex, personal, intimate, and possibly fragile. Specifically in projects that address personal and private topics and experiences, documentary filmmakers aim to protect the relationship of trust they have, over time, managed to build with a participant, and are wary to let an outsider enter this relationship, for instance, by being present on set for direct or participating observation, or for interviewing the participant. The fear is that the outsider might invite a different reading of, for instance, the aims, intentions, level of honesty, and professionalism of the filmmaker, and disturb the relationship, and thus the working conditions and the project.

The challenges to access discussed above prevent, for instance, the option of participants keeping written or taped diaries or taking photographs to mediate their understanding of the experience of being filmed or interviewed for a documentary project. They also prevent the researcher from entering production sites and filming locations to observe the participant and her interactions with the filmmakers.

In addition, being involved in a documentary project can be an intense experience. Having a crew around to film can turn an everyday situation upside down and be quite demanding. In any case, for most participants it will be an exceptional situation, which demands more energy and feels more intense than any other 'ordinary' day. If at the end of such a day the participant is also asked to reflect on it, one runs the risk of fatigue getting in the way of that reflection. Rather than serving to answer the question of one's contribution to a documentary project, such data might illustrate the effect of such a day on a participant; as a consequence, such data would harm the validity of the research outcomes.

Accepting that the production spaces are off limits for observation and interrogation, alternative ways of tapping into the experiences of documentary participants are needed. Also, to prevent participant fatigue, it seems doing this retrospectively after the experience, or at least after filming is completed, when the collection of material can no longer be affected, and the anxiety associated with filming has passed, is most viable. As discussed above, in past research, documentary participants have been asked to remember experiences through interview accounts. These interviews took place shortly (Sanders, 2012) or somewhat longer (Nash, 2009) after their actual participation. To overcome some of the disadvantages of this method, such as not memorizing all events and a focus on the most salient ones, rather than asking participants to recount their experiences in general, asking them to reflect with the help of filmed material might prompt them to remember details that might otherwise get lost, or evoke and elicit thoughts and ideas in ways that interviews cannot. What I propose there is a way to 'get closer' to the production process than through mere recollection or recounting in the form of participant interviews. And that is through visual methods and, more specifically, through using both the film text and the raw footage recorded with a participant, as a more direct link to the production process.

Visual research

In ethnography, there is a long tradition of using film and video for research purposes. Buckingham sketched a 'broader "shift to the visual"', to the use of visual methods, in many disciplines (2009: 633). In various social sciences, such as education and therapy, video-assisted conversations have been used to address previous interactions or experiences (Burford and Jahoda, 2012; Pomerantz, 2005; Rowe, 2009; Welsh and Dickson, 2005). Interestingly, the first efforts in using video for therapy were conducted in TV studios, because that was where the equipment and the expertise were available (Welsh and Dickson, 2005).

Welsh and Dickson (2005) discuss the use of video-recall methods in various fields of research and in clinical practices. Here, actions such as therapy sessions or research sessions are videotaped, and the participants are then asked to view the tape and comment on what they see; these comments may relate to their own behaviour, the behaviour of others, or both. Welsh and Dickson (2005) describe this method as an extension of direct observation, with the advantage of eliciting subjective meanings and emotions, as well as notions of purpose or intent, and significance. Also, personal aspects, such as cultural identities, might be taken into consideration in understanding experiences of participants in media productions (Welsh and Dickson, 2005). Pomerantz (2005) distinguishes video-recall, aimed at 'reconstructing' earlier thoughts and feelings, from video-stimulated comments, aimed at eliciting present thoughts and ideas. She discusses the possibility of clarifying one's actions, pointing to significant elements researchers might overlook, as well as providing evidence of researchers' inferences through video-stimulated comments, as gains of this method.

While there are advantages in combining the analysis of an interaction with comments on that interaction by an interactor, several challenges face those who research individuals' accounts and narratives, specifically when these individuals are talking about previous interactions and experiences (Pomerantz, 2005). It will be difficult to determine whether comments on previous interactions relate to the interaction as it originally occurred or to the reviewing of the interaction. Also, thoughts, feelings, and interpretations, which are experienced mentally, occur in messy ways: thoughts and ideas can replace each other like waves on a beach; intuitive associations and mental leaps may be impossible to convey in coherent and linear conversational sentences. In addition, sharing thoughts and interpretations in a research setting invites making them accessible to an outsider, who might need more information about the original interaction (Pomerantz, 2005). Also, interlocutors might not share a common language. Finally, as Pomerantz (2005) mentioned, contrary to the original interaction, in a review setting, the participant knows the outcome of an interaction and might adjust thoughts and interpretations in line with the outcome. This obscures the relationship between the experience of the original interaction and the reflection on it through comments on video-replay of the action.

Notwithstanding such disadvantages and challenges, video-recall and comment methods do have something to bring to the research on documentary participation. They provide opportunities for a reflection on experiences which usually remain hidden and unaddressed, and they confront the participant with a representation of the events, avoiding a singular reliance on memory and recollection. They also provide an opportunity to include material usually discarded but potentially rich in clues about the participant's involvement with the project and the crew. In addition to the participant reflecting on the documentary itself, I therefore propose to invite the participant to review and respond to raw material shot with her. I also propose to analyse the raw material.

Pink (2001) discusses the distinction made between research film and 'creative' film: the former is supposed to be a neutral or 'objective' representation of the phenomenon being studied, which might serve as research data; the latter a narrativized and edited account, subjective to the maker's selection and construction. Raw documentary footage would be situated somewhere in between. It might include shots conceived for the film but not included, for instance, because it contains slips of the tongue and other mistakes, which provide entry points for discussing the construction of participation; these might be regarded as part of the creative footage. It might also include test footage (set-ups, rehearsals), including negotiations and extra-textual interactions between participant and filmmaker(s), which might in turn refer to interactions not recorded. Such footage might be regarded as research data. Both however, as Pink (2001) argues, might serve as research material: 'In the broadest sense a video is "ethnographic" when its viewer(s) judge that it represents information of ethnographic interest' (p. 79). Raw footage will provide opportunities for the participant to recount interactions and other elements of her participation in the project and for the researcher to ask questions about these. Previous research suggests that participants 'relived' experiences while watching them a few days later as they were displayed on video (Lingel and Naaman, 2012). Similarly, reviewing taped experiences might help 'get closer' to the original experiences than just talking about them in an interview format or on the basis of the final film. This brings me to my three-level method for studying documentary participation.

A three-level method for documentary participant studies

In trying to understand the nature and meaning of participation in documentary production, one needs to somehow capture the participant's thoughts, ideas, and reflection on the experience. Given the media-saturated world we live in, Holliday argues for examination of both text and experience to study any culture: '[But] more important than either of these is the interplay of both with each other' (2000: 509), as the 'consumption' of cultural texts informs our understanding of our identity and in turn informs the production of such texts. I argue that to understand documentary participation, studying the experience as well as texts capturing that experience is desirable. And although Buckingham (2009) points to the need to distinguish between audience research and media production research, this research seems to be in between, as participants are contributors to creative production and thus co-creators, but only partially, with respect to their contribution (Sanders, 2012); for the remaining parts, they are audiences. Their responses to the resulting film, however, might provide powerful insights into their perspectives on the experience. The use of both raw footage and the resulting film will encourage the participant's talk about and reflection on the experience, assuming that raw footage provides an alternative form of access to the production process. Because raw footage might be messy and there might be a lot of it, a selection might be made based on a rationale relevant to the research. I propose a three-level method to investigate participants' experiences: video comments to the film; analysis of raw footage; and video comments to raw footage in interaction with the researcher.

Video comments on the film

The finished film presents, among others, a selection of all the material shot with a participant, her actions and interactions with the filmmaker, and her contribution within the context of the whole narrative, possibly intercut with selected material with other participants. This is the represented interaction, the interaction as represented by the filmmaker through the film. This represented interaction constitutes the public face of the participant, the one that is accessible for the audience. The participant will have an idea about this representation, which might be quite nuanced. As discussed above, a specific motivation might underlie the participant's contribution. This representation itself, however, does not suffice to address the experience of the participant in the production process. Watching the whole film rather than just scenes containing the represented interaction leaves open the option of other material being, or becoming, relevant to the perspective of the participant. Therefore, watching the whole film might be a fruitful experience to try and understand the represented interaction and how the participant relates to it.

Wood (2007) developed a method to describe the various ways in which female viewers of daytime television talk shows interacted with the television text. She recorded the responses of these viewers, produced as they were watching. Wood (2007) differentiates three ways in which these women spontaneously interacted with and related to the content of the programme. She distinguishes primary responses, which include the use of second-person pronouns, directed at a participant, as well as 'minimal responses' such as 'yeh, mhm', and the completion of the sentence of a studio participant; secondary responses, which interrogate and comment on the broadcast text; and tertiary responses, which invoke personal experiences, and relate the text to oneself. Although documentaries are not aimed at a sense of interaction with the audience at the text level the way that talk shows are, I consider Wood's a worthwhile method to elicit and invite an initial response to one's representation within a film. This text-in-action method might be used with a participant as 'audience' of the programme she participated in. Pink pointed to the need to not just elicit comments, but to engage in dialogue with the respondent to try and understand how 'informants situate themselves as viewers of the footage' (2001: 89). Hence, a dialogue might be conducted with the participant to understand how she relates to the represented interaction. However, to prevent participant fatigue, I propose to limit this first level to video comments and possibly a few prompts to keep them going, and to reserve interaction with the participant for the third level, discussed below.

Investigating the participant's response to the viewing of the film she participated in and inviting her to comment out loud hopefully elicits her initial subjective understanding of her appearance in the programme and her participation in the project. Specifically, it invites reflection on her own participation and contribution to the narrative as a whole. Viewing the film at home rather than in a research setting might further facilitate this. Apart from the represented interaction, material generally exists that remains unused or was never intended to be used, which I have described above as raw footage. This material might contain many clues for further discussing and understanding the participant's involvement in the documentary project. The second level of my method therefore includes analysing raw footage.

Analysing raw footage

Any media-production comes into being in a process of decision-making and selection: what will be included (images, text, artefacts, audio, video, links), to which extent, and in which configuration? In the production of media of representation, there usually is a discrepancy between what is recorded and what is eventually used in the film. Raw material concerns images and sounds surrounding the edited takes included in the media text, including 'mistakes' and successive takes. Test material might include rehearsals and set-ups. The interactions captured here might be referred to as the original interaction, as it is not represented and not edited. Such material can include clues to the negotiations between media-maker(s) and participant with respect to their collaboration and the participant's contribution. Negotiations might concern issues of disclosure, representation, and address; they might concern re-enactments, interview questions, and scenes to be included or excluded; they might include discussions of authenticity, spontaneity, performance and motivation; they might concern production practicalities; they might include clues for understanding the relationship between filmmaker and participant. A careful analysis of this material might give insight in all these aspects as well as raise further questions about the involvement of the participant in the production process, as it might refer to interactions and experiences not recorded. That is one reason to include it in this method. However, combining levels one and two provides for a third level. Here the participant views and comments on the raw footage or a selection thereof, in interaction with the researcher, who then has the opportunity to pose questions and prompts.

Video comment on the raw footage

The third level I propose consists of participant video comments to raw footage in interaction with the researcher. This might take the shape of a dialogue or an interview. Interview accounts are, after all, constructed in interaction; it is in the mutual response of interviewer and interviewee that narratives are constructed and meaning is created (Holstein and Gubrium, 1995; Rapley, 2004).

After having analysed the footage, the researcher now invites the participant to comment on the original interaction represented in the raw footage and respond to further questions, queries, and prompts. Comments and responses to questions and prompts together construct a rich account of and reflection on the experience of participating in a documentary project. This way, a level is added which allows for further analysis and understanding of the experience of the participant in documentary production, as raw footage will include specific clues for understanding the participant's involvement in and contribution to the project. The researcher might decide to limit this level to outtakes of the raw footage based on the analysis at level two, or some other rationale relevant to the research. As discussed above, the interaction with the researcher in the form of questions, queries, and prompts is reserved for this level, to prevent participant fatigue.

Recoding the research

Levels one and three of the method proposed here include the participant and researcher watching material. Both levels might be recorded for research purposes. Video rather than audio recording allows for the analysis of the interaction and dialogue between researcher and respondent as well as of their body language. Specifically because the participant is watching video material in which she is featured, and can point to or even imitate behaviour displayed in the video material, it seems valuable to video-record the reviews.

Conclusion

In this chapter I have argued for the inclusion of documentary participants in production studies research. I have proposed a three-level method for researching documentary participation, including video comments on the documentary film, an analysis of raw footage, and video comments on raw footage in interaction with the researcher.

The method proposed here brings with it a number of challenges. First of all, it seems more common to have respondents or informants produce creative material as data for reflection on experiences or perspectives (see, for instance, Luttrell and Chalfen, 2010; Packard, 2008). Indeed, there is a need, as Buckingham (2009) argues, to reflect on the research methods and materials themselves, to try and understand how the configuration of the research enables respondents to speak and share, while acknowledging that in the end, the research is the researcher's work – as it should be.

Second, the raw footage I propose to use was never recorded to be included in a research project such as the one proposed here. This invites practical and ethical considerations. On a practical level, I believe many production studies projects depend on the collaboration of the community under investigation. Some researchers might be able and willing to conduct participating observation, but many researchers will not be able or might not be willing to do this. So collaboration and consent are necessary and arguably desirable. Hopefully, the idea of using raw footage is considered less risky than having someone observe a shoot. In the digital age we live in, it might be necessary to arrange beforehand the safeguarding of the material with the makers, before it is deleted. Of course, sensitive material might be included in the raw footage, but it is up to the researcher to convince those involved that it is not her aim to judge behaviour on an individual level but to understand what is going on. These practical issues make the method more suitable for smaller projects, such as individual documentary films, than for more institutionalized practices, such as documentary and reality TV series.

On an ethical level, there is the need to negotiate the use of raw material with both the legal and moral owners, and get their explicit consent to use it in the research context. In addition, as the research report forms another form of representation, this time of the documentary participant as research respondent, a member check seems desirable to allow the represented to comment on the representation and correct blatant mistakes and omissions. Such research practices have been used in the social sciences for many years. Also, to protect individual respondents, research might be published on the basis of anonymity. Finally, there is the question of what this raw material might be exactly, and how, if necessary, a selection might be made and accounted for. This will have to be addressed at the level of individual research projects.

Despite these considerations, I believe including participants in production studies and including raw footage in our research methods will provide an additional opportunity to investigate and understand the complexities of documentary film production. The material exists and is, at least in theory, readily available. Although it is important to not understand this material as representing any kind of unmediated reality or to be comprehensive or transparent in any way, despite its possibly spontaneous character or lack of immediate purpose (Buckingham,

2009), it does provide rich data for studying documentary participation, and is potentially full of clues about the practice of media making and the involvement of 'ordinary people'. I therefore believe using it would enrich our research into documentary production and, possibly, other non-fiction genres.

Notes

1. Grindstaff (2014) uses the concept of 'ordinary celebrity' to describe the celebrity of non-professional actors whose 'fame' tends to be temporary and related to a specific programme or event rather than it being sustained and intertextual.
2. These observations are based on conversations with documentary filmmakers and producers, held both formally and informally, over the course of the past 15 years or so. Whether they are valid for other non-fiction productions remains to be seen.

References

Andrejevic, M. (2004) *Reality TV: The Work of Being Watched* (Lanham, MD: Rowman & Littlefield Publishers).

Bonner, F. (2003) *Ordinary Television: Analyzing Popular TV* (London: Sage Publications Ltd.).

Boyle, R. and Kelly, L. W. (2010) 'The celebrity entrepreneur on television: Profile, politics and power.' *Celebrity Studies*, 1(3), 334–350.

Buckingham, D. (2009) '"Creative" visual methods in media research: Possibilities, problems and proposals.' *Media, Culture & Society*, 31(4), 633–652.

Burford, B. and Jahoda, A. (2012) 'Do video reviews of therapy sessions help people with mild intellectual disabilities describe their perceptions of cognitive behaviour therapy?' *Journal of Intellectual Disability Research*, 56(2), 179–190.

Caldwell, J. T. (2008) *Production Culture: Industrial Reflexivity and Critical Practice in Film and Television* (Durham, NC: Duke University Press).

Curnutt, H. (2009) '"A fan crashing the party": Exploring reality-celebrity in MTV's Real World franchise.' *Television & New Media*, 10(3), 251–266.

Dornfeld, B. (1998) *Producing Public Television, Producing Public Culture* (Princeton, NJ: Princeton University Press).

Galletta, A. (2012) *Mastering the Semi-structured Interview and Beyond: From Research Design to Analysis and Publication* (New York: New York University Press).

Grindstaff, L. (2009) 'Self-serve celebrity: The production of ordinariness and the ordinariness of production in reality television' in V. Mayer, M. J. Banks, and J. T. Caldwell (eds), *Production Studies: Cultural Studies of Media Industries* (pp. 71–86) (New York: Routledge).

Grindstaff, L. (2014) 'DI(t)Y, reality-style: The cultural work of ordinary celebrity' in L. Ouellette (ed.), *A Companion to Reality Television* (pp. 324–344) (Hoboken, NJ: John Wiley & Sons).

Gross, L., Katz, J. S. and Ruby, J. (eds) (1989) *Image Ethics: The Moral Rights of Subjects in Photographs, Film, and Television* (New York: Oxford University Press).

Hearn, A. (2006) 'John, a 20-year-old Boston native with a great sense of humour: On the spectacularization of the self and the incorporation of identity in the age of reality television.' *International Journal of Media & Cultural Politics* 2(2), 131–147.

Hemmingway, E. (2008) *Into the Newsroom: Exploring the Digital Production of Regional Television News* (London, New York: Routledge).

Hew, K. F. (2011) 'Students' and teachers' use of Facebook.' *Computers in Human Behavior* 27(2), 662–676.

Holliday, R. (2000) 'We've been framed: Visualising methodology.' *Sociological Review* 48(4), 503–521.

Holstein, J. A. and Gubrium, J. F. (1995) *The Active Interview* (Thousand Oaks, CA: Sage Publications).

Lacey, S. and McElroy, R. (2010) 'Real performance: Ordinary people and the "problem" of acting in constructed documentaries.' *Studies in Documentary Film* 4(3), 253–266.

Lange, P. G. (2007) 'Publicly private and privately public: Social networking on YouTube.' *Journal of Computer-Mediated Communication* 13(1), 361–380.

Leurs, K. H. A. (2012) *Digital Passages: Moroccan-Dutch youths performing diaspora, gender and youth cultural identities across digital space*. PhD thesis (Utrecht: Utrecht University).

Lingel, J. and Naaman, M. (2012) 'You should have been there, man: Live music, DIY content and online communities.' *New Media & Society* 14(2), 332–349.

Luttrell, W. and Chalfen, R. (2010) 'Lifting up voices of participatory visual research.' *Visual Studies* 25(3), 197–200.

Marquis, E. (2013) 'Conceptualizing documentary performance.' *Studies in Documentary Film* 7(1), 45–60.

Mayer, V., Banks, M. J., and Caldwell, J. T. (eds) (2009) *Production Studies: Cultural Studies of Media Industries* (New York: Routledge).

Nash, K. (2009) *Beyond the Frame: A Study in Observational Documentary Ethics*, PhD thesis (Armidale: University of New England).

Packard, J. (2008) '"I'm gonna show you what it's really like out here": The power and limitation of participatory visual methods.' *Visual Studies* 23(1), 63–77.

Patterson, N. (2013) *Focusing on Reality TV: Exploring Women's Participation in Talent-based Competition Shows*, PhD thesis (Simon Fraser University).

Pink, S. (2001) *Doing Visual Ethnography: Images, Media and Representation in Research* (Thousand Oaks, CA: Sage Publications).

Pomerantz, A. (2005) 'Using participants' video-stimulated comments to complement analyses of interactional practices' in H. te Molder and J. Potter (eds), *Conversation and Cognition* (pp. 93–113) (Cambridge University Press).

Rapley, T. (2004) 'Interviews' in C. Seale et al. (eds), *Qualitative Research Practice* (pp. 15–33) (London: Sage Publications).

Roberts, G. (2011) 'Opening Pandora's (Black) Box: Towards a methodology of production studies.' *Wide Screen* 3(1), 14 [accessed 23 January 2013]. Available from: http://widescreenjournal.org/index.php/journal/article/view/14.

Rosenthal, A. (ed.) (1988) *New Challenges for Documentary* (Berkeley, CA: University of California Press).

Rowe, V. C. (2009) 'Using video-stimulated recall as a basis for interviews: Some experiences from the field.' *Music Education Research* 11(4), 425–437.

Sanders, W. (2012) *Participatory Spaces: Negotiating Cooperation and Conflict in Documentary Projects*, PhD thesis (Utrecht: Utrecht University).

Shufeldt, M. and Gale, K. (2007) 'Under the (glue) gun: Containing and constructing reality in home makeover TV.' *Popular Communication* 5(4), 263–282.

Silverstone, R. (1985) *Framing Science: The Making of a BBC Documentary* (London: BFI Publishing).

Turner, G. (2010) *Ordinary People and the Media: The Demotic Turn* (Los Angeles: Sage Publications).

Welsh, D. P. and Dickson, J. W. (2005) 'Video-recall procedures for examining subjective understanding in observational data.' *Journal of Family Psychology* 19(1), 62–71.

Winston, B. (1988) 'The tradition of the victim in Griersonian documentary' in A. Rosenthal (ed.), *New Challenges for Documentary* (pp. 269–287) (Berkeley, CA: University of California Press).

Winston, B. (1995) *Claiming the Real: The Documentary Film Revisited* (London: British Film Institute).

Wood, H. (2007) 'The mediated conversational floor: An interactive approach to audience reception analysis.' *Media, Culture & Society* 29(1), 75–103.

14
A Cultural Biography of Application Software

Frederik Lesage

> Photoshop's goal isn't entertaining unless you think the national pastime of bitching about Photoshop is a sport. Photoshop has no points or leaderboards because Photoshop is a tool and the perception of tools is that you must be willing to supply blood, sweat, and tears in order to acquire the skills to become any good at using them.
> Bullshit.
>
> (Lopp, 2012)

Lopp's dilemma

In a blog post from 2012, Michael Lopp compares the Valve-designed videogame Portal to Adobe Systems' digital-imaging application software Photoshop. While both appear to be very different kinds of digital media objects, Lopp argues that they share certain characteristics in terms of user experience and that because of these shared traits designers of Photoshop stand to learn how to improve its user experience by studying Portal's design. In the above quote from the post, Lopp rather colourfully takes issue with the argument that, because Photoshop is generally classified as a tool, it somehow requires a different kind of engagement on the part of its users from the kind of engagement required by games. By challenging this classificatory distinction, Lopp concludes: 'game designers and application designers might exist in different universes, but there is no reason one universe can't teach the other' (Lopp, 2012).

While the following paper does not deal with questions of user experience design that are Lopp's principle concern, his comparison of Photoshop and Portal serves as a useful starting point to introduce a reflection on how cultural categories and practices mediate (and are mediated by) things over time. Photoshop's status as a 'tool' rather than as a 'game' touches on the more fundamental problem of how creative practitioners are enabled and constrained by classificatory orders of their materials and practices. At stake in 'Lopp's dilemma' (as I would like to refer to it in this chapter) is the challenge of understanding how, and to what extent, the order of software objects enables and constrains media work. It is entirely possible that the reason why so little academic attention has been paid to software for media work like Photoshop is that its status as a tool within fields of cultural production has never been scrutinized. Highlighting the contingency of such a categorization may help to correct this oversight. In this chapter I set out to demonstrate how cultural biographies of software serve as a useful conceptual and methodological framework for an investigation of application software for media work, specifically a case study of Adobe Photoshop's categorization as a tool.

Biographies of things: practices and categories

As an approach, cultural biographies of application software work as a kind of infrastructural inversion (Bowker and Star, 2002). They encourage the researcher to study 'taken-for-granted' things with a view of examining how they change over time. Anthropological approaches to the cultural biography of things (Kopytoff, 1986) have been adapted to conduct media and software ethnographies (Silverstone and Haddon, 1996; Lash and Lury, 2007; Pollock and Williams, 2008; Lesage 2013). In this chapter I set out to develop the biographical approach specifically as a means of examining the mediation of categories and practices related to software for media work. This approach is of particular value in our case because it emphasizes how our understanding of software should not limit itself to the dominant or taken-for-granted categories and practices associated with it. What drives the biographical account is not, therefore, to ascertain the reason for a particular software application's success or failure but to better understand the politics of value (Appadurai, 1986) that shape (and are shaped by) software objects. My objective is not to wade into the ongoing debates around the ontology of things. I will heed Bijker and Pinch's (2012: xxvi) recommendation to lean towards 'ontological agnosticism' regarding the technologies under examination leaving the actors to draw the boundaries between technical and social instead of assuming that these boundaries 'are pre-given and static' (Bijker and Pinch, 2012: xviii).

Kopytoff's own approach to the study of things depends on a dialectical back-and-forth between ideal categories that unfold 'processually'

(Kopytoff, 1982: 69) instead of 'an all-or-none state of being' (Kopytoff, 1982: 73). Assigning a cultural category to a thing (for example, assigning Photoshop to the category of tool) must therefore be understood as a phase in Photoshop's existence that can be supplanted by another phase. Where the following approach differs somewhat from Kopytoff's is that it emphasizes how the meaning of a category can itself shift over time. Positioning things into different cultural categories is part of creating and maintaining social order (Couldry, 2012) including what stands at the margins of said order (Star, 2010). Much of the way in which this classification takes place should be understood as part of contingent socio-cultural processes of differentiation or what is sometimes referred to as 'boundary making'. Too often in research on cultural and media work, technological order and transformation are conceptualized as exogenous forces that influence cultural fields or media industries. The highly influential Production of Culture perspective, for example, emphasizes how technology can 'profoundly destabilize and create new opportunities' (Peterson and Anand, 2004: 314). Such an emphasis overlooks the ongoing and uneven processes of mediation involved in negotiating endogenous *and* exogenous technological forces at the symbolic and material levels.

Categories, as Lucy Suchman puts it, have politics. It is at the intersection of categories and practices that one is able to contest or reify these politics. This is especially relevant to our understanding of creativity and art:

> One could imagine...a system of painting that trained artists to follow a 'simple' scheme of primary colors. But our sense of artistry in a field is precisely the ability to move, in more and less articulable ways, effectively through the circumstances in which one finds oneself. This is not done through reductions but through complex forms of highly skilled practice, involving an ability to bring past experience to bear in creative ways upon an unfolding situation. (Suchman, 1994: 185)

Discrepancies inevitably appear between ideal classificatory orders and the actual order of categories shared between practitioners. For example, Jonathan Sterne (2007) shows how the theoretical distinctions between 'instrument' and 'medium' for the study of sound and music are difficult to sustain in the practical settings in which actual musicians practice music making, especially in the case of digital sound production. One should also be careful to avoid the assumption that practices escape any kind of classificatory order. Nick Couldry (2012: 44–46) shows how certain practices can serve as anchors that reinforce a particular order for other practices and argues for a more considered approach to categories and how they order practice in the media (Couldry, 2012: 60–63). The way in which value is attributed to/through categories does not stem from one singular source but is heterogeneous. To examine the texture of a category and the politics of its articulation entails tracking how practices are entangled in these categories. One must therefore ask how categories are generated, maintained, and undermined through practices within different and at times overlapping orders of worth.

The primary qualities of a 'tool' that differentiate it from something else, how we might define its ideal category, are its functional qualities (Feenberg, 2005: 211). The source of Lopp's dilemma, as I have characterized it here, is whether acquiring such qualities through practice requires a 'supply of blood, sweat, and tears' or some other particular intensity and quality of affective and cognitive engagement on the part of cultural subjects.

The framework deployed for examining how these socio-technical designs and users' interpretations of these designs come together or diverge is based on the concept of 'double articulation' signifying that the cultural value of application software lies 'both in its meaning as an object...and in its content' (Silverstone, 1994: 123). This framework allows us to address what Wajcman and Jones' call the 'tripled dimensionality' of modern media technologies:

(1) the social shaping of the design of communications technologies 'as technologies' (which may entail the role of media organizations and policy);
(2) the recognition of the role of communications technologies as 'mediums' *pace* medium theory and STS *with their own situational social consequences*; and
(3) the recognition of discrete cultural forms (such as television programmes) borne by communications/media technologies. (Wajcman and Jones, 2012: 687)

The articulations are part of a continuing trajectory that includes what one 'does' with application software for media work (including, in this case, the images produced using Photoshop) and how this 'doing' is subsequently represented and validated. To return to Lopp's dilemma, classifying Photoshop as a 'game' intuitively seems to 'transgress' or 'misunderstand' its proper place within the dominant implicit categorical order of cultural production. This intuition arguably stems from the way in which Photoshop and Portal both fall under the category of application software but that Photoshop falls under the subcategory of 'office productivity software' (analogous to a word processing application like Microsoft Word) while Portal falls under 'multimedia content'. The categorical distinction between the two is therefore based on occluding dynamic subject-object relations in favour of a specific set of relations: the former privileging production, the latter consumption. It is only through an analytics of mediation that one can look past these types of occlusions (Born, 2010: 87–88). For example, a biography of Photoshop that conforms to the conventional understanding of its categorical order and proper use through practice would likely constitute an account of its design and use as a tool for digital imaging by focusing only on its place within media production workflows. Adobe Photoshop is widely understood to be the de facto standard for digital imaging across most fields that require such work. The following account does address digital imaging as practice but it also examines two other overlapping practices in an attempt to seek out the multiple and potentially contradictory articulations of Photoshop as a tool by studying its dual roles as a thing 'to be consumed' and as 'the means – as media – for the continued stimulation of consumption' (Silverstone and Haddon, 1996: 45).

My investigation into the mediation of categories and practices that are part of Photoshop's biography does not simply address customization through use or a people's preference for one application over another. Instead, it examines the slippages between, on the one hand, articulations of the category of 'tool', and on the other hand, the practices through which Photoshop appropriates, and is appropriated by, different cultural practitioners who convert/are converted back into collective representations of media work. While a more detailed examination of each of these practices (or any other relevant practice, for that matter) is beyond the scope of this chapter, the following sections provide an overview of imaging, playing, and developing Photoshop. The choice of these three practices stems from a media ethnography of Photoshop undertaken between 2011 and 2014. The initial fieldwork included semi-structured interviews with twenty-three practitioners and document analysis with the objective of generating a long-term picture of Photoshop's biography. The research design for the interviews used purposive sampling to identify people who worked in a wide range of different disciplines and who used Photoshop over an extended period of time (in twenty-two of the twenty-three cases, for more than ten years). The interview guide was designed to elicit a semi-autobiographical account of the participants' experiences of using Photoshop over the course of their career. The document analysis focused mainly on Photoshop's representation in the media and in technical documentation. The population of documents selected included magazine reviews and discussion forums (see Lesage, 2014) as well as textbooks and instruction manuals. Interview transcripts and collected documentation were subsequently thematically analysed in order to identify certain themes running through the material (see Lesage, in press, for details). A second phase of the research involved participant observation of using Photoshop in personal and pedagogical contexts that were identified over the course of the thematic analysis (for an example of the results of this second phase, see Lesage and Smirnova, 2015).

Imaging

The original version of Photoshop, designed by Thomas and John Knoll in the late 1980s, first shipped commercially as part of software accompanying scanners designed by Barneyscan. While Photoshop's name implies that it was initially designed specifically with photographers in mind, a more accurate account of its reason for being is as a tool for imaging. Imaging is a practice that, much like broadcasting in relation to television (Williams, 1990), predates Photoshop by many years. While a comprehensive history of imaging is not possible here, for the purposes of this study I define it as the practice of producing reproducible visual material for the purposes of its circulation and/or commoditization. As personal computers gained popularity in the workplace in the 1970s and 1980s, it became clear that these new technologies could play a significant role in *digital* imaging. But without a single standard digital image format and with such a wide variety of disciplines practicing some form of imaging it seemed unlikely that one tool could be able to accommodate everyone.

The Knoll brothers, one a graduate student in computer science and the other employed by Industrial Light and Magic to help develop special effects for film and television, originally set out to improve how raster images could be displayed on a computer screen. With the help of Adobe Systems, one of the leading technology companies in desktop publishing at the time, the brothers redesigned the application in order for it to be used as a means of preparing digital images for print (Pfiffner, 2003: 118–119). Rather than attempting to be a tool for one specific field of media work, Photoshop was initially designed to classify digital imaging as a practice that included: (1) creating digital special effects on a still screen image with a personal computer (see also Manovich,

2013: 124–147) for more details); (2) creating, editing, and outputting images for print with a personal computer; and (3) to be a photographer's 'darkroom on the desktop' (Adobe Systems Incorporated, 1990:1). As the original *Adobe Photoshop User Guide* stated:

> ...the Adobe Photoshop program is extraordinary photo-retouching, image-editing, and color painting software for pixel-based images. Whether you are a professional or a novice, with the Adobe Photoshop program you'll quickly be able to enhance, retouch, and compose scanned images, original artwork, and other pixel-based graphics. (Adobe Systems Incorporated, 1990)

The metaphor used to articulate the interface for dealing with such a wide variety of features was the 'toolbox'. There was a toolbox that contained painting tools, one for editing tools, the type tool, the fill tool, etc. Photoshop was designed as more of an open-ended collection of features or commands, each one a different tool.

Because Photoshop's own version of imaging was so broad and so conducive to the circulation and absorption of additional functions, it was able to weather the multiple transformations that imaging itself would undergo over the following years. Under its 'feature mountains' (Fuller, 2001), one could find in the more recent versions of Photoshop the sedimentation left behind by multiple 'paradigm shifts' and 'revolutions' in digital imaging in the form of features and commands including some for desktop publishing, digital video, 3D animation, and web design. As an artifact of imaging over the past quarter century, Photoshop was a testament to the explosive growth and ubiquity of digital imaging as a consumer-oriented practice in creative disciplines or industries like photography, graphic design, prepress, animation, scientific visualization, videogame design, and web design.

Playing

Although Photoshop was not designed as a game, some Photoshop enthusiasts created their own games based on using Photoshop. Referred to as 'Photoshop Tennis' or 'Photoshop Battles' (for example, see https://www.reddit.com/r/photoshopbattles/), These types of games were typically played online with the use of mailing lists or discussion forums and involved producing a kind of 'cadavre exquis' by circulating an image between players who modify the original image through a digital imaging application.

As one practitioner interviewed for the research put it, Photoshop Tennis in the early 2000s represented a significant form of entertainment for those interested in digital imaging prior to the explosive growth of social media:

> ...there was a time when there [were] some real expert Photoshop people. People so good that the rest of the Internet would wait for Friday morning where they would pair two Photoshop experts from around the world in two different places and they would say: 'You start!' (H.A.)

These games served to build cultural reference points for demonstrations of technical skill and expertise. So much so that Photoshop Tennis was used at the turn of the millennium as proof of Photoshop's status as the global 'common language' (Shreve, 2001) among designers. The name of the game would soon be rebranded as Layer Tennis (referring to the way in which a raster image in Photoshop is separated into layers to enable editing). The change was more than likely in response to Adobe's reticence towards the use of the term Photoshop to refer to anything other than their branded product. Adobe acquired notoriety for jealously protecting its intellectual property and the trademark for Photoshop was no exception:

> Trademarks must never be used as slang terms.
>
> Correct: Those who use Adobe® Photoshop® software to manipulate images as a hobby see their work as an art form.
>
> Incorrect: A photoshopper sees his hobby as an art form.
>
> Incorrect: My hobby is photoshopping.
>
> (Adobe Systems Incorporated, 2015a)

In 2009, Adobe partnered with Coudal Partners, a Chicago-based design firm credited with inventing Photoshop Tennis (as is often the case, the question of who should be credited for inventing the game is unresolved; Clarkson, 2004: 2–3), to offer an Adobe-sanctioned version of the game in an attempt to promote their new cloud-based service Creative Cloud (which included Photoshop, see next section below). As stated on the official Layer Tennis website:

> Creative Cloud is the weapon of choice for Layer Tennis players and creative people everywhere. (Coudal Partners Incorporated, 2015)

Much like posting product reviews of Photoshop (see Lesage, 2014), games like Layer Tennis simultaneously represented an opportunity for Adobe to configure the kind of consumer it wanted for its product while also affording a space for people who used Photoshop to 'convert' and 'incorporate' it publicly, connecting individuals to wider contexts of 'shared meanings and the claims and counterclaims of status and belonging' (Silverstone and Haddon, 1996: 65). An examination of how these affordances for play could be articulated as a form of pedagogy may help to better understand the dynamics of the articulation between play and Photoshop-as-tool.

Interviews and participant observation conducted over the course of the fieldwork yielded a second, less visible and more individual form of play. Interviewees related playing with Photoshop an opportunity to explore its potential outside the confines of the everyday workflow. Play therefore enabled one to shed 'one kind of order and to grasp a different reality defined by its own rules and terms of trade and action' (Silverstone, 1999: 60).

One topic that received considerable attention in the document analysis and interviews was the significance of teaching and learning as part of using Photoshop (see Lesage and Smirnova, 2015, for more details). Teaching and learning Photoshop is a massive industry in itself in which one finds large corporate players like Pearson as well as relatively smaller players such as Lynda.com. There are conferences, forms of accreditation through certification, and international associations all built around teaching and learning the application. Although much of the learning encountered in my interviews constituted what might be described as self-directed, informal learning on the part of practitioners – using books, online tutorials and personal projects to develop skills – teaching and learning Photoshop in more formal contexts was also a fairly common practice. Some applied their knowledge of Photoshop to train friends or family or organized workshops in their workplace. When describing his approach to teaching others to use Photoshop, one male designer affirmed the importance of play as part of learning:

> I think it's great to play. To really use it as an opportunity to do lots of silly stuff, make loads of mistakes and everything and just to take down any kinds of inhibitions that might be there about the program itself. (G.G.)

While not understood as a game per se, this type of open-ended play with Photoshop was not only a form of release but also a necessary step in the development of a more complete and skilful deployment of Photoshop's extensive features as part of a practitioner's work:

> (T.R.): You can tell an amateur just based on the work they produce in Photoshop.
>
> Interviewer: In what sense?
>
> (T.R.): Like they used all the special effects on their default settings, something like that. Bevel, emboss, all the standard settings, they haven't actually gotten in there and played around with it and found something that doesn't look like it's just canned straight out of Photoshop.

Play, therefore, helped establish distinctions between work and leisure, between being 'on the clock' and experimenting during one's spare time, between the serious and the enthusiastic. Play was in fact a significant practice for teaching and learning Photoshop-as-tool but also possibly one that was not explicitly recognized as such. Playing Photoshop was essential to be qualified as a proficient practitioner, but not a sufficient condition. Recognizing the importance of play as a means of developing Photoshop skills sheds a different light on the significance of games like Layer Tennis and Adobe's more recent efforts to foster this type of structured collective play. The growth of the Web since the early 1990s and the subsequent popularity of social media platforms represented a new way for practitioners to collectively develop and impart their skills including through play. Adobe's sponsorship of Layer Tennis could be understood as part of a larger social media strategy to commoditize and control how practitioners shared their work and their techniques online. A more ambitious push in this direction involved Adobe's purchase of the social networking platform Behance in 2012. The official announcement explicitly referred their objective to create a 'creative meritocracy' that would ensure that creative 'tools [were] integrated with the way we discover, inspire and collaborate' to ensure that creative work was 'organized, properly credited, and more easily discovered' (Behance Network Team, 2012). Anyone interested in registering to play Layer Tennis could now do so by creating a Behance account.

Developing

Having examined both imaging and play as practices in a processual account of Photoshop's biography as tool, I now turn to an overview of

Photoshop's role in the practice of developing (a practice that includes designing and marketing).

The first Adobe-licensed version of Photoshop shipped in 1990. Adobe would eventually purchase the rights to the software from the Knoll brothers in 1995 for $34.5 million, cementing the brothers' place in the pantheon of software developers who found (a relative amount of) fame and fortune from the sale of their design.

A significant aspect that shaped Photoshop's role as a tool of/for development was that its original design included 'plug-in filters'. This feature meant that users could install additional tools developed by third-party developers onto their own version of Photoshop. Adobe also released Photoshop's software development kit (SDK) as a way to foster the development of more 'plug-ins'. This design was in keeping with the logic of an ever-expanding toolkit of features and commands in an attempt to cover as broad a definition of digital imaging as possible (see 'imaging' above). Thirteen major versions were released since Photoshop's launch under Adobe as well as numerous incremental improvements (for example, the significant Photoshop 5.5) and the release of plug-ins and peripherals.

For more than two decades, Adobe Photoshop was sold to consumers, like most consumer-oriented application software at the time, as a shrink-wrapped individual license agreement. While Photoshop was undoubtedly one of Adobe's flagship products, it was by no means its only one. By 2003 Adobe's development strategy shifted to bundling their creative productivity applications like Photoshop, Illustrator, and InDesign into a 'Creative Suite', thereby encouraging customers who used different products to also purchase and use other Adobe applications for their work. This strategy was an attempt to produce what could be characterized as an 'insurrectionist' position – creating an operating system within the user's personal computer's operating system. The model of the suite created a nesting doll effect by connecting multiple feature toolkits together.

But just as Adobe continued to develop an ever larger and more elaborate structure around its digital imaging tool, a number of significant transformations in the broader information and communication technologies industry led to important changes in the practice of developing application software itself. These interrelated transformations included: (1) the continuing growth in popularity of software-as-a-service (SaaS) as a software business model; (2) considerable technical improvements to how one could access digital resources via Internet on a continuous or semi-continuous basis (what is often referred to as 'cloud-computing'); (3) the shift away from desktop computers as the dominant computational hardware for general consumers; and lastly (4) the birth of a new cultural category for software known as the 'app':

> In a time of location-based media capable of receiving content, processing content, and sending content anywhere at any time, apps have become synonymous with mobility and the ubiquity of computing – to a larger extent than the hardware devices that carry them. (Matviyenko, 2014: xviii)

With the launch of Apple's App Store in 2008 and the subsequent growth of similar platforms for purchasing and downloading apps, developing apps (and 'crowdsourcing' app developers; see Dyer-Witherford, 2014) surfaced as a key concern among large consumer-oriented tech firms. The emerging definition for 'app' represented a new articulation for the category of application software that included subcategories like productivity tools, games, and social media.

In 2013, Adobe Systems announced that it would no longer sell individual perpetual licenses for Photoshop beyond the most recent version as part of its Creative Suite 6. Instead, consumers would gain access to Adobe's suite of creative applications through a new online 'ecosystem' called the 'Creative Cloud'. A letter to stockholders from 2010 by Adobe's directorship already foreshadowed the shift to a SaaS approach for the Creative Suite: 'as the line between designers and developers blurs, demand is growing for a new generation of tools and services to make it easier for the two roles to work together' (Narayen et al., 2010).

When examined from the perspective of its status as a tool for digital imaging, the shift resembled a regular software upgrade: there were few significant changes to the interface with similar menus with nearly identical features, Photoshop also remained a distinct application that could be accessed either individually or as part of a suite of other more-or-less familiar applications.

It would be unwise to claim to know what the long-term implications of this transformation will be with the events still so recent. Adobe System's gamble was met with short-term financial success: it reported meeting its predictions of quarterly sales of over $1 billion in June of 2013. Recent reports placed the number of subscribers to Adobe's Creative Cloud at 3.5 million with revenues from subscriptions nearing $3 billion (Manjoo, 2015).

One of the changes that had potentially significant long-term implications was the way in which Creative Cloud altered the way in which users upgraded their software. Upgrading represented a kind of interweaving between practitioners and the technologies they used to perform their tasks (Ashton, 2011: 319). Moving from one version of a traditional Photoshop license to another afforded consumers the opportunity to critically reflect on the changes taking place at an individual and collective level (Lesage, 2014). With the Creative Cloud, upgrading became more a process of opting out than opting in.

A second potentially significant change was the way in which Photoshop was articulated as a tool. By moving to the Creative Cloud, Adobe signalled that some of the functional qualities of their creative applications were as a tool for development rather than purely for digital imaging. Just as importantly, Adobe launched its Adobe Creative SDK, advertising itself as a way to provide 'the world's best creative tools...for all developers to use in their apps and websites' (Adobe Systems Incorporated, 2015b). Both changes represented at once the potential for Adobe to extend its reach as a dominant software provider for cultural and media production and the potential that its established user-base turn to or develop software alternatives.

Conclusion

Tech reporters and early adopters are not the only people one can accuse of getting swept up in new media hype. As researchers, we often seem to find ourselves asking how the latest technological innovation will 'fit' into our current understanding of media work. We are easily tempted to study the latest digital media invention or controversy while leaving more established objects overlooked or under examined. The obviousness of Photoshop's status as a tool for media work over this past quarter century may have been the reason for the dearth of studies on the topic in our field.

In this chapter I set out to demonstrate how a biographical approach usefully provided insights into the changing symbolic and material relationships that tied practitioners to the tools of their trade. Practices and categories were continually negotiated between developers and users. In a sense, Photoshop always remained a tool but the functionalities that served as qualities for its activation as tool through practice continually shifted over time. Although it is not a substitute for established traditions of media production research, cultural biographies of things like application software give media researchers a way to explore some of the interstices that cut through much of contemporary media work. With this in mind, below are three lessons I learned from this research that could apply to further media production research.

The first lesson is that biographies of software for media work do not exist in a social or technological vacuum. Their lives are shot through with material and symbolic transformations that dynamically unfold over time. It is therefore important that media researchers develop conceptual and methodological frameworks that capture the 'processual' aspects of a thing's historical becoming.

A second lesson is that media researchers must be aware of the tensions that exist between how their theoretical models conceptualize an object and how that same object is symbolically and materially ordered through practice. The practices of imaging, play, and development do not fall neatly into a cultural field or media industry. But as I demonstrated above, an analysis of these practices provides insights into how an object is articulated as a tool for contemporary media work. The answers to questions like 'How and when does an object come into being?', 'Who and/or what is it for?', 'How is it (mis)used?' are at the heart of the politics of value for infrastructures of media production and consumption and require further investigation.

The third and final lesson is that the principle challenge for this type of research involves developing a framework that acknowledges the dominant symbolic and material articulations of the object while also leaving room for alternative, contradictory, and/or singular articulations (Lesage, 2013). There is no magic formula for examining how uneven constellations of categories and practices mediate an object, but it is essential that we subject the resulting asymmetries of power to a critical analysis.

References

Adobe Systems Incorporated (1990) *Adobe Photoshop User Guide* (Mountain View, CA: Adobe Systems Incorporated).
Adobe Systems Incorporated (2015a) *Adobe trademarks*. http://www.adobe.com/ca/legal/permissions/trademarks.html (accessed on 1 March 2015).
Adobe Systems Incorporated (2015b) *Adobe Creative SDK*, https://creativesdk.adobe.com/ (accessed on 1 March 2015).
Appadurai, A. (1986) 'Introduction: Commodities and the politics of value' in Appadurai, A. (ed.), *The Social Life of Things: Commodities in Cultural Perspective* (pp. 3–63) (Cambridge: Cambridge University Press).
Ashton, D. (2011) 'Upgrading the self: Technology and the self in the digital games perpetual innovation economy.' *Convergence 17*(3), 307–321.
Behance Network Team (2012) 'Behance and Adobe: Serving the future of the creative world', http://blog.behance.net/teamblog/behance-adobe-serving-the-future-of-the-creative-world (accessed on 1 March 2015).
Bijker, W. E. and Pinch, T. (2012) 'Preface to the Anniversary Edition', in W. E. Bijker, T. P. Hughes, and T. Pinch (eds), *The Social Construction of Technological*

Systems: New Directions in the Sociology and History of Technology (pp. xi–xxxiv) (Cambridge, MA: MIT Press).

Born, G. (2010) 'Listening, mediation, event: Anthropological and sociological perspectives.' *Journal of the Royal Musical Association*, 135(1), 79–89.

Bourdieu, P., Castel, R., Schnapper, D., Chamboredon, J.-C., and Boltanski, L. (1990) *Photography: A Middle-brow Art* (Cambridge: Polity Press).

Bowker, G. C. and Star, S. L. (2000) *Sorting Things Out: Classification and Its Consequences, Inside Technology* (Cambridge, MA: MIT Press).

Clarkson, M. and Coudal Partners Staff (2004) *Photoshop Secrets of the Pros: 20 Top Artists and Designers Face Off* (Alameda, CA: Sybex).

Coudal Partners Incorporated (2015) 'Season Tickets: The LYT Newsletter. Layer Tennis', http://www.layertennis.com/newsletter (accessed on 1 March 2015).

Couldry, N. (2012) *Media, Society, World: Social Theory and Digital Media Practice* (Cambridge: Polity Press).

Dyer-Witherford, N. (2014) 'App worker' in S. Matviyenko and P. D. Miller (eds), *The Imaginary App* (pp. 127–141) (Cambridge, MA: MIT Press).

Feenberg, A. (2005) *Questioning Technology* (New York: Routledge).

Fuller, M. (2001) 'It looks like you're writing a letter.' *Telepolis*, www.heise.de/tp/druck/mb/artikel/7/7073/1.html (accessed on 1 March 2015).

Kopytoff, I. (1986) 'The cultural biography of things: Commoditization as process' in A. Appadurai (ed.), *The Social Life of Things: Commodities in Cultural Perspective* (pp. 64–91) (Cambridge: Cambridge University Press).

Lash, S. and Lury, C. (2007) *Global Culture Industry: The Mediation of Things* (Cambridge: Polity Press).

Lesage, F. (2013) 'Cultural biographies and excavations of media: Context and process.' *Journal of Broadcasting and Electronic Media* 57(1), 81–96.

Lesage, F. (2014; online first) 'Reviewing Photoshop: Mediating cultural subjects for application software.' *Convergence*, http://con.sagepub.com/content/early/2014/08/13/1354856514545711 (accessed on 1 March 2015).

Lesage, F. (In press) 'Middlebroware.' *Fiberculture*.

Lesage, F. and Smirnova, S. (2015) 'Introducing Photoshop: Mediating application software for cultural work.' *Canadian Journal of Communication* 40(2), 223–241.

Lopp, M. (2012) 'Two Universes: Rands in Repose', http://randsinrepose.com/archives/two-universes/ (accessed on 1 March 2015).

Manovich, L. (2013) *Software Takes Command* (New York: Bloomsbury Academic).

Matviyenko, S. (2014) 'Introduction' in S. Matviyenko and P. D. Miller (eds), *The Imaginary App* (pp. xvii–xxxvi) (Cambridge, MA: MIT Press).

Narayen, S., Warnock, J. E., and Geschke, C. M. (2010) 'To our stockholders', http://www.adobe.com/aboutadobe/invrelations/pdfs/fy09_lettertostockholders.pdf (accessed on 1 March 2015).

Peterson, R. A. and Anand, N. (2004) 'The production of culture perspective.' *Annual Review of Sociology* 30(1), 311–334.

Pfiffner, P. (2003) *Inside the Publishing Revolution: The Adobe Story* (Berkeley, CA: Peachpit Press).

Pollock, N. and Williams, R. (2008) *Software and Organizations: The Biography of the Packaged Enterprise System or How SAP Conquered the World* (London: Routledge).

Shreve, J. (2001) 'Anyone for Photoshop Tennis?' *Wired.com*, http://web.archive.org/web/20130504212945/http://www.wired.com/culture/lifestyle/news/2001/09/47132 (accessed on 1 March 2015).

Silverstone, R. (1994) *Television and Everyday Life* (London and New York: Routledge).
Silverstone, R. (1999) *Why Study the Media?* (London: Sage).
Silverstone, R. and Haddon, L. (1996) 'Design and the domestication of information and communication technologies: Technical change and everyday life' in R. Mansell and R. Silverstone (eds), *Communication by Design: The Politics of Information and Communication Technologies* (pp. 44–74) (Oxford: Oxford University Press).
Star, S. L. (2010) 'This is not a boundary object: Reflections on the origin of a concept.' *Science, Technology & Human Values* 35(5), 601–617.
Sterne, J. (2007) 'Media or Instruments? Yes.' *OffScreen 11*, 8–9.
Suchman, L. (1994) 'Do categories have politics? The language/action perspective reconsidered', *Computer Supported Cooperative Work* 2(3), 177–190.
Suchman, L. (2012) 'Configuration' in C. Lury and N. Wakeford (eds), *Inventive Methods: The Happening of the Social* (pp. 48–60) (London: Routledge).
Wajcman, J. and Jones, P. (2012) 'Border communication: Media sociology and STS.' *Media, Culture & Society* 34(6), 673–690.
Williams, R. (1990) *Television: Technology and Cultural Form*, 2nd ed. (London: Routledge).
Woolgar, S. (1991) 'Configuring the User: The case of usability trials', in J. Law (ed.), *A Sociology of Monsters: Essays on Power, Technology and Domination* (pp. 57–99) (London: Routledge).

Epilogue
C.W. Anderson

Both individually and as a whole, the chapters in this excellent volume have much to recommend them. Many embrace a level of personal introspection that is sadly rare in today's scholarly publishing ecosystem. The reflexive nature of the first two chapters, penned by both a founding figure of the ethnographic newsroom research tradition (Schlesinger) and a more recent contributor to that same tradition (Ryfe), makes them particularly helpful for scholars trying to forge their own journalistic research paradigms. Likewise, Munnik's later chapter details the steps he took when initial avenues of ethnography were closed to him, making it an essential starting point for fledgling ethnographers. The middle sets of chapters, by Willig, Berkowitz and Liu, along with Slaatta, Munnik, Gynnild, Perrin, Lowrey and Erzikova, and Bruun, develop media production research along a variety of important axes and zero in on some recent advances in both theory and method. The final section, with chapters by Alacovska, Sanders, and Lesage, is perhaps the most expansive, drawing production research on news and journalism into dialogue with a variety of other fields (genre film, documentary, and even software production).

Taken together, then, the chapters collected in this volume go a long way to fulfilling the editors' goals of 'advancing media production research.' Indeed, in many ways the book performs a useful ground clearing and consolidation function, both opening up new avenues for future research and clearly spelling out what it is that media production researchers already know. For the remainder of this epilogue, I want to expand on three of the latent themes I see embedded in the book: drawing them out in the hopes of pushing the conversation forward to the (hopefully!) *next* volume of *Advancing Media Production Research*.

First, several of the chapters in this book raise the important question: what is the space of media production research? Where does such production, and such research, occur? Schlesinger actually alludes to this conundrum when he discusses his 1994 book with Howard Tumber on crime, which takes not simply media production but the entire policy and publicity apparatus as a whole as its research target – what we might call the 'media ecosystem through which crime is produced and publicized.' Likewise, Ryfe's provocative chapter on time discusses the advantages and disadvantages of a networked ethnographic approach, and also indirectly confronts the relationship between the research field and time. Ryfe is correct, of course, in his contention that the more time in the field the better. However, there are also different ways to conceive 'the field' in which we spend this time – we can see it as a network, for instance, or we can consider the more content-focused approach of Berkowitz and Liu, or we might adopt Lowrey and Erzikova's media ecology perspective. All of this, of course, takes us outside the realm of ethnographic research per se. Nevertheless, all these different strategies revolve around reframing the notion of the *space* of journalism research and thus relate back to some classic ethnographic questions of *where* to go and for *how long*.

A second question raised by many of the chapters in this book: what is the relationship between the theory we borrow and the empirical findings we give back? As media production scholars, we are indebted to a variety of different practices and fields of study; we are magpies which happily poach from a variety of different domains, including field theory (Benson and Neveu, 2005), political economy (Pickard, 2015), science and technology studies (STS) (Boczkowski, 2004), sociology (Waisbord, 2013), anthropology (Boyer, 2014), and cultural studies (Zelizer, 2009). This eclecticism has, by and large, been to the advantage of media production research. And yet, are we only borrowers? Might there be something about studying media production as *media production* that makes it different from studying the production of shoes, aircraft carriers, or scientific facts? And if there is a difference in the object of study, perhaps there is also something we can give back to these more prestigious fields from which we draw. Does the theory–application relationship always only have to go in one direction? These questions are raised, though not answered, by a number of chapters in this book.

Finally, I want to return to the question of production research and time, but this time thinking about time as *history* rather than as *time in the field*. One of the methods for grappling with media production in the digital age is to expand the fields we consider to be part of 'the digital' – to wrap our intellectual arms around a larger space, we might say. A second strategy, however, is to rethink our notion of time, and thus perhaps continue to rethink our notion of ethnography. In this age of rapid technological churn, of collapsing institutions and obsolete media products, perhaps the most important substance we can add to our media production research is the notion of history – the path through which the spaces we study came into being for the short period of time in which we were there. This is ethnography, but it is ethnography with a different relationship to time (Anderson, 2015). The chapters in this excellent book have prepared the ground for this type of scholarship; perhaps we will see more of it in the future.

References

Anderson, C. W. (2015) 'Up and out: Journalism, social media, and historical sensibility.' *Social Media and Society* 1(1).
Benson, R. and Neveu, E. (2005) *Bourdieu and the Journalistic Field* (Cambridge, UK: Polity Press).
Boczkowski, P. (2004) *Digitizing the News: Innovation in Online Newspapers* (Cambridge, MA: The MIT Press).
Boyer, D. (2014) *The Life Informatic: Newsmaking in the Digital Era* (Ithaca, NY: Cornell University Press).
Pickard, V. (2015) *America's Battle for Media Democracy: The Triumph of Corporate Libertarianism and the Future of Media Reform* (Cambridge: Cambridge University Press).
Waisbord, S. (2013) *Reinventing Professionalism: Journalism and News in Global Perspective* (Cambridge: Polity Press).
Zelizer, B. (2009) *The Changing Faces of Journalism: Tabloidization, Technology and Truthiness* (Cambridge: Polity Press).

Index

academy, 24, 28, 47
  productive demands of, 48
  tenure requirements of, 42–43
access, for production research, 5, 14, 25–26, 28, 30, 33, 40–41, 44, 70, 76, 122, 132–135, 137–143, 147–150, 153, 154, 158, 166, 172, 195–196, 201, 204–207, 209
Actor Network Theory, 96
administrative research (as distinct from critical research), 24–25
Adobe Photoshop, 217–218, 220–230
applied linguistics, 161–162
articulation (of cultural objects), 220–221, 225, 228
audience studies, 131–132, 141, 144
authenticity, 204–205, 211

backstage information, 134–135, 137–138, 142, 161–162, 173
Benson, R., 54–55, 56, 58, 82, 97, 99
biographies, 161, 172, 191–192, 229–230
  of things, 218, 229–230
Born, G., 40, 148, 182, 187
Bourdieu, P., 13–14, 34, 53–57, 61–62, 72, 82, 96–102, 103–109, 150, 195
British Broadcasting Corporation, 20, 24–26, 29, 33, 39–40, 147, 149, 159, 184
  BBC journalism, 20
  BBC Scotland, 148–150, 154–155

Canadian Broadcasting Corporation, 148
capital, 14, 53–56, 59–61, 72, 100, 103, 106, 108, 109, 187
  cultural, 60
category
  core (in grounded theory), 126
  cultural, 217–221, 228–230
  genre as, 188, 194
CBS News, 41

collaborative practice, 161
computer logging, 167
content analysis, 61–62
Creative Cloud, 224, 228, 229
creative cycling theory, 116, 121–126, 128
creative economy, 5, 28–30, 32, 34
creative industries, 6, 8, 16, 29–30
creative labour, 9, 31
crime journalism, 26
cultural consumption, 53, 57, 104
Cultural Enterprise Office, 30, 33
cultural industries, 10, 15, 24, 34, 95, 96, 109, 133
cultural meanings, 71–72, 74, 75, 76, 77
cultural omnivore, 61
cultural practices, 9, 31–32, 45, 131, 169, 172–173, 189, 217–218
  political economy of, 106
culture, *see* cultural industries; cultural meanings

documentary, 14, 21, 149, 186, 192, 200–209, 211–214, 233
Domingo, D., 38, 40
doxa, 54

ECREA, vii, 3
elite informants (also elite interviewing), 59, 131–134, 137, 139–144
email, 44, 140–141, 148–149
  in negotiating access, 40–41, 148–149
  use by journalists, 44
ethics, 7, 30, 75, 97, 136, 140, 142–143, 152, 192–194, 200–202, 213
  in documentary production, 200–203
  ethics review boards, *see* institutional review
  of journalists, 170
  in travel writing, 183–185

ethnographic teamwork, 21–30
ethnography, 9, 13–14, 39–41, 96, 99, 183, 233–235
  definition, 3–5, 26, 38, 45, 132
  ethnographic self/selves, 147, 151–153
  ethnographic studies, 3–5, 11, 21, 57, 59, 62, 222, 225
  as method, 10, 38, 45, 167, 173, 207–209, 221
  network, 9, 26, 44, 91–92, 234
  of news production, 3–5, 10–12, 20, 38–41, 45, 70, 79, 233–235
  "speaking, ethnography of", 194
exclusive informants, 134–144
experience, professional (value of in research), 14, 147–150, 153
  of cultural production, 8–10, 28–31, 195–196, 218
  field, 80, 82, 133
  of participants in media production, 201–214
  of production research, 4–5

field theory, 13, 53–63, 69, 72, 76, 95–109, 195, 234
first wave of media sociology
  see production studies, first wave of

Gans, H., 4, 33, 39–41
genre, 3, 103–105, 107–108, 142, 181–197, 201, 233
  communication and genre, 193
  genre system, 188–194
  genre-specific worlds, 181
  of interview, 131–136, 144
Glasgow, 147–148, 158
grounded theory, 100–101, 115–129

habitus, 53–54, 61
Hermeneutics, 182, 188–190
history, as approach to research, 234–235
Home Office, 26–27

IAMCR, vii, viii, xi, 3, 12
ICA, vii, 12
Ideograph, 69–72, 74–76
Imaging, digital, 217, 221–230

impact, as measure of research value, 23–24, 31–32
inovation
  focus by researchers on, 229
  in journalism, 86–88, 121, 125
  in research method, 12–14, 191
Institutional review, 41, 68, 75, 143
interpersonal power in interviewing, 134
intertextual chain, 162, 166–172
interview
  critique of as poor predictor of practice, 11, 47
  for employment, 48
  by journalists, film-makers, 74, 164, 201, 205, 211–212
  as research method, 7–9, 25–26, 29–30, 33, 39, 45, 57, 59–63, 76, 90, 119–120, 131–144, 150, 154–155, 167, 196, 203–207
  transcripts, 45, 119

journalism, 10–12, 20–22, 38–49, 68–77, 81, 88, 103–106, 147, 153, 162, 166, 173, 223–235
  culture of, 10, 45–49, 70, 72
  disruption of, 7, 10–12, 21, 41–42, 45, 81–82, 117
  ethnographic research on, *see* ethnography, of news production; newsroom, studies of
  field, 53–54, 59, 72, 103
  Studies (as research field), 10, 15
journalistic self, 152, 157–158

keylogging as research method, 168
Kopytoff, I., 218–219

language awareness, 162, 168–170
Layer Tennis (also 'Photoshop Tennis'), 223–225
Lazarsfeld, Paul: critical and administrative research, *see* administrative research
legal agreements (for research and publication of research), 40, 142, 213
level of analysis, 69, 90

Index 239

media consumption (also media reception, cultural consumption), 22, 32, 53–57, 60–63, 95–97, 101, 104, 187–191, 209, 230
media production practices, 3–4, 12, 15, 20, 38, 44, 54, 57, 59–63, 80–83, 87–88, 96, 115, 147, 157–158, 167–168, 182–183, 190–195, 197, 214, 218, 220–222, 226–227, 229–230
media reception, *see* media consumption
media strategies, organisational, 26–27
media system, 55–58, 61–62, 71, 83, 88, 135
media-centrism, 26, 27, 150
mediatization, 15, 55, 58, 221
memory, 9, 76, 90, 151–152, 154, 157, 158, 204, 206, 208
 collective, 73–74
metadiscourse analysis, 166, 169–171, 173
methodology, 57, 76, 90–91, 124
 innovation in, 193
multi-method research, 6, 161, 167, 171–173
mythical narrative, 72–73, 76

nationalism, 71–72
New York Times, 40
news, *see* journalism
 ecology, eco-system, 13, 40, 44, 79–81, 84–88, 234, *see also* ethnography, network
 online, 41, 120
 professionals, 117, 119, 121, 122, 123, 128
 texts, 69–72, 152–153
newsroom(s), 12, 14, 38, 40, 41, 44, 45, 46, 121, 127, 149, 155, 166
 environment of, 42, 45, 76, 118, 123, 148, 149
 studies of, 3, 11, 39, 40, 41, 43, 45, 49, 53, 60, 62, 69–70, 71–72, 72, 76–77, 79, 118, 150–153, 158
newswriting, 161, 166, 171–172
non-fiction, 201–205, 214
Nordic Noir, 183

observation, *see* ethnography
organization ecology, 79–80, 82–90

paradigm, 54, 69, 118, 123, 173
participants, in research, 47, 151–152, 154–155, 159, 170, 186–187, 200–204
 non-professional, 205–212
play, 105, 223–226
poetics, 181–183, 190–191, 193–195
policy, 6, 24, 28, 29, 30, 163
policymakers, 6, 26, 29, 32, 163, 170
political communication, 56, 82
political economy, 9, 10, 15, 186, 234
 of academia, 42, 43, 47
politics, 10, 23, 27, 30, 54, 55, 56, 62, 71, 75, 106, 107, 132, 138, 141, 219, 230
 of media, 22, 26, 27
population
 of media organisations, 79–92
 of minority groups, 154–155
power, 5, 6, 9–10, 21, 98–99, 107, 109, 132–134, 182, 186, 187
 media, 6, 22, 53, 55, 56, 58, 71, 103–106, 135–136
 relationships with informants, 135–136, 139, 143, 144, 204
 in research context, 10, 14, 23, 25, 26, 117, 127, 154, 161, 163, 207, 213
process perspective, 161
production, 12, 14, 22, 53
 of culture perspective, 9, 15, 58, 231
 media, 6–8, 54–56, 59–63, 106–109, 125, 127, 142, 181, 183, 185–188, 190, 204–206
 news, 41–44, 68, 70, 72, 75–76, 79, 84–88, 103–104, 120–121, 165–167, 172–173
production studies, 3–4, 8–12, 15, 20, 22, 25–26, 28, 31–33, 38–40, 47, 53, 55–59, 63, 69–70, 76–77, 80–83, 92, 95–102, 115–118, 124, 1 28–129, 131–140, 143–144, 147–150, 154, 158, 181–182, 190–192, 195–197, 200–202, 209–213, 233–234

production studies – *continued*
  first wave of, 5, 11, 21, 22, 25, 32, 39
  second wave of, 21, 22, 26
professional vantage point, 70, 153
Progression Analysis, 14, 159, 161, 166–169, 173
public discourse, 162, 171
public understanding, 163, 170

qualitative research, 3, 69, 76, 124, 126, 131, 132, 135, 139, 144, 154

raw footage, 201, 207, 209, 211–213
Reality Television, 200, 201–202, 203, 204, 205, 213
reception studies, 62, 95, 187, 189, 190, 191
recontextualization, 161
reflexivity, 13, 23, 106, 131, 152, 154
  of media producers, 58, 142, 194
  sociology, 53–55, 57, 61, 63
  visible/visibility, 61, 151, 158
representation, technologies of, 201–204, 208, 210–211, 213
research question, 132, 134–137, 143, 144, 150, 155–156, 158
research teams and teamwork, 25, 26, 30
review by sources prior to publication, 40, 143
Russia, 13, 60, 81, 83, 85–88, 92

Scandinavian crime fiction, 183, 191, 195–197
Scotland, Scottish Government, Scottish Parliament, 27–30, 147–150, 154–155
screenshot recording, 168
self-presentation, 201, 203, 205
Sociological approaches
  genre, 181, 186–187, 193–195
  news production, 70
  organisational, 79, 81–83
  see Bourdieu, Pierre
sources
  journalists', 26–27, 147, 150, 156–158
spontaneity, 202, 204–205, 211
stancing, 161–165, 169–171
status, 85, 132–135, 139–142, 144 218, 224, 228–229
storytelling, 70, 72–74, 151–152, 163, 165
  research, 27–28, 141, 142, 150–152
  writing, 166–168
survey, 11, 14, 59–60, 62, 104–105, 203
symbolic power, 55–58, 60, 103

technological change, 7, 22, 73, 79, 117, 119, 203, 229
  see also journalism, disruption of
test footage, 201, 208
text (re-)production, 161–162, 166–167, 170–172
text-in-action, 210
textual studies/analysis, 9, 45, 71, 76–77, 182, 197
theory, 13, 56, 69, 115, 234
  field, see field theory
  grounded, see grounded theory
  travel guidebooks, 183–185
triangulation, 172
Tuchman, G., 4, 15, 33, 39, 79

UK, 4, 5, 13, 22–23, 26–27, 34, 42, 60, 192
UK Film Council, 29–30, 33
upgrading, 228–229
USA, 4, 13, 39, 60–61, 71, 73, 81, 83–88, 92
Usher, N., 10, 40

variation analysis, 169